D1152598

**OAKHAM SCHOOL
LIBRARY AND INFORMATION SERVICE
ASHWELL ROAD
OAKHAM LE15 6QG**

Return on or before the last date stamped below.

1 9 FEB 1996

WITHDRAWN

OAKHAM SCHOOL LIBRARY

T

R32459K 0183

The Guinness Book of Fakes, Frauds & Forgeries

Richard Newnham

GUINNESS PUBLISHING

Editor: Honor Head
Picture Editor: Alex Goldberg
Design and Layout: Cathy Shilling

© Richard Newnham 1991

Published in Great Britain by Guinness Publishing Ltd,
33 London Road, Enfield, Middlesex

All rights reserved. No part of this publication may be
reproduced, stored in a retrieval system, or
transmitted in any form or by any means, electronic,
mechanical, photocopying, recording or otherwise,
without prior permission in writing of the publisher.

Typeset in Bembo and Gill Sans
by Ace Filmsetting Ltd, Frome, Somerset
Printed and bound in Great Britain by
The Bath Press, Bath

'Guinness' is a registered trade mark of Guinness
Publishing Ltd

A catalogue record for this book is available from the
British Library

ISBN 0–85112–975–7

The right of Richard Newnham to be identified as
Author of this Work has been asserted in accordance
with the Copyright, Designs & Patents Act 1989.

OAKHAM SCHOOL LIBRARY AND INFORMATION SERVICES

ACCESSION No: DATE: 1\95

R32459

Introduction

The tale of a fake, fraud or forgery must move in on the listener and take possession, just as a good film or play does. It will also allow things to emerge from the telling that were not known before – about material objects, about the place these have in our lives, the way they are made and loved, bought and sold; or about the ideas and beliefs of science, literature and the arts. Most importantly of all, such a tale will underline a truth (often a very complicated one) about human beings. Every story in this book is, in the end, about people.

A word on how fake, fraud and forgery will be used as terms. Let's say an artist invents a drawing that a recognized master-artist might have done, and produces this as the master's own drawing. The result is a fake. Forgery, by contrast, is the term for when the artist copies an already existing drawing by the master. And fraud is whatever improper use is made of what has been faked or forged.

That at least is how this book understands and applies the three terms. For specialists they often have quite other meanings. In ceramics, for example, a faked piece of china is an existing piece altered to seem something it is not, perhaps to look older or made by another factory. Again, lawyers will narrow the meaning of forgery to give the word a special sense (if that artist had signed the drawing 'Picasso', the signature would not be a forgery because a drawing is not a document). Nor are fake, fraud and forgery by any means the only terms we could use. This collection of stories, however, applies them in the manner just described, to books and archaeological finds, to lab data and counterfeit bank notes, to a play, a sculpture, an autograph letter – whatever the item may be. If an item exists or once existed, it can be forged; if not, it is said to be faked.

Here and there the term 'fraud' gets an extra meaning. As well as referring to an improper use of something, a fraud can also be the person most directly involved. 'Faker' or 'forger' are sometimes awkward or incorrect for that.

The stories are grouped in four sections – *Distortions and Deceptions: Ideas* (fraudulent science and medicine, history, literature); *Feats and Counterfeits: Money* (notes and coins, cheque frauds, fund-raising schemes); *Trick or Treat? Objects* (art, archaeological finds, manuscripts); and *A Question of Identity: People* (impostors and false claimants).

Choosing the stories found fewer options available than were expected. Science does its work in the open, in front of fellow professionals. The test of replicability (will an experiment run for a second time under identical conditions to those of the first experiment repeat its results?) is everywhere demanded. Scientific constants are laws which never alter. Matter behaves according to named effects that when they change at all do so only with wide general agreement. As a result, although there is any amount of bad science, if the work itself is worth doing then scientific fraud is rare. Medicine too does not tolerate fraud for long, though with the healing sciences an extra point must be remembered: the so-called 'placebo' effect. A patient getting treatment will usually be open to psychological suggestion. The worthless pill or the impressive box of tricks can achieve results that are hard to measure or account for, even though medically they occur. To sum up – science may be bad, but that does not make it fraudulent; medicine may be good, but that does not make it genuine. In consequence the stories from both areas quickly chose themselves.

With religion, every Messiah is somebody's anointed one. To go looking for fraud among what in the Near and Middle Eastern world alone would have been identified as thirty-two named pseudo Messiahs by the year 1707 would soon cause offence. So there are no stories here about faked relics, spurious miracles or idols with feet of clay.

Large-scale city swindles – fraud in its meaning of financial wrongdoing – generally involve too many technicalities for an outsider to stay interested in what is happening. Politics seems too close to half-truths to force any one particular fraud into the book. If both these judgments are wrong, then certainly those two areas of life would fill a volume on their own.

Finally the question of morality. Several stories here are shocking and surprising. In the worst cases it is hoped that the facts condemn the guilty out of hand (three stories show a killer at work). But once beyond such extreme cases the moral question becomes slippery, and the book avoids passing judgment. Faked art, for example, by one view gives the taste of its age a valuable stimulus. By another view it has at last compelled art dealers to accept the practice of selling under guarantee. Certainly, any lesson that teaches that there is a difference between the false and the genuine will be worth learning.

A further shock may be felt as, one by one, the stories reveal how seldom people in authority seem to learn any lesson at all. Can't 'they' do something to stop such ridiculous and shameful things from happening? it may be asked. The answer is no, they can't. Every imposture related here, and most of the money tricksters, idea peddlers and object fakers too, could be matched to a similar story told in the ancient world. Authority in this regard never learns: so much the better for true creativity must be our conclusion.

Picture Acknowledgements

Archiv für Kunst
Ashmolean Museum (Oxford)
Associated Press
Ullstein Bilderdienst
Bodleian Library (Oxford)
Bridgman Art Library
British Museum
Camera Press
E.T. Archive
Hulton Picture Library
Images Colour Library
Keystone (Hamburg)
Mary Evans
Museum of Fine Arts (Boston)
Národní Muzeum v Praze

Popperfoto
Rex Features
Roger Viollet Collection
Ann Ronan
Royal Library Windsor
St. Paul's Bibliographies, Winchester
UPI-Bettmann Archive
Victoria & Albert Museum

Special thanks to:
Catherine Cheval
Jocelyn Clapp
Simon Conti
Jürgen Raible

Author

At the start of his career in publishing, Richard Newnham had as his first assignment an author who believed that Shakespeare's plays were in fact by Marlowe. His later publishing projects, while seldom matching the theme of fakes, frauds and forgeries quite so exactly, have given him a background from which to tackle the present work. Richard Newnham has edited books on most non-fiction subjects, including art, archaeology and literature, and is an advocate of science popularization. His own book *About Chinese* (Penguin 1971, new edition 1987) is established as the layman's introduction to that language. He lives in Oxford.

Acknowledgements

For help at the planning stage, thanks are due to David Battie, of Sotheby's, London and to his colleagues Andy Hooker (musical instruments) and John Michael (postage stamps); to Walter Gratzer, of the MRC Cell Biophysics Unit, London; and to Chris Howgego and Nick Mayhew at the Heberden Coin Room, Ashmolean Museum, Oxford.

Useful comments on the text were made by Nicolas Barker, of the British Library; Lorna Carney, law student of St Hilda's College, Oxford; Peter Claxton, of Lloyds Bank plc; Martin Dodsworth, of the Department of English, Royal Holloway and Bedford New College, London University; Walter Gratzer; Anne Stevenson, poet, of County Durham; Doreen Stoneham, at the Archaeological Research Laboratory, Oxford; Michael Valentine, company director, and David Walker, theatre designer, of London.

CONTENTS

DISTORTIONS AND DECEPTIONS
IDEAS

'An idea whose time has come' has been used to describe an innovation that takes root at once. Some ideas, by coming too early, are rejected by their contemporaries as fraudulent. They are not always early or fraudulent in the same amounts. Dr Anton Mesmer, born in the 18th century, was ahead of what quite soon after his death became a respectable area of healing. James Graham's thoughts on fertility (the better ones at least) had to wait for two centuries after the man himself was gone. And Dr Albert Abrams's 'radio waves' of the 1920s were such a swindle that not even the usefulness of modern radio diagnosis can excuse him.

Many bogus ideas catch a contemporary spirit only too well. This was true for all Europe with James Macpherson's Ossian, that pseudo-Gaelic heritage he brought to light. In England, George Psalmanazar arrived just as a boom in travel writing was beginning to build: he described a land so remote and bizarre that few people dared contradict what he said. The same trick was played on the world in our own time by Lobsang Rampa, the monk from Tibet.

A fraudulent idea often does its most serious damage internally – to professionals who need to trust their colleagues. A sense of betrayal is one result. Nazi influence badly undermined German archaeologists, as the story of Herbert Marwitz shows. In the Soviet Union Stalin gave Trofim Lysenko the power to tear genetics apart. The case of Cyril Burt, exposed in the 1970s for what was either negligence or wilful deception with his data on intelligence, sparked off an anger among colleagues both for him and against him in the matter of his guilt.

Protocols of the Elders of Zion:
a witches' sabbath

The twenty-four short texts which compile the Protocols fill some seventy pages of a booklet innocently enough. Yet ever since their first appearance in a Russian newspaper in 1903 they have seemed to invite questions. What exactly are 'Protocols'? Who were the 'Elders' and why were they 'of Zion'? The texts had been translated from the stolen French minutes of a secret meeting in Paris. How had the Russian interest come?

Conspiracy

As with many mysteries, the Protocols of the Elders of Zion relate to an age-old and quite simple idea. Already in the 12th century it was believed that there existed a secret organization run by the Jews against Christianity. The 18th century gave this a new twist: Jews had taken over Freemasonry and were screening their activities behind it. That 'explained' the French Revolution. One sequel to that revolution brought the Jews civil rights in Europe, and because this was the doing of liberals and democrats they naturally supported such parties. The Jews moreover lived in towns, where they needed to show enterprise. So if something went against the conservative landed interest and was modern and urban, it was Jewish.

By the 1880s Russia had extended this idea to account for all political opposition to the Tsar. Alexander III and his son Nicholas were fanatical anti-Semites. And Russia was where most Jews lived – five million of them. The authorities set out to ensure that, in Russia at least, they did not gain the rights granted to European Jewry. Witch-hunts were sponsored via pogroms led by the 'Black Hundred', an infamous name for local paramilitary rightists. The anti-Semitic writer Osman-Bey 'uncovered' a network of Jewish committees, each led by a rabbi and staffed by what he described as terrorists, that stretched along the entire frontier. These were in fact help agencies for Jews leaving the country. Jewish emigration from Russia reached 100,000 a year.

One of the worst pogroms took place in 1903 just before the Protocols appeared. Book publication followed in 1905, as part of a work by Sergei Nilus. Looking to explain 'Zion' and 'the Elders', Nilus later said that the original minutes stolen from a meeting in France were those of the first Zionist Congress and its Elders in 1897. But this is best read as a warning not to trust Nilus: the Congress was held in Basle, Switzerland, and conducted itself in German, not French. Although the Protocols hit the mood of the time (they were read in all the 600 churches of Moscow) it was 1917 before they became internationally known. By then the top Bolsheviks were seen as religious-Jewish to a man. What had explained the French Revolution now explained the Russian one.

The supremacy of Judaism

The Protocols on this Judeo-Masonic or Judeo-Bolshevik conspiracy do not make a good summary, but anything is better than the full original text with all its repetitions. Two themes (an attack on liberalism and an account of the means whereby Jews will attain world domination) come in the first nine Protocols; a third theme, prophesying the world state that will result, occupies the remaining fifteen. The drift of argument has five recurring points. (1) Old-fashioned aristocratic rule has gone, and the controlling force is now gold. (2) The Gentiles must be reduced to desperate unthinking beasts by 'our' people (who are 'the Snake'). We will achieve this by forcing on them drink, depravity and opinions supplied by us alone. (3) Discontent, both social and international, must be fostered. The 'oratorical contests' of parliament have already confused voters. Workers must be kept in unrest, war must be frequent. (4) The collapse of Christian faith opens the way to Judaism. 'Our' Elders are perhaps within a century of their goal. (5) When the Messianic Age is attained, a firmly controlled world social economy will reflect the fact of human inequality. A Jewish ruler, selfless and incorruptible, will go among the crowd accepting its petitions but surrounded by security police.

Who believed it

On Tsar Nicholas's death in 1918 this apocalyptic vision circulated among the White armies. Many landed gentry officers took it as explaining the events that were shattering their world. Abroad, the Protocols began a long career among other people equally bewildered. In England the *Morning Post* and *The Times* took them seriously; Henry Ford's *Dearborn Independent*

PROTOKOLY ZE SHROMÁŽDĚNÍ SIONSKÝCH MUDRCŮ

'A secret organization run by the Jews.' For the *Protocols of the Elders of Zion* that was what lay behind the traumatic changes of modern life. The book has been translated into more than twenty languages – here is the Czech version (1927).

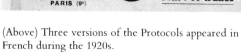

(Above) Three versions of the Protocols appeared in French during the 1920s.

Tsar Alexander III (above right) was a rabid anti-Semite. (Right) Sergei Witte, Russia's minister of finance. Was he the target of the Protocols?

Psalmanazar (left) got people believing in a land that never existed – or at least not as described by him. (Below left) The dress style of its inhabitants, and (below) the book that made him famous.

M.ʳ George Psalmanazar

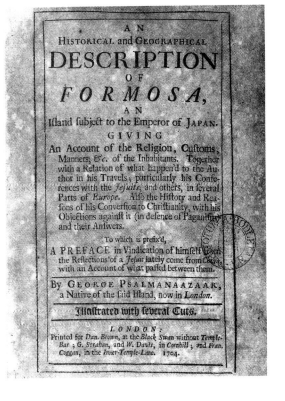

AN
HISTORICAL and GEOGRAPHICAL
DESCRIPTION
OF
FORMOSA,
AN
Island subject to the Emperor of JAPAN.
GIVING
An Account of the Religion, Customs, Manners, &c. of the Inhabitants. Together with a Relation of what happen'd to the Author in his Travels; particularly his Conferences with the *Jesuits*, and others, in several Parts of *Europe*. Also the History and Reasons of his Conversion to Christianity, with his Objections against it (in defence of Paganism) and their Answers.

To which is prefix'd,
A PREFACE in Vindication of himself from the Reflections of a *Jesuit* lately come from *China*, with an Account of what passed between them.

By GEORGE PSALMANAAZAAR, a Native of the said Island, now in *London*.

Illustrated with several Cuts.

LONDON:
Printed for *Dan. Brown*, at the *Black Swan* without *Temple-Bar*; G. *Strahan*, and W. *Davis*, in *Cornhill*; and *Fran. Coggan*, in the *Inner-Temple-Lane*. 1704.

THE SINGULAR

TRAVELS, CAMPAIGNS, VOYAGES,

and SPORTING ADVENTURES

OF

BARON MUNNIKHOUSON,

COMMONLY PRONOUNCED

MUNCHAUSEN:

As he relates them over a BOTTLE, when
furrounded by his FRIENDS.

A NEW EDITION, confiderably enlarged, and
ornamented with four Views, engraved from
the BARON's Drawings.

OXFORD:

Printed and fold by the BOOKSELLERS of that
UNIVERSITY, and at CAMBRIDGE, BATH
and BRISTOL; in LONDON by M. SMITH, at
No. 46, FLEET-STREET, and by the BOOK-
SELLERS in PATER-NOSTER-ROW.

MDCCLXXXVI.

Other writers than Raspe were soon adding stories to the Munchausen collection. This
edition of 1786 was the last to be compiled by Raspe alone, and is an extremely valuable
book today.

did as much in America. Three French periodicals ran versions – for France it was not so long ago that the Dreyfus affair had revealed the degree of her anti-Jewish feeling. In Germany a decade or more later Alfred Rosenberg and Josef Goebbels would make use of the Protocols, by then transformed within a myth that went far beyond them into darkness. With the 1920s' readership in mind, Prussian conservatives subsidized a first publication (they need not have worried: the book was reprinted five times in its first year).

The Protocols were soon shown up as faked, or more correctly as plagiarized. A writer on *The Times* found in 1921 that they derived from some fictional dialogues composed in 1864 by a French lawyer called Maurice Joly. The Frenchman's aim had been to criticize Napoleon III, who was then on the throne. This was forbidden, however, and so he put his attack in the form of conversations between a liberal (Montesquieu, the great 18th-century political philosopher) and a man speaking for despotism at its most cynical: the Italian Machiavelli, who represented Napoleon III. Whoever devised the Protocols had used these dialogues, reversing Joly's message but following his words and ideas over whole stretches of the work.

That, then, was the source of the Protocols. Who wrote them or thought them up will probably never be known. Sergei Nilus is no candidate. As a dispossessed landowner turned Russian Orthodox convert, Nilus detested modernism enough to qualify for the job, but his role was only that of a middle-man. Far more likely to have instigated the Protocols was Pyotr Ruchkovsky, head of the foreign branch of the Tsarist secret police. Ruchkovsky offers two possible explanations. The first is that he was plotting to discredit a French faith-healer called Philippe who had won favour at the Tsar's court. Freemasons appear in the Protocols as screening the Jews, and Philippe belonged to a group known as the Martinists (they were not in fact Freemasons, but the Tsar was not to know). However, if this was Ruchkovsky's plan it rebounded on him. The second possibility sits better.

But why

Sergei Witte, the Russian minister of finance, was a noted modernizer of the economy. Those whose wealth was tied up in land hated him; a slump in 1898 even brought losses to those who had benefited from Witte's changes. The Protocols order that slumps be used to foster unrest among the workers. They also show the gold standard as ruinous – and Witte had adopted gold for Russia. At the time, a sworn enemy of Witte (though not of the Jews, for he was one himself) was the French writer Elie de Cyon. It is known that Ruchkovsky arranged for de Cyon's villa to be burgled: his men were looking for anti-Witte papers and may have found an adaptation of Joly's book in the items they took away. Ruchkovsky may then have given it Russian life as the Protocols. This would have been a neat trap, as de Cyon would have been unable to reveal himself as the author. It is also elegant because his name sounds very like 'Zion'. But if this does explain the Protocols it does not explain Ruchkovsky's motives: Witte was his patron, not his enemy.

As we will probably never have an author proved certain-sure for a book that is still obtainable, it remains to ask how genuine was the Jewish world conspiracy which the Protocols describe. One testimony is on record. After World War II, the leader of the Nazi Higher SS in central Russia (a man qualified to speak) confessed to what the Holocaust had taught him: 'Contrary to the opinion of the National Socialists that the Jews were a highly organized group, the appalling fact was that they had no organization whatsoever. If they had had some, these people could have been saved by the millions; instead they were taken completely by surprise.'

George Psalmanazar:
the island inventor

One idea about sin is that we atone by experiencing the sin again and again in a kind of reversed-out form. Several characters in Dante's medieval portrayal of hell suffered this. So, more recently, did George Psalmanazar (?1679–1763).

In 1704 a book went on sale in London that described a part of the world no one knew much about: Formosa, the present-day Taiwan. Those who voyaged there were mostly Dutch traders – 'a very distant place' summed up the general feeling about Formosa. The book did well. Travel literature was popular at this time, and the writer's eye for detail, his heavily religious message and the fine drawing of the dozen or so plates made this an attractive package. It appealed to all who liked lists and catalogues, especially as the subjects described came close to what they met in their own lives: estates, crops, manners and customs. Readers were disposed to trust an account of such things, and felt themselves taken gently by the elbow:

> The Rich Men and Nobles build their Houses of four-square Stones; but others build the outer-part of plain Timber, while the inner-part is adorn'd with Painted Wood, or fine Earthen Ware Gilded and Painted, which the Natives there call *Porchellano*, but the English *China-Ware*.

Now and then the tone could be mildly naughty. Formosan society allowed men to take several wives:

> And the husband sends for one of them whom he has a mind to lie with that Night; and in the Day-time he sometimes Visits one of them, sometimes another according to his fancy. This kind of Life is sweet and pleasant enough, as long as every one of them is of an agreeable humour; but if the Husband begins to love one Wife more than another, then arises Envy and Emulation.

Whatever had to do with the country's physical and material existence, from the site of its gold mines to the dress worn by its people, received a measured description. It was when the writer turned to the government and above all the belief-systems of Formosa that his personal attitude towards his material started to show.

Climate of acceptance

England in 1704 was a land unsure of its rulers. Religion, too, had a half-century of crisis to add to the doubts. Titus Oates, the instigator of two witch-hunts that saw the throne threatened by Catholics, was still alive when the book appeared; Jesuits were specially feared as symbols of the Inquisition. Questions of faith had just been reopened by the problem of a successor to Queen Anne, none of whose many children survived.

The book played on this general unease, and made some helpful suggestions. Formosan law required all foreigners on arriving there to first trample on a crucifix: the Catholics among them of course refused, which allowed Christians of other churches to enter freely and be tolerated. The book went on to tell how Jesuits plotting in nearby Japan had ruined the work of converting that land to Christianity, and showed the schemers justly punished 'with terrible slaughter'. Killing was indeed a theme never far away for the writer. Each year a religious cult on his Formosa took the lives of 20,000 boys aged under nine years. This figure had been cut to 18,000 by a Moses-like leader named Psalmanazar – 'the author of peace'. However, as critics of the book pointed out, even this number would soon depopulate the island.

The book's critics included Father Fontenay, a Jesuit missionary then visiting London, who gave the writer a hard time over some elementary mistakes. (One was that Formosa came within the Chinese empire, not within that of Japan.) Father Fontenay easily spotted that much of the information had been taken from an account by a Dutch missionary called Candidius. Next, Bishop Burnet wanted proof that the writer was indeed from Formosa as he stated. It was a face-to-face challenge but the bishop had his demand thrown back at him – how would My Lord prove himself an Englishman to someone out there? Psalmanazar asked. 'They would say you looked as like a Dutchman as any who ever traded to Formosa.'

The road to fame

This quick thinking showed that Psalmanazar clearly was from somewhere. His birthplace may have been Avignon (the strange surname was his own choice, and a family for him has not been traced). He spoke good French and had had an education: a talent for languages is apparent, for example, in the sketch he gives of 'Formosan', the language. (The book shows this to use a script with symbols reading right to left as in Hebrew, and everything else is well described in the style of a pocket grammar.) Psalmanazar claimed that after a Jesuit schooling, he went north in search of his father, travelling penniless and on a passport forged to declare him Japanese. His father once found could offer no support, so at Cologne Psalmanazar enlisted in the Duke of Marlborough's forces.

By late 1702, however, word of this strange Japanese who performed prayer rituals each evening had reached his officer. An accomplice now enters the story – William Innes, a Scottish army chaplain, who also questioned Psalmanazar. Innes saw through him at once but suggested they might usefully team up. Together they devised a cover story: the boy was from Formosa, not Japan, and after escaping Jesuit persecution had been baptised a Protestant by the chaplain himself. Duly written up, this tale was sent to the Bishop of London. Innes was ordered to get the boy discharged and bring him immediately to England.

This imposture did more than hold – it became easier with practice. Almost the first thing the two offered their host the Bishop was a Formosan translation of the catechism, in the spirit of paying for his very considerable support. Psalmanazar in fact spoke Latin when among the clergy and wanting to be understood; Formosan he reserved for other occasions. All England was tricked by the imposture. The Archbishop of Canterbury and Sir Hans Sloane at the Royal Society obediently fell into line behind it. The Dean of Christ Church invited Psalmanazar to Oxford for six months, where he finished the book on Formosa that was to create such interest and, by one account, also wrote learnedly about coins. Religion served him well as a Protestant; so three years later he produced yet more anti-Jesuit material in his *Dialogue between a Japanese and a Formosan*.

By about 1707 his accomplice Innes had used Psalmanazar's fame as a route to another and better job for himself. He was appointed chaplain-general to the army in Portugal. There was some unpleasantness over his parting with Psalmanazar, and without Innes to guide him the young man began to lose his sureness of touch. The critics of his book would not go away; towards 1710 Psalmanazar gradually became seen as a figure of fun. Another five years brought a return to the days of hand-to-mouth existence. He dropped out of the limelight, did some tutoring and worked as clerk to an army regiment.

The long atonement

Psalmanazar's life after the fraud, most noticeably after 1728 when he had been badly ill, was one long atonement. It proved to be the mirror image of his crime: those months that a boy had given to faking came back now as a middle-aged man's sentence to toil year after year on the genuine article. George Psalmanazar contributed to several reference books, putting in a daily stint of what was always careful and thorough work done for these giant compilations. They were often badly managed: the *Universal History*, which used him for eleven major sections, had a 'monstrous bulk' that meant dropping an article he had long laboured over. This concerned the style of the biblical Psalms: he had learnt Hebrew in order to translate them, and now another man beat him into print with a version nowhere near as good. Psalmanazar missed out repeatedly. A *General History of Printing*, all his own work, was credited in the book to its printer alone. His five essays on miracles were described as by 'an obscure layman'. And when the time came to confess to his youthful fraud, even that piece of public knowledge was somehow stopped short. An article on Formosa he wrote in 1749 for a geography encyclopedia smuggled in a reference to the 'pretended native called Psalmanazar still in England' who had been taken advantage of when young and vain. This article then went again to the Dutch missionary Candidius for what it told of the island. All else about himself, however, he left for his *Memoirs* (published in 1764) to report.

Little wonder after such days that Psalmanazar needed his evening tincture ('ten to twelve drops of opium in a pint of punch'). Yet by his final years the half-century of drudgery did bring some reward. He was a lovable man. Children greeted him in the street, the novelist Smollett put him into *Humphry Clinker*, there was a glow of respectful admiration on all sides. Samuel Johnson sat with him at the alehouse in Old Street, Clerkenwell. On these occasions the learned doctor did not contradict what he heard. 'I would as soon have thought of contradicting a bishop,' said Johnson shrewdly.

William Henry Ireland:
playwright for a day

Eighteenth-century England was rich in Shakespeare discoveries – the poet's will was found in 1747, pieces of a mulberry tree said to have been planted by him were circulated from 1756, the Jubilee held at Stratford-upon-Avon and at London's Drury Lane Theatre in 1769 began what we now call Bardolatry. The world expected 'a rich assemblage of Shakespeare papers to start forth from some ancient repository'.

William Henry Ireland (1775–1832) began life in search of a parent's approval. The head of the family, Mr Samuel Ireland, was an antiquary and bookseller. This father is on record as saying he did not believe the boy to be his, also as promising that at the age of 21 he would hear the truth about his birth. Meanwhile all Mr Ireland's love was for Shakespeare. He led the family's regular playreading sessions, and in summer 1793 allowed William Henry on a buying trip with him to Stratford. The boy dreamt of fame as a writer. He had no talent, said

Samuel, but how marvellous it would be if they were to unearth even just a signature of the Bard's!

One year later William Henry saw the way to recognition open before him. He began to fake a series of Shakespeare finds. At the office where he worked was some old rent-roll parchment and a wax seal. William Henry used these along with a deed of James I's time for his handwriting model to fake a mortgage document (the property was in Blackfriars) which on one side involved Shakespeare and an actor called John Heminge. Heminge's name he signed with his left hand. For an authentic Shakespeare signature he went to one of his father's books – it was edited by Edmond Malone, the great lawyer and literary critic – that included facsimiles. The fake passed scrutiny at the Heralds' Office.

The finds came together as a series over the next two months (December 1794–January 1795). They were done in bookbinder's marbling ink on blank pages taken from books of the Tudor period. The list included correspondence between Shakespeare and the Earl of Southampton, a letter and love-poem to Ann Hathaway, two theatre contracts, Shakespeare's spiritual confession, a letter to him from Queen Elizabeth, and revisions to several known Shakespeare plays in addition to two historical dramas never before seen. William Henry's cover story was that a 'Mr H' had chosen him to sort out old papers at the family estate, in return for a right of use (on condition that Mr H's name stayed a secret).

For and against

Mr Ireland put the finds on show and people flocked to see them. Literary figures such as the biographer James Boswell and the poet laureate Henry Pye declared the items genuine. The royal family was friendly, the Duke of Clarence particularly so. But many heavyweight scholars stayed away, not caring to make instant judgments, and as 1795 went on the doubts began.

William Henry lived through some desperate moments. A visitor dropped the mortgage seal; until it was repaired, anyone could see how it had been split open and refilled during the faking process. At the office a colleague caught him pen in hand. Soon after Mr Ireland published the series in December 1795, a genuine signature of John Heminge was discovered, looking not at all like the one on the mortgage.

By early 1796 the press was in full cry after the Irelands. That January they were condemned by the *Oracle*, whose editor had previously supported their discoveries; another paper, the *Monthly Mirror*, called the finds 'a gross and indecent imposition'. Verses satirizing them appeared. Most worrying of all for Mr Ireland, Edmond Malone was known to have a detailed criticism of the finds almost ready for publication. This put the foremost judge of Shakespearean authenticity on a collision course with *Vortigern*, one of the new historical dramas found at 'Mr H' s' home.

Birth of a play

Vortigern, a play in five acts, had been arriving in batches from William Henry during the previous year. Unlike the other items it did not involve him in faking an authentic-looking handwritten manuscript, just a transcript in modern-copy form. Drury Lane Theatre took the new play for production initially in 1795, but had held it over to the spring of 1796. Since the other finds were by then widely suspected of being fakes, the play's credibility became a key issue. *Vortigern* would tell the public whether or not to believe the Irelands.

Drury Lane Theatre's decision to buy *Vortigern* was cynical. Sheridan, the famous playwright who owned the theatre, said to his actor-manager J. P. Kemble that it would be good box office. However, the cast did include at least one supporter: Dorothea Jordan, who was playing the female lead. Mistress of the Duke of Clarence (by whom she would have in all ten children, the 'Fitzclarences'), this spirited Irish actress took to William Henry. When the production became delayed, a meeting was called at the theatre to look into why there were no sets ready and no original of the script, but Kemble did not turn up and Sheridan spoke only of getting his money back. Dorothea Jordan fixed another meeting the very next day, this time at the Palace. Clarence liked to meddle in Drury Lane business. He stated that the play was definitely by Shakespeare, and told Mr Ireland to keep back the original script until work on the sets began. It seems this royal nod was enough – luckily, since there *was* no original script, only William Henry's modern copy. Rehearsals continued, with the opening night agreed for the 2nd of April. As this date approached the play's supporters were much relieved when twenty of Britain's great and good signed a statement backing the finds. Also in February, they received word that Malone's criticism would not be out for a while.

Vortigern tells of an English warrior's bid for the throne of King Constantius, whose murder he has arranged. His own daughter Flavia loves the rightful heir. She, a brother and the court jester run away to join anti-Vortigern forces from Scotland in opposing the Saxon troops led by Hengist and Horsus, who seemingly have rallied to the tyrant but are planning to replace him. Various subplots involve Flavia's distracted mother and two further brothers. The play ends with the Saxons killed, the lovers united, and Vortigern himself (despite wishing to die) spared for his daughter's sake.

Malone's criticism came out just two days before *Vortigern*'s opening. There is no reason to suspect that the rescheduling was intended to hurt the play, and anyway the 400-page book by Malone needed more time to be read than that allowed. Samuel Ireland noted this fact, and added a comment to the *Vortigern* playbill: Let the public be judge.

The age was reinterpreting its Shakespeare. After the 1660 English Restoration his plays had been asked by French classicism and performance style in England to do impossible things, for example, to have one constant time and place for different scenes, and to speak in rhymed verse throughout. Shakespearean characters were seen as too 'nervous', so Juliet was made to wake up before Romeo's death and the tragedy of King Lear was given a happy ending. From the 1740s actors such as Garrick and Macklin began a rescue job. However, the alterations did not stop with them, because Shakespeare editors were beginning to ask what exactly a 'true' text of the plays might be. Malone was among the first to compare one text with another (the differing 'Folios' and 'Quartos' problem), and he had published his own Shakespeare edition only a few years ago, in 1790. Scholars argued hotly over the technicalities, with prominent members of society like the Duke of Clarence taking sides. So Shakespeare, as well as *Vortigern*, was in the public eye.

The public decides

Hours ahead of the opening performance some 2500 people were already packed into Drury Lane Theatre. It would soon be hard to separate supporters from opponents. Acts 1 and 2 went well enough, but any 18th-century production with a claim to being serious risked being let down by the cramped theatre building itself, which overheated the audience's response to events on stage. Actors would play to this. When the on-stage events in *Vortigern* that night started to go wrong, Kemble and others of the cast helped them along.

Act 3 brought outbreaks of laughter at one actor's high-pitched voice. In Act 4 the man playing Horsus chose to die too far down stage and became trapped under the drop-curtain, which was so heavy that he cried out. Pandemonium erupted as a drunken man left his box to drag him off. Most damaging of all was Kemble's delivery of his speech in the last act where Vortigern looks on death – he managed to speak the line 'And when this solemn mockery is ended' in such a way as to refer clearly to the play itself. The ensuing uproar stopped only after Kemble had insisted on silence, and the fact that there was any applause at the final curtain was due to Dorothea Jordan, a house favourite, who spoke an Epilogue. Clarence then made himself 'wonderfully ridiculous and conspicuous' among the play's supporters, while oranges were thrown at the drunken man.

Vortigern never had a second performance, yet for its time the play was at least as serviceable as Shakespeare's *Richard III*, mangled in 1700 and staged in that version throughout the century. The final Vortigern monologue, properly spoken, would sound impressive. It begins:

O! sovereign death!
Thou hast for thy domain this world immense:
Church-yards and charnel-houses are thy haunts,
And hospitals thy sumptuous palace;
And when thou wouldst be merry, thou dost choose
The gaudy chamber of a dying King.

There were plenty of scholars who disagreed with Malone, and most actors liked heavy historical drama. They could well have had more from Ireland – his other history play, *Henry II*, was completed and a *William the Conqueror* was in draft. None of this would be staged today, but it must be considered an achievement for a boy scarcely 20 years old.

Malone found it simple to destroy the Ireland discoveries. Impossible dates and events made them easy game (Elizabeth writes to a Globe Theatre not yet built). The bizarre 'Olde Worlde' spellings were clearly over the top, and Malone pointed out other yet more foolish errors of language in this pseudo-Shakespeare.

To show that the finds were false and not by Shakespeare might be easy enough, but no one was any the wiser as to who in truth had done them all. Samuel Ireland held to his belief about William Henry: the boy lacked talent, he was too stupid for fraud. One month later young Ireland announced that he alone could vouch for the finds. When this brought no result from the man who had yet to acknowledge him as a son, he wrote again: he himself was their author. Samuel at once replied with a pamphlet stating Malone to be wrong and denying any fraud: the finds were genuine. He never gave up that view of them, and never spoke to William Henry Ireland again.

MUNCHAUSEN/RASPE

No two people agree on which Munchausen story is the best. Some like their Baron to be the huntsman whose long-serving hound literally runs itself off its legs. For others he must be abroad tending the Sultan's bees, a task that takes him to the moon when one of them escapes. Many Munchausen adventures happen at sea. This is a place where giant fish are apt to swallow live men, game-birds and other exotic creatures, all of which survive happily.

What is never in doubt, though, is that here is one of the world's great liars. Baron Munchausen made up every word he wrote. His name itself stands for a fanciful and ridiculous piece of boasting.

This in a double sense is incorrect. Hieronymus Karl Friedrich, Freiherr von Münchhausen was born in 1720. He was soon a soldier: many of his fellow Germans served the Empress Anna of Russia, and Münchhausen fought against the Turks in the campaigns of 1738–40. He married in 1744, was promoted to captain in 1750. Ten years later, still young, he retired to his estates at Bodenwerder, north Germany, and led a life of hunting and entertaining. That he had a racy sense of humour, that his soldiering gave him material for anecdotes which he told with a straight face, is on record. But this does not make him 'Munchausen', nor does it make him an author.

How different was the life-story of Rudolf Erich Raspe (1737–94), creator of the Munchausen myth. The two men came from the same part of Germany and may well have met. But Raspe, to start with at least, was a thief. After leaving university already deeply in debt, he wrote a book on geology and managed somehow to get a library job. More writing followed, on arts subjects as well as science. In 1767 he was appointed keeper of the collections (which included very valuable gems) to Frederick of Hesse-Cassel, from whom he methodically stole. The post paid badly; his debts mounted; not even marriage to a Berlin banker's daughter could clear them.

This was a time when people fawned and cringed before their patron. Raspe added a whining all of his own. Finally he was rewarded with a lucrative appointment abroad, but when this news got out his creditors besieged him. Lodging his wife and children in Berlin, he borrowed yet again from his father-in-law. Then there was Frederick's collection of gems to hand over to the next keeper. For years Raspe had been stealing items from it; now his own huge catalogue that he had compiled of the gems made these thefts possible to detect. He appealed in vain to the prime minister, decided it would be contemptible to declare himself a bankrupt, and chose instead to flee the country. By summer 1775 he was in England.

Raspe's life thus far makes him look pathetic and unproductive. As an author, however, he shows quite another side. The geology book he wrote, for example, the *Specimen Historiae Naturalis*, became a classic. Its second edition had already won Raspe election to the Royal Society in London. He made some important discoveries for mining, and his technique for 'stoping' (angled steps that allowed more than one miner to work the same face) was taken up in Cornwall. With the arts, Raspe was the first German to champion Ossian's poems – that Scottish ballad source so powerful for the romantic imagination. He translated plays, wrote a history of oil painting, and after a while could handle almost any topic in his near-perfect English. Soon he would be ready for Munchausen.

When the Royal Society heard about his theft they expelled him (King George III applied pressure) but there were prominent people who did not much like the Anglo-German tide then running at court, and they adopted Raspe. Matthew Boulton, the steam-engine entrepreneur, gave him a job as assay officer for a tin mine near Camborne. Buried away down in Cornwall, through contact with an Oxford printer he wrote the work that made another man famous.

The first seventeen 'Munnikhousen' stories had an edition dated 1786. Raspe added a further five, the Sea Adventures, to a third edition of that year. His way of storytelling (a dry staccato to which the everyday and the impossible both march in step) might be the real Baron's too. Far more likely it was Raspe himself speaking. Style is the man. His Cornish neighbours knew him as an eccentric; the German warrant posted for his arrest described a beaky pointed nose, red hair under a stumpy periwig, a hasty walk. And in the 18th century only a scientist, more particularly one with practical skills, would tell of a winter's journey like this:

> One effect of the frost which I then observed, is rather an object for philosophical speculation. I travelled post night and day, and finding myself engaged in a narrow lane, I bid the postilion give a signal with his horn, that other travellers might not meet or stop us in the narrow passage. He blew with all his might, but all his endeavours were in vain. He could not make the horn speak.

After the coach has in fact met one coming in the other direction, so that the two can only proceed by taking themselves to pieces and reassembling once they are past each other, the party at last reaches the inn. Seated by a warm fire they suddenly hear:

> *Tereng, tereng, teng, teng!* We looked round, and now found the reason why the postilion had not been able to sound his horn. His tunes were frozen up in the horn, and came out now by thawing.

Rudolf Raspe invented only a few of his stories, at most three or four of them. The others had long been in common ownership. Touches of that winter journey, for example, are found in the Greek writer Plutarch (1st century AD), also in Castiglione and Rabelais (16th-century Italy and France). Some are medieval tales collected as 'pranks' (*facetiae*) or by the monks in their chronicles. A man's adventures inside a giant fish are narrated in the Welsh Mabinogion first written down in the 12th century. Many such stories came together in a Berlin magazine that Raspe knew, so strictly speaking what he made of them now was a double fake.

After a slow start *The Adventures of Baron Munchausen* took off. Eight editions appeared before the end of the century, although from the fourth edition onward other writers regularly added new stories and Raspe dropped out. It soon became a world-famous book. What hurt the real Baron was that it was immediately translated into German: people turned up at his house expecting more tales, or just to stare. Münchhausen's adored wife died – the couple were childless and he had a miserable old age, his humour and friendliness gone too. The unwanted fame made him self-conscious and morose. Another disaster proved to be his remarriage late in life: the new Baroness was a vicious, scheming woman. Only his faithful huntsman Rösemeyer, struggling to keep sightseers off the estate, remained to cheer him.

Alessandro Cagliostro:
master mason

The composite put together by a French police spy and added to later by the Papal Inquisition describes Alessandro Cagliostro (1743–?95) as an impostor, forger, swindler, thief, pimp, seducer, alchemist, heretic, fake soothsayer, quack and dabbler in the black arts. Not surprisingly, his own account of himself differs – he denied even being that person physically. We may choose what we want to believe about Cagliostro. Certainly he was a man of many faces, and first impressions of him seldom tally. One picture alone holds Cagliostro steady in a frame, and that is Freemasonry.

Brotherhood

Despite the rites and rituals, the good works and its biblical origins in the building of Solomon's temple, Freemasonry is not a religion. The stonemasons' guild went through medieval times as a craft union and then became 'operative' Freemasonry, the Knights Templar being the earliest members drawn from outside a guild. 'Speculative' or lay masonry grew up in the 17th century; tools of the stonemason were its symbols (a pair of compasses stood for man's conscience, a chisel for education, and so on). Masonry of this kind spread from Scotland and England to the Continent and to America. France and Italy opened lodges (masonic meeting houses) in the early 18th century; Germany did so from 1738. Both Benjamin Franklin and George Washington were freemasons. Leaders and monarchs from Charles Martel to Frederick the Great favoured the cult, and so did many of the French aristocracy in Cagliostro's time. This membership profile may seem odd. After all, freemasons were bonded by democratic ideas of acting together against unjust authority (they called each other 'Brother'), so might be thought to oppose inherited power. Their ideas were non-violent, however, and did not square with the revolution that was soon to bring down the *ancien régime*. Anyone dealing with the masons needed to remember this.

Getting started

Cagliostro was born as Giuseppe Balsamo, in Palermo, Sicily (the name Cagliostro appears only later and is from a distant relative of his mother's). Balsamo the father, a merchandise dealer, soon died and the boy was looked after by an uncle; in 1756 Giuseppe entered a monastery, where as a a novice he learned some chemistry and medicine. From that entry date it is twelve years to the next firm sighting of him. His own account of those first years tells a very different story. Cagliostro claims that he was born as the son of the sherif of Mecca and received instruction there from one Altotas. Master and pupil (he says) then travelled through Egypt, going later to Malta – that much is known historical fact – where the young man met the Grand Master of the Knights Templar order and became a Christian. While on Malta he heard about Freemasonry. Rome, 1768, is also a fixed point for Cagliostro. He got married; in the Holy City various important contacts were made (he claimed the Pope was one of them) but soon he resumed his travels, now with Lorenza his wife and in western Europe. The couple survived on their wits, partly also on Lorenza's sexual attractiveness – she went with the men Cagliostro picked out. They had frequent changes of address, also it seems of name. By 1776 the two of them were in London. Cagliostro was initiated into 'Esperance Lodge N°. 369', a group that met at the King's Head public house in Brewer Street, early in 1777. This lodge belonged to the Order of Strict Observance, which had fraternal ties to Europe. It funded Cagliostro to act as its representative on the Continent. He and Lorenza went first to Germany where they raised more funds – but the money was for a brand of Freemasonry that was largely his own invention. In Leipzig at a banquet given in his honour fifty people heard an account from their guest of the 'Egyptian Rite'.

Light rays and magic mirrors

This 'Rite' may have been a blatant fraud, yet it came close to succeeding. For Freemasonry, Egypt was already a colour on the spectrum. Certain orders believed as did the patriarch Enoch that a 'lost word', an innocence untouched by formal religion, would come to light and would be in a language spoken in the Holy Land that was not Hebrew. Also some of the masonic symbols came from Egypt, for example the five-pointed star, as well as pre-Judaic number magic which later became the cabbala. And it had been in the Egyptian desert that hermits had experienced the Early Christian mysteries whose content was much like the Freemasonry's own anti-authoritarian message. Cagliostro performed tricks probably learnt from Egyptian magic and medicine while he was on Malta (or from Altotas, by the other version of his early life). In particular he liked the mirror, the converging lens and the opaque crystal ball, which were used at Nile Valley temples to foresee the future.

Putting all this together, along with the brand of faith-healing that made him a celebrity for non-masons too, Cagliostro moved from Leipzig to the Baltic, and from there via Russia and Poland back south to Strasbourg in Alsace. At almost every city on this route he managed to set up an Egyptian Lodge. Only in Russia, at St Petersburg, did he fail in this when one of his confederates betrayed him.

The Egyptian Rite admitted all Christian brothers or sisters (it was unisex, another drawing card) who had already been initiated into Freemasonry's three degrees, and bestowed on them a further three. Men took the names of the prophets, women those of the sibyls. Initiation required a vast and pompous ceremony. The Great Copt, Cagliostro himself, presided as Grand Master; the Grand Mistress was Lorenza, Queen of Sheba. A pupil or 'dove', often a young girl, summoned the spirits who then put each initiate's suitability to the test. It was a

(Left) Alessandro Cagliostro. When he left Strasbourg in 1783 his supporters lined the street, but doctors considered him a charlatan.

COMTE de CAGLIOSTRO.

'I have shown you the Truth,' said Cagliostro (below) to his fellow masons. In fact his version of Freemasonry, although it used the masonic symbols, was largely bogus. A Paris lodge in 1740.

(Opposite) Countess Marie du Barry, Louis XV's mistress. Did she see her death at the guillotine in Cagliostro's magic mirror?

Samuel Ireland (right). He promoted the Shakespeare finds of 1794–5 and never doubted that they were genuine.

Edmond Malone (below), the foremost judge of what was and what was not Shakespeare.

William Henry Ireland (below right) perpetrated a series of manuscript fakes, also two completely new plays by the Bard.

MALONE.

London Published at the Act directs, Aug'.1,1815, by G. Jones.

31

MILTON vindicated

From the CHARGE of

PLAGIARISM,

Brought againſt him by

Mr. LAUDER,

AND

LAUDER himſelf convicted of ſeveral FORGERIES and groſs IMPOSITIONS on the Public.

In a LETTER humbly addreſſed to the Right Honorable the EARL of BATH.

By JOHN DOUGLAS, M.A.

Rector of Eaton Conſtantine, Salop.

Turno tempus erit magno cum optaverit emptum
Intactum Pallanta, & cum ſpolia iſta, diemque
Oderit.——— VIRG.

LONDON:

Printed for A. MILLAR, oppoſite Catharine-Street, in the Strand. MDCCLI.

Milton was vindicated from Lauder's charge of literary theft by Dr. John Douglas's all-seeing eye.

dove who betrayed Cagliostro in Russia: after a crystal-gazing performance at St Petersburg, she told the audience how she had been paid to learn her lines. Elsewhere the lenses and mirrors did much better, although Madame du Barry, Louis XV's favourite, was so horrified by what she saw in the glass – her imminent death at the guillotine perhaps – that she fainted away and refused ever to come near Cagliostro again.

Practices, promises

We do not know much about the Rite as formal doctrine. Cagliostro did put something on paper about it, but only fragments and bad copies report what he said. His source may have been a Jutland merchant who knew Egypt and who stayed on Malta during the 1770s; or he may have unearthed it from manuscripts he bought in London. Certainly the Rite offered an attractive package of benefits: health and vitality would be restored by it, life extended to 5777 years, riches and beatific visions were promised. The forms of the Rite centred on cabbalistic signs and numbers: '3' was the base figure, which gave three 'directives' and six 'commands', a temple with storeys and rooms in threes where the initiate spent thirty days away from the world, each day's time being given over to prayer, meditation and consecration of ritual instruments in the ratio of 3:6:9. Once initiated, however, lodge members enjoyed mixed-sex meetings, lively affairs at which the women were swathed in white shawls and were colour coded to help with subsequent grouping-off. The Queen of Sheba directed such evenings, with Cagliostro seated on top of a ball. Wine was served and thirty-six 'geniuses of truth' wore masks, which led to a good deal of flirting until they were removed. The proceedings continued until after three a.m.

In this as in everything, Cagliostro seemed so convinced by what he did that others believed in him too. It was the faith-healer's secret given another use. If the idea is to admire him, his years in Strasbourg (1781–3) were a triumph. We hear more about faith-healing there than about Egyptian Rite. Cagliostro cured rich and poor alike in the city. The wife of an eminent Swiss financier suffered from a type of hysteria and was also unable to have children; within a year she was a healthy mother. The Chevalier de Langlois, close to death, took Cagliostro's pills and recovered. An aged uncle of Cardinal Rohan came through scarlet fever after his doctors had given up the old man as incurable. Beyond a doubt Cagliostro took money from patients such as these, but he seems not to have done so from the poor. Eventually the medical establishment of Alsace grew jealous of his fame. The registered practitioners banded together and made a longer stay in Strasbourg difficult for 'the charlatan'. As he left, crowds lined the streets and a woman called out 'The good Lord himself is abandoning us!'

Errors of judgment

Not long after this rejection by orthodox medicine came a breach with orthodox Freemasonry, though here Cagliostro himself must take the blame. In February 1785 a Paris congress of masons met to find ways of settling the disputes within the movement and somehow uniting its many different orders. Cagliostro decided that his moment had arrived. He argued that the Egyptian Rite alone could save Freemasonry, and commanded his brother masons (more particularly the group known as 'les Philalèthes', who had organized the congress) to burn their archives and join him. 'You claim to seek the Truth – I have shown it to you', he informed them. The Philalèthes stalled, the other delegates talked on and on; Cagliostro finally gave an ultimatum that was ignored. He lost his temper and walked out, saying: 'I had reserved happiness for you which you were to share with the elect. Now I abandon you to your own devices.' This was naïve behaviour and bad politics. Many of the highest nobility of France were among these brother masons; with revolution in the air they were not likely to surrender their one safe refuge to a hothead, nor would a movement set against authoritarianism much care for his arrogant tone on the subject of truth.

Cagliostro made thousands of converts to his Rite. That same year in Paris a craze for him began that equalled the success accorded only recently to Mesmerism. And yet the February congress in Paris was a kind of farewell. A year later, in 1786, after Cagliostro's friendship with Cardinal Rohan saw him charged and acquitted in a famous law case involving Queen Marie Antoinette's necklace, the authorities banned him from France and put about the black version of his character. He returned, now a celebrity, to that wandering existence where the story had started.

After three years Cagliostro decided to visit Rome. This was another error of judgment: Freemasonry had by now become heresy, banned in the Catholic dogma. Cagliostro attempted to set up an Egyptian Lodge in the city, was arrested, tried by the Papal Inquisition and condemned to be executed. The sentence was commuted to one of life imprisonment, and he died at the San Leo prison probably in 1795.

LAUDER

In 1747 the *Gentleman's Magazine* astonished the world with a series of articles showing that much of John Milton's epic poem *Paradise Lost* consisted of borrowings from other authors. Milton, said the writer of the articles, 'W.L.', had raided various poets of his day who wrote in Latin. One of them (Jacob Masenius, an obscure 17th-century German) gave *Paradise Lost* its overall design. Masenius even supplied the opening

Of man's first disobedience, and the fruit
Of that forbidden tree, whose mortal taste
Brought death into the world, and all our woe,

when he wrote

Principium culpæ, stygiæque tyrannidis ortum,
Et quæ sera pramunt miserandos fata nepotes,
Servitio turpi scelerum, poenaque malorum
Pandimus.

Then there was the Dutch poet Hugo Grotius, whose lines in *Adamus Exsul*

Lacusque vivi sulphuris semper fluunt
Et ampla vacuo spatia laxantur loco

became in *Paradise Lost*

And lakes of living sulphur always flow,
And ample spaces.

Borrowings of this kind looked bad for Milton's claim to have done 'things unattempted yet in prose or rhyme' with his poem.

What began the year as a curious footnote – England's great poet had after all been dead for over seventy years – grew into a full-scale controversy. People wrote to the magazine arguing the case. That August 'W.L.' revealed himself to be one William Lauder. Few readers were any the wiser; but it was 1748 before one of them ventured to enquire where exactly in *Paradise Lost* that sulphur passage might be found.

The story ran and ran. Lauder was introduced to Samuel Johnson, who felt that the affair was worth taking further in the public interest. Their plan was to publish the Grotius poem complete with Milton's borrowings shown, and Johnson agreed to write a few words as a prospectus for subscription orders. This plan later became a more saleable idea. Lauder enlarged and expanded the magazine articles to deal with eighteen poets, and this, his *Essay on Milton's Use and Imitation of the Moderns*, with Johnson providing the preface, came out at the end of 1749. Public interest was by then enormous.

The *Essay* did not disappoint its readers. Lauder quoted an eight-line passage in Masenius and showed how Milton put it word for word into

Paradise Lost. Other liftings were from the modern Latinist poet Caspar Staphorstius. He gave Milton the beautiful Morning Hymn sung by Adam and Eve that has the lines:

Witness if I be silent Even or Morn
Him first, him last, him midst and without end.

In Staphorstius this read:

Aurora, redeunte nova, redeuntibus umbris.
Hunc primum, & medium, & summum, sed sine carentem.

So it continued with the many other poets. Lauder noted entire images taken over for *Paradise Lost*: the comparison of Satan to a tower, the serpent as a ship, its eyes likened to carbuncles, and so on. Nothing escaped Lauder.

What was all this really about? Lauder was an Edinburgh classicist and would-be schoolteacher. His career took a blow when a Latin version of the biblical Psalms by Arthur Johnston, which Lauder had edited and which the authorities were to adopt for Scotland's schools, ran into a little local difficulty. It seems to have been scarcely more than that – one schoolmaster disliking another schoolmaster's book. However, Lauder took it seriously enough to send both book and criticism to Alexander Pope for his assistance with the problem. The great man was no help at all: he put Johnston into his poem the *Dunciad*, apparently with the sole aim of showing him to be a lesser man than Milton. In fact Pope was settling scores with a third party and was not interested in either of these writers, but for Lauder the unfavourable reference spelled an end to the Psalms project. His author had been set up against Milton and made fun of – where was the answer to that?

Today a psychologist would describe Lauder as the victim of a delusional system. This mode of life allows its victim to behave quite rationally, so long as such behaviour serves to maintain an absurd and obsessive fiction. Lauder was acting as though to hit at Milton would make good every setback he himself had ever suffered, the Psalms project of course but also the two teaching jobs he had applied for without result.

His Essay survived a few weeks only. Dr John Douglas, in a careful piece of detective work entitled *Milton Vindicated from the Charge of Plagiarism*, proved in the following spring that Lauder's so-called borrowings were faked. Those lines of Masenius and other poets came not from their obscure authors but from a Latin translation of *Paradise Lost*, Milton's poem itself. What Lauder had done was to place them as his discoveries. He had thought such minor authors would not be easily found and checked. (In Masenius's case this was so. Douglas needed the help of readers of the magazine to sleuth him out.)

Lauder was clever, learned and evasive but he made some mistakes (that 'sulphur' passage occurred nowhere in *Paradise Lost*). Between the magazine and the Essay versions, tell-tale alterations of the pretended sources jumped out to Douglas's all-seeing eye. 'Te primum, & medium, & summum' for example had become 'Hunc primum . . .', as a better match for Milton's 'Him first, him last, him midst'. Douglas could not resist teasing Lauder for this – did the man need forged evidence, when the real evidence was so damning? That question was the one touch of sarcasm he allowed himself in *Milton Vindicated*.

Disowned now by his publishers, forced by Samuel Johnson to write an apology, Lauder nonetheless held to his delusion. He announced his regrets for having tricked the general public 'instead of a few obstinate persons for whose sake alone the strategy was devised'. Milton-worship, as before, was to blame. Douglas's sensible line on the wider issue – that great writers when they borrow do so not for lack of imagination but at the prompting of their own sound judgment – was lost on William Lauder. For several more years he continued to denounce Milton, then with his daughter Rachel emigrated to Barbados, where he ran a shop before dying in poverty.

Anton Mesmer:
the animal magnetist

The commissioners wrote a long report in 1784, but their final message was clear and damning: 'This non-existent fluid can serve no useful purpose. Moreover we feel constrained to point out that the manipulations may prove harmful in themselves and may be deleterious to the onlooker through the faculty of imitation. Therefore to proceed with these methods in the presence of others cannot fail in the long run to be unwholesome.'

A separate attachment to the report went more fully into the meaning of 'unwholesome'. It meant sex.

Franz Anton Mesmer (1733–1815) believed he was making one discovery but in fact came closer to making another and far more useful one. Louis XVI closed him down, or tried to do so. This places Mesmer in the company of productive scientists seen by their own time as fraudulent.

Born at Iznang, south Germany, Mesmer studied religion, law and philosophy before getting his medical degree at Vienna in 1766. Marriage to a rich widow allowed him a fine house and frequent music parties (the Mozart family were friends; Wolfgang Mozart's first opera had its première at the Mesmers). Wealth and position not only left time free for research but spared him the need to rush out with results, which suited his patient style of working. He also set up a medical practice.

The scientific instrument behind Mesmer's discovery was the magnet. It came his way when a lady visitor to Vienna fell ill and a treatment by magnetism was sought for her (belief in such treatment went back two centuries to the alchemist and sage Paracelsus). Mesmer was intrigued by this 'treatment', and after the lady was cured, he began testing magnets on different parts of the body to observe their health effects. When Mesmer used them in his practice he had immediate success. He was commanded abroad to Bavaria, where he cured a councillor Osterwald of total paralysis and fading eyesight. Osterwald wrote of this: 'I shall not expect any doctor in the world to believe more than that I imagine myself to have recovered perfect health.'

Mesmer's equipment (two standard magnets, one above, the other below the affected part) aimed to create a magnetic stream that might infuse the body's system with 'harmony'. Later, other magnetized objects (cups, beds, clothes, even musical instruments) were used to enhance this stream, and magnetized bathing followed. Mesmer also built the baquet: a series of rods projecting from bottles filled with magnetized water held by patients against the site of their pain.

Theoretically, Mesmer's guiding principle of a 'universal fluid', a latent energy released by magnets which the body could tap, does not seem totally absurd to modern science. Radiation fills many pages in today's medical textbooks, and gravity effects are studied too. Furthermore, his equipment and procedure got results, if we are to believe the reports of the gout, spasms, insomnia, pain in the ears, liver disorders and menstrual problems cleared up or made bearable. Patients flocked to his door. But he was too honest to form an initial theory and leave it at that.

What honest observation seems to have told him, within a year or so of his first success, was that it mattered little if the magnets were omitted from the treatment. The same relief of symptoms came if he simply stroked the patient, following the line of the nerves. This obviously was a different kind of energy at work – animal magnetism. Mesmer spent many years questioning that idea, but in essence the questions came down to this: did animal magnetism exist in everyone or only in himself? He concluded that every human being has the power to create the will to get better, especially with the support of others, and that the physician's duty is to help this desire for better health to come about. 'It is not a secret remedy and I wish to train medical men in my methods', he wrote in 1779.

Dangers might lurk within such animistic or 'suggestive' treatments. Mesmer noted how the greatest relief often came after the patient had pushed a disorder to extremes, even going into convulsions in the process. This 'theory of crises' (his own term for it) sounded too like exorcism for comfort. It also led to doctor-dependence. He cured the blind pianist Maria Theresia Paradies of a dead optic nerve. After some time living with him she could see once more, but she then would not leave his house and a scandal resulted. The girl was ordered home and Mesmer, already under fire from the university school of medicine, had to leave Vienna. Maria Theresia lost her sight again.

Vienna might not want him, but Paris was eager for new medical notions. Queen Marie Antoinette offered to support Mesmer. Mesmer told the queen he wanted the top medical experts on his side rather than a lot of money, 'where a matter of such vital moment to humanity is under discussion'. As things turned out he got far more money than he could handle, and at cost to his true aims. Even the most illustrious of his supporters (they included General Lafayette, hero of the American revolution) failed to win over the medical establishment; King Louis opposed the Queen in refusing to help animal magnetism become a treatment known to the wider world. Mesmer's supporters, who were aristocrats and middle-class people, then went to the marketplace with him. A fund raised 340,000 livres and was oversubscribed, while branches of an organization called the Société de l'Harmonie opened to hold meetings throughout France. This was a triumph; but a triumph for 'Mesmerism' rather than for a measured and scientific use of the man's discovery. Regrettably, too, his naivety seemed to send him over the top. His stage-managed group 'suggestion meetings' became music and light shows with Mesmer presiding in his robe. It all looked fraudulent enough, yet he still had his supporters – a play satirizing the cult in November 1784 was hissed off the stage after only one performance.

Well before that date the king had set up a commission to investigate Mesmer and his works. The commissioners included Benjamin Franklin (inventor of the lightning conductor), Antoine Lavoisier (one of the founders of modern chemistry), and Dr Joseph Guillotin, who recommended the method of execution that bears his name. Their report tried to appear objective but missed the essential point about Mesmer's discovery. For the commissioners, because nothing could be seen or felt or smelt, therefore nothing in animal magnetism existed. Eighteenth-century science did not allow for personality or suggestion, the items of most concern to Mesmer.

'How, then, are we to deal with nervous disorders outside anything we know about?' one doctor in Lyons enquired impatiently. 'With hot and cold baths?' Protests of that kind, voiced by patients and those in the profession who had reason to thank Mesmer, told the king he was wrong. But from enemies came easy jibes: a cartoon showed Mesmer wearing a donkey's head (he had in fact once magnetized a horse). After two years Mesmer left Paris and went back to Vienna, was accused of being a revolutionary, and deported. He spent his final two decades quietly in local practice, unwilling to leave his native south Germany even when Berlin belatedly woke up to his achievements.

Anton Mesmer's life is rich in irony. The discovery he was close to making lay in someone else's grasp even before the commission report ended animal magnetism. One of his students, Maxime de Puységur, had found while treating a shepherd boy magnetically that the boy went into hypnosis. He sleepwalked, obeyed orders, woke up when told to. Others reported observations that took this further: patients who heard commands while asleep and performed them once awake again.

Hypnotism gained its basis for medicine in 1847 with experiments published by the English scientist James Braid proving the role of suggestion in healing mental disorders. Later Jean Charcot, organizer of the Paris clinic that actually treated hysterical patients by hypnosis, was able to support with facts the theory of emotional energy which, by the 20th century, had led to psychoanalysis.

James Macpherson:
the maker of Ossian

One of Samuel Johnson's reasons for touring Scotland in 1773 was to ask about the Gaelic poems newly discovered and enjoying a huge success in translation. He found no traces of their originals and on returning to London that November he decided to attack: 'The editor, or author, never could show the original; nor can it be shown by any other. Whence could it be had? It is too long to be remembered, and the language formerly had nothing written. He has doubtless inserted names that circulate in popular stories, and may have translated some wandering ballads.'

Adding that such passing-off was 'insolence' and 'stubborn audacity', Dr Johnson put these comments into his book of the tour. The translator of the poems, Macpherson, wanted to challenge him to a duel. Johnson was by now far too old to fight, but he bought a large oak stick in case of an assault (Macpherson was a big man).

Europe looks north

None of this could slow the Celtic Revival that was at its height. Genuine or not, poems sung by Scotch and Irish bards as they brooded at the lakeside or over their fallen heroes were what Europe wanted. Art and literature looked to the Noble Savage, to a code of behaviour as grand as that of Greece or Rome but untouched by artifice and imitation. 'Back to Nature' was the slogan of the time. At one point in Goethe's novel *Werther* (1774) the hero presses his face to the grass, knowing that among wild plants and tiny insects he will feel God's presence. Verse drama became a particular target for dislike, especially the plays of Corneille, Racine and their followers outside France. In style, something fresh was sought – a measured prose to stride forward with a natural diction, speeches that came from the heart.

Politically Scotland caught the mood. The Jacobite rebellions, with Highlanders fighting as far south as Derby, aroused sympathetic interest for the Gaels. Famine and emigration seemed their fate. It was via the Western Islands that Christianity first reached the British

Franz Anton Mesmer – 'in the company of productive scientists seen by their own time as fraudulent'.

James Macpherson (opposite), creator of the legendary Celtic bard Ossian in the 18th century (portrait after Reynolds).

The poet Goethe (right) soon became an enthusiast for the faked Ossian. A 19th-century portrait.

Samuel Johnson (below), firmly convinced of Macpherson's guilt with the Celtic poems. Portrait after Reynolds.

Lobsang Rampa of Tibet, after taking over the body of Cyril Henry Hoskins.

mainland, yet the Gaelic Scots were still without their Bible. Even wearing the tartan was banned.

James Macpherson (1736–96), the son of an Inverness farmer, hailed from this newly discovered country. He spoke the local Gaelic, had attended two universities without graduating, and wrote mild imitative poetry with some ease. From 1758 he worked as a tutor in Edinburgh but was dissatisfied with this and looked for an escape. A meeting with the author John Home led him to describe some pieces by the 3rd-century Highland bard Ossian that he had collected. Home knew no Gaelic and asked for a sample translation. Insisting that no English version would do them justice, Macpherson eventually produced fifteen items which were sent to Hugh Blair, Edinburgh's professor of literature, and then on to London where they were much admired. In 1760 these were published as *Fragments of Ancient Poetry collected in the Highlands*. Blair wrote an introduction hinting at another work, a 'heroic poem' of considerable length, that might be recovered and translated 'if encouragement were given'. It was: a subscription raised £60 and Macpherson promptly made two trips to the Highlands and Islands. The announced heroic poem *Fingal* came out in 1761, followed two years later by *Temora*. One way and another these books absorbed the fifteen early Fragments. Hugh Blair supplied a long dissertation that went into almost every subsequent Ossian – and there were many over the next century.

Ossian the Scot

If this body of poetry were to appear credible in its context, Macpherson had to bring off some tricky historical footwork. First he needed to establish it as Scottish. The Irish Gaelic tradition laid claim to both Cuchullin and Cairbar, his protagonists in the two long poems. Granted, much of this tradition was shared; but he still had to show that the Irish had taken over characters who were already known to the Scots. That meant reversing the course of history: an Irish colonization in about AD 500 of what is now Argyll became instead a Caledonian migration into present-day Ulster somewhat earlier. So he made the first poem tell of Fingal, king of Scotland, going to aid the Irish against Scandinavian invaders, and the second poem tell of a second call there, this time to rid the throne of an Irish usurper Cairbar. This neatly confirmed a Scottish presence; however, because the poems were from the 3rd century Macpherson found it necessary to put back the historical date of the Norse (Scandinavian) invasion by some five hundred years.

Scotland now owned an early literature. Blair's dissertation, and the copious text notes that both he and Macpherson wrote, battened down the poems as history. They also underlined what made Ossian irresistible for the modern era. This poetry had no religion, whether Druid or Christian, none of those ridiculous Greek gods, but instead 'the mythology of human nature'. Despite its early date readers would find 'tenderness and even delicacy of sentiment', as well as the moral that victory over an enemy is achieved by moderation and generosity. The poetic style was never abstract; 'even a mountain, a sea or a lake is particularized'.

Today it takes an effort of imagination to taste Ossian like a cool spring water hitting the jaded 18th-century palate. We might try Cuchullin's chariot on the move:

> It bends behind like a wave near a rock; like the sun-streaked mist of the heath. Its sides are embossed with stones, and sparkle like the sea round the boat of night. Of polished yew is its beam; its seat of the smoothest bone. The sides are replenished with spears; the bottom is the footstool of heroes.

And, riding it, Cuchullin the chief:

> The look of his blue-rolling eye is wide, beneath the dark arch of his brow. His hair flies from his head like a flame, as bending forward he wields the spear. Fly, king of ocean, fly! He comes, like a storm along the streamy vale.

The measured lines could be from the King James Bible or from Milton.

Macpherson's success was instantaneous, but many readers found the poems doubtful and he tried to reassure his public with indications that the Gaelic originals would appear when time permitted., The fact was, however, that even had they done so, no one knew enough to judge such material. Palaeography, the science of ancient scripts, hardly existed away from the classics. Samuel Johnson, who stated in his tour book that there were not five hundred lines in all Gaelic which could be shown to be a hundred years old, underlined this lack of technical skill, because that statement was quite wrong. Today we can point to Macpherson's oldest source for Ossian. He went to collectors of the day (Fletcher, Maclagan, MacNicol and Stone) for some passages, but the most authentic material was in *The Book of the Dean of Lismore*, a transcription of 30 poems into a local phonetic Gaelic made in about 1512. Macpherson only based four Ossian passages on this collection. He thought badly of *Lismore* for being too modern, for having too many allusions to the manners and customs of the 15th century to pass muster.

This is a double irony. First of all, the Fingal in *Lismore* is a homespun hero who chats with St Patrick, far more believable and authentic a character than any Macpherson ever painted. Secondly, when the pressure to show his critics some kind of a Gaelic source grew intense it was *Lismore* that Macpherson came up with. Or so his publisher later said – apparently the manuscripts were at his shop but no one asked to see them. An expert, the Reverend William Shaw, scoured the Highlands for Ossian, finding the very earliest poems to be all of *Lismore*'s time and all passed on by mouth (he came to dread the fiddle fetched from the corner cupboard).

Macpherson soon gave up the Celtic revival for a career in politics. He continued to promise sight of his Gaelic sources, and was not best pleased when in 1784 a body known as the Highlanders of India sent him £1000 towards the work. Only in 1807, some years after his death, did a number of Gaelic poems appear in copy form. Originals were never produced for them, and more than one critic believed that the Gaelic had in fact been translated from the English. By then it was becoming clear that only scraps of genuine material, drawn from sources in themselves patchy, would ever be traced. Yet the belief that the search was for a single long epic poem lingered on for another hundred years.

No matter if faked

The 18th century may not have known what it was looking at but it knew what it liked. Ossian was taken up all over Europe. An Italian version appeared in 1763, a German version the year after. The poems were Napoleon's favourite campaign reading – there were three French translations, and they also went into Danish, Dutch, Polish, Russian, Spanish, Swedish and Modern Greek.

Qualities sought by the age and found in Macpherson were a romantic wild scenery together with a mood of morbid sentimentality. Both were backdrops for the *génie*, a cross between talent and spirit, the key 18th-century term. Above all, Macpherson had melancholy. A single line of Ossian catches this: it is said of the Celts that 'they went forth to the war but they

RAMPA

The book appeared on the shelves during the late 1950s. Its author, Lobsang Rampa, born to a high family in Tibet, at the age of seven was ordered by astrologers to become a monk and study medicine. His story of life at the lamasery races along: the dormitory pranks, chanted prayers, memory-training sessions (some under hypnosis) and trips to gather herbs are told with great freshness. Above it all, the wise figure of his guru, the Lama Mingyar Dondup, hovers watchfully.

The most memorable episode came with the drilling operation that opened his 'third eye'. This made Lobsang into a clairvoyant:

> The instrument penetrated the bone. A very hard, very clean sliver of wood which had been treated by fire and herbs was slid down so that it just entered the hole in my head. I felt a stinging, tickling sensation apparently in the bridge of my nose. It subsided and I became aware of subtle scents which I could not identify. Suddenly there was a blinding flash. For a moment the pain was intense. It diminished, died, and was replaced by spirals of colour. As the projecting sliver was being bound into place so that it could not move, the Lama Mingyar Dondup turned to me and said: 'You are now one of us, Lobsang'.

This notion that there might be a psychic centre with some physical equivalent in the brain was well established, and the pineal gland was a favourite choice. This gland was nicely placed in the brain's frontal area, right where the Tibetan drill cut through bone. The benefits from that operation were immediate:

> It was fascinating meeting the boys I knew so well, yet had not known at all. Now I could look at them and get the impression of their true thoughts.

Lobsang Rampa's tale went on to describe flying by kite, levitation of the body, astral travel, and friendship with the Dalai Lama himself. Best of all was the book's clear promise of more to follow.

Three British publishers had turned down this winner before it was finally accepted. Then the problem was how to present it: fact or fiction? Numerous experts were consulted: some felt the writer had copied other accounts, or that he was from Tibet but had let his fancy take over. One academic called the entire thing a fraud – the author clearly knew no Tibetan. Undeterred, in 1956 the publishers went ahead. The Third Eye enjoyed a huge success (45,000 copies sold by the end of 1957 and editions in twelve countries). It earned its author £20,000; the reviewers by and large were kind. Early in 1958, however, a number of Tibetan scholars, among them the explorer Heinrich Harrer who had personally tutored the Dalai Lama, grew angry at what they saw as a fraud and hired a detective to shadow the man who had written the book.

Cyril Henry Hoskins (b. 1911) was shown to be the son of a plumber from Plympton, Devon. He left that area in 1937 to work for a firm of surgical instrument makers. During the first years of World War II he moved to Surrey, shaved his head, grew a beard, changed his name and claimed to have been brought up in China. In time this version of Hoskins took on added shape: he had been a flying instructor with the Chinese airforce and endured terrible privations in a Japanese prisoner-of-war camp. That was what his neighbours reported.

So with book two already on its way, the fragments of a double identity needed to become one believable author. In April 1958 Hoskins stated himself to be a Tibetan lama occupying what was originally the body of a Western man. There had, truly, once been a Mr Hoskins, those neighbours in Surrey had not made him up; but he was gone.

This body-possession by the Lama Lobsang Rampa had happened nine years earlier, as Hoskins, climbing a tree to photograph an owl, had fallen to the ground and was concussed. On recovering, he saw crossing the Thames Ditton lawn towards him the figure of a lama in saffron robes who entered his body. As a reward the Englishman had his Karmic debt cancelled. The lama severed Hoskins' astral cord and watched the now spent astral corpse float off. Lobsang Rampa then cut his own cord (which stretched all the way to Tibet), tied the loose end to the end protruding from his host's physical body, and took possession.

All of that went into Rampa's third book, The Rampa Story. As can often be the case, his second book had disappointed; but he went on to write fourteen more. They were unstoppable, exactly what the '60s required – a mix of astrology, medicine, occult practice and fantasy travel. Now and then he dropped this formula: You – Forever and Wisdom of the Ancients attempted to teach the reader. But with Tibetan Sage (1980) he was back at his childhood adventures, roaming the caves beneath the Potala palace and seeing visions of past and future, his faithful guru hovering beside him. As for The Third Eye, the book has never been out of print.

always fell'. Readers who cried over characters like Richardson's Pamela or Goethe's Werther, who admired Rousseau or Madame de Staël, spotted at once that there was something for them in Ossian. Melancholy might be as out of place in the 3rd century as were Macpherson's bows and arrows and other trappings of chivalry; but it inspired three generations of writers, artists and musicians.

Albert Abrams:
the 'distance healer'

In 1911 the American Medical Association was threatened with legal action by the author of a new book because they refused to advertise it in their official magazine, the *Journal*. The AMA backed their editor and the case was called off. It had been a quiet and respectable first encounter in what for the *Journal* would later prove to be a long war.

Dr Albert Abrams (1863–1924) had a faultless medical background. Born in San Francisco, Abrams obtained his degree from Heidelberg in 1882 and went on to study further at Berlin, Vienna, London and Paris. He returned from Europe to practise, then was appointed head of the medical clinic at Cooper Medical College in his home city. At some point in his mid-forties, however, he decided to change direction with his career.

Toward a system

By 1910 Dr Abrams had devised a new treatment which he called 'Spondylotherapy' and began touring the country to give instruction courses in it. The therapy centred on percussion (or tapping) of the spine, already a method used by osteopaths and chiropractors for back trouble. His courses at $200 were a success, as was his writing. The book rejected by the AMA sold out of five editions. In 1912 Abrams founded an association for the study of Spondylotherapy which evolved into the American Assocation for Medico-Physical Research, a focus for people who felt that orthodox medicine was letting them down. A house journal was published to spread the word.

With money and organization behind him, Albert Abrams could move on from tapping spines. It was the age of radio and telephony and to an inventive mind these demanded an equivalent in medicine. Abrams came up with the idea that the electron now supplanted the cell as a basic unit of biology. Though no one had stated it in such round terms, this insight was not entirely his own. Others already advanced the theory that disease caused changes in the electrical potential of the skin. The prime scientific requirement for any new theory – a means of quantifying or measuring its data – was close at hand if not yet quite achieved. Both the AMA journal and its British equivalent gave space to wave-theory discussions. Abrams drew on all this for a comprehensive two-part medical system of his own that in 1920 became known as ERA – the Electronic Reactions of Abrams.

Golden vibrations

Both parts of his system had a specific machine and the first task specified was diagnosis. If all disease came from a disharmony of electronic oscillation, then the Abrams 'Dynamizer' would detect and measure the fault. This apparatus performed diagnosis without the patient being present: a single drop of blood squeezed onto blotting-paper represented the entire individual. To find the 'vibratory rate' of the disease, the skin reactions of a healthy person had to be measured too. This person stood stripped to the waist, facing west, and wired in at the forehead by a lead running from the apparatus which housed the blood sample.

When all was set, the physician tapped the healthy person's abdomen to sound out 'areas of dullness': these determined the disease from which the patient who had supplied the blood sample was suffering, and its site. Abrams later managed without the blood – just the patient's own signature would do. He claimed that his machine could tell from an autograph the sex and even the religion of someone whom the physician had never met.

For ERA to be comprehensive there needed to be some kind of treatment. The second machine was an 'Oscilloclast', which worked by applying radio-wave impulses at the same frequency as that of the diagnosed disease. Disharmonies were vibrated out of even the most delicate tissue; this was far safer than using drugs. The Oscilloclast could treat eight patients at a time. They were given private cubicles in which they rested on comfortable couches as the 'units' were tuned to the 'wave' of whatever disease each arrived with. The affected sites were then neutralized by a dose of their own vibration. The AMA noted that treatment could be very lengthy. It quoted the case of a woman whose blood-drop sample had just been diagnosed to show she had cancer of the left breast. Her physician wrote: 'I am sure that I can help you. You would have to come to my clinic daily for from four to six weeks. My fee is $150 per month payable in advance.'

The two-part Abrams Electronic Assembly was leased on a franchise basis, not sold. A Dynamizer and an Oscilloclast each cost the lessee $250 per year, plus a postal start-up course at $200. Every piece of apparatus was securely sealed and the lessee had to sign an agreement never to open it. At ERA's peak in mid-1923, a lessee might take from $1000 to $2000 a week; an estimated 3500 machines were running that year. Abrams' personal wealth was put at more than two million dollars.

Before 1923, however, the AMA had gone to work to discredit Abrams. It encouraged its physician members to supply ERA operators with specimens of blood purporting to be from patients who were ill but which were actually taken from animals. (In that spirit, 'Miss Bull' wrote to her ERA operator in Albuquerque, New Mexico, who diagnosed her as having an infection of the left frontal sinus; 'Mrs Jones' was declared to be suffering from a skin ailment and stomach trouble. The samples for both women came from a male guinea-pig.) The Association broke open an Abrams box and found inside a condenser, a rheostat, an ohmmeter and a magnetic interrupter wired up to no purpose. Doctors were encouraged to trust their own eyes and skills: why rely on a drop of blood and a machine to diagnose tonsillitis or bad teeth?

Judgment

In its obituary notice for Dr Abrams, the AMA *Journal* called him 'the dean of all 20th-century charlatans'. From today's viewpoint, with many more candidates, the title is open to question. It may also seem cowardly of the AMA – if the doctor was that bad he should have been closed down.

To see authority as ducking the issue, however, makes everything look too simple. Wireless waves were believed to offer unique possibilities for medicine. Nor were they an American fad alone. The leading London clinician Sir Thomas Horder lectured on Abrams' methods in

1924 and briefed his physics colleagues to stay close to them; other top British doctors, including a BMA vice-president, worked with wave machines. Later developments gave good reason for authority to be shy of choking off new growth too hastily. By the 1960s diagnostic radio pills were in use throughout the world to bring to light diseases of the digestive system.

William Summerlin:
a man and his mouse

Dr William Summerlin (b. 1938) worked at the Sloan-Kettering Institute, New York City, during the early 1970s. His long-term research sought to find out why the body rejects tissue other than its own or that of a closely related donor. By 1974 he believed he had the answer to this problem of 'self' and 'non self'. A study he was running on mice claimed that if the donor tissue prior to being grafted is held for some weeks in a nutrient solution, this changes the composition of markers (proteins known as antigens) on its cell surfaces and makes the donor tissue more acceptable to the host – in less technical language, it crosses the immunological barriers. Summerlin's research was of great importance to the understanding of cancer, as well as to organ transplants and the grafting of skin after burns, and had been highlighted by his boss Robert Good among the many projects at Sloan-Kettering. His five-year grant application to the National Institute of Health looked to receive a total of $629,000 as funds.

Cosmetic change

One morning in March 1974 William Summerlin was making ready to go and see Dr Good. It promised to be an important session, a complete review of his work, in fact. At least the outlook for his funding was good. He could report a successful talk in Boston earlier that month – there was a chance of the grant application going through. But he was somewhat nervous about his current study.

From the cages in his lab Summerlin selected white mice that had been grafted with skin cells taken from black mice. A side-effect of culturing tissue in nutrient was that the cells could lose colour during the weeks of immersion: this seemed to have happened with the patches grafted onto the mice he selected. Today of all days, they must be seen to be taking well. As he stood in the elevator, Summerlin pulled a felt-tipped pen from his lab coat and touched up the patches to make them more distinctly black. Then, the ground floor reached, he went out into 68th Street and over to the building where Dr Good would be awaiting him.

The two men had known each other for some five years. In the 1960s Robert Good had done excellent work on bone-marrow grafts in children which, by involving an immune deficiency, could lead on to discovery of a cancer therapy. Recently, though, he had become an administrator, advising the President on cancer research funding. Good was new at Sloan-Kettering, having come to run the institute just eighteen months previously from Minnesota, where he had met William Summerlin. His young colleague had worked on burns, then on human skin grafts at Stanford, where he claimed that his new technique managed without the aid of drugs as immuno-suppressants. Good, always the talent spotter, prised him away first from Stanford and later (on leaving there himself) from Minnesota University.

Success pressures

New York was a big step up for the younger man. As the equivalent of a full professor, Summerlin now had an experimental lab and staff for his own work and was also the sister hospital's head of dermatology. Almost immediately on being appointed, Summerlin at a meeting of science writers sponsored by the American Cancer Society had announced his results from the human skin-graft studies, where they made headline news.

To back up this work on tissue acceptance, Summerlin had reported some exciting findings about transplants. Adrenal glands first nourished outside of the host were not rejected for at least six months. He also told of human eye corneas transplanted into rabbits: where the cornea slice had been grown in culture it was accepted by the rabbit and survived for six months, whereas when freshly-cut immediate transplants were made the animal rejected them. He showed rabbits which had one eye clear (the accepted graft) and one eye cloudy (indicating rejection). Robert Good moreover confirmed the grafts as edge-to-edge, that is, tied in to the host's blood supply and hence exposed to its immune defences rather than made in the centre of the host's eye and less at risk. Summerlin was obviously doing work of enormous potential.

However, by March of 1974 and Summerlin's review meeting several doubts were heard. Summerlin was a physician, not an eye surgeon. Even more damagingly he lacked a background in animal experiments: at Minnesota he had worked alone using his own mouse colony instead of strictly controlled pedigree animals. For some months reports had been coming in that other scientists were unable to replicate his successes when they ran identical experiments – a researcher in Summerlin's own lab had ready a paper saying so. Dr Good was therefore anxious for the meeting that day to reassure him about his protégé.

Summerlin's account of his work and the display of some of its results took forty-five minutes. Good barely glanced at the animals. When it was over, Summerlin went back to his own lab and handed the dozen featured mice to an assistant for return to their cages. The assistant noticed a difference in two of them: the black grafts were darker than before, and a quick scrub with alcohol at once showed why. He told another assistant about the ink that had come off; the information went to one postdoctoral researcher, then to a second; and finally back across the street to Robert Good's office.

No mix-up

As Good himself put it, there had been plenty of problems about Summerlin's science but until then he had never doubted his veracity. It seemed as though the man himself scarcely realised what he had done wrong. Summerlin did not deny colouring the mice he had just shown his boss. Nor was this the first odd incident. The previous autumn, others working on the corneal transplants had become convinced that rabbits he was showing as grafted in both eyes had in fact received only one graft (which no matter whether it was of fresh or of cultured cornea the animals uniformly rejected). Summerlin, told of their doubts, thanked his colleagues and carried on showing the single-grafted rabbits as double grafts that proved the success of his theory. This could not conceivably have been a mix-up on his part, if only because any animal given and rejecting a freshly-cut immediate transplant in one eye would have been in the lab for weeks while the cornea slice for its other eye was being cultured.

William Summerlin was put on temporary suspension that same March morning. In May a peer review committee (the usual internal inquiry by colleagues not involved in the matter) looked at all aspects of his work. He was offered and accepted a year's leave of absence on what were stated to be medical grounds. This marked the end of his research career. Summerlin now practises medicine in Louisiana.

Balance sheet

There is another point that belongs with our thoughts about the affair. The one surviving mouse to have a skin graft endure beyond six months, nicknamed 'Old Man', came with Summerlin from Minnesota and was a C3H grey onto which some skin from a white A strain mouse had been grafted. Old Man turned out to be a descendant of a cross between those very lines C3H and white A. Any hybrid will far more readily accept a graft from one or other of the strains involved in its crossing: the fact is elementary science. With this mouse so important to his work, we may wonder that Summerlin apparently knew nothing of its descent.

It is hard to decide where Summerlin's fraud most hurts science. He does not seem to have sought money or power beyond the needs of his project. His peer review allowed him a personal statement: Summerlin pleaded overwork from his twin office responsibilities and the added pressure of fund-raising on his own research. The committee did not ignore Good's role in that publicity drive, further remarking on his slowness to act on criticisms of Summerlin. But an institute's director has other things to do than police his colleagues. Amid the shared-out blame and fuzzy liabilities the truth may be that Summerlin was a researcher too much in a hurry, and that his fraudulent science was simply bad science made to carry too many expectations.

Cyril Burt:
intelligence expert

Psychologists have the job of explaining human behaviour. The life and work of one of them, however, only leaves more questions to answer. That man is Cyril Burt (1883–1971).

Burt came from a background likely to value scholastic achievement. His doctor father slaved in a struggling country practice; on his mother's side were Welsh grocery folk. Close by the Burts in Warwickshire lived some eminent families. There was Sir G. O. Trevelyan, the historian, and the family of Sir Francis Galton, a cousin of Charles Darwin. Galton started the branch of study he called eugenics and which is best known for its belief that ability is something that careful breeding can pass on. He has an important part in this story.

Cyril Burt won a scholarship to Oxford while at his charity-foundation school. He studied classics, though one university lab offered a voluntary option and he began some psychology. This led to work on a national survey – Burt's part had to do with intelligence – in which he met the psychologist Charles Spearman and a scientist involved in human measurement data, Karl Pearson. Both these men were developing new mathematical ideas about their subject.

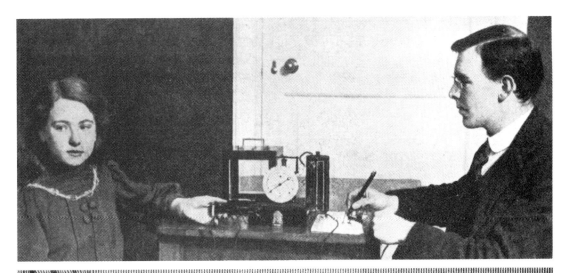

Cyril Burt (top) using a chronoscope to measure a child's speed of thought. Burt was in favour of intelligence testing. Today it is often intelligence itself that is seen as the greater fraud in his story. Sir Francis Galton (above) coined the term 'eugenics'. Its adherents claim that sound marriages produce gifted children. Galton strongly influenced Burt.

Dr William Summerlin (right) in 1973. Fund-raising for his important scientific work led him into experimental fraud. (Below) One of the mice 'coloured' with a pen in March 1974 to make it appear more clearly a successful skin-graft subject.

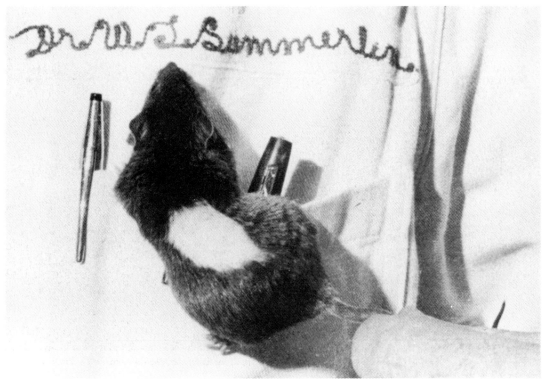

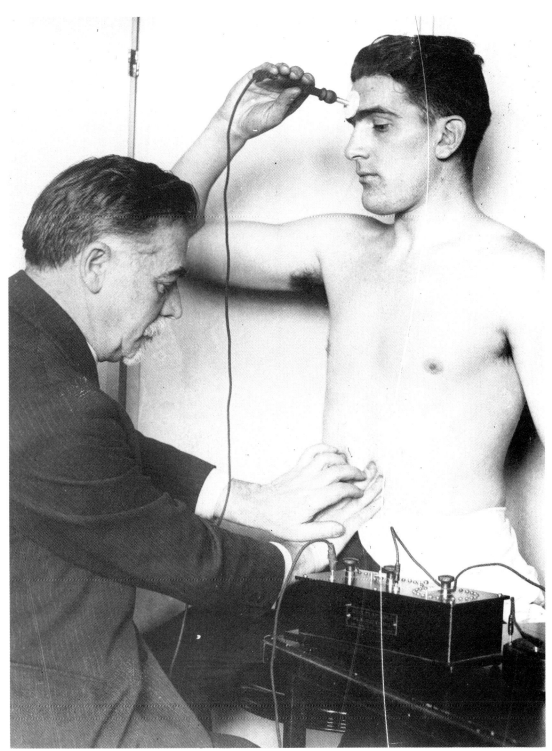

As his patient faces west, Dr Albert Abrams sounds out the 'areas of dullness', an essential item in his diagnosis. California, February 1922.

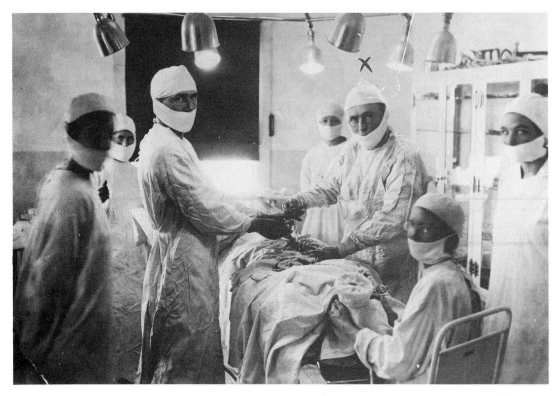

'Doc' Brinkley (above, marked 'X') performing a
goat-gland transplant operation at Milford, Kansas.
(Right) Brinkley with a patient in 1920.

There was a meeting with Galton too. In 1908 an award took Burt to Germany for some months, and sideline became main track for him from then on.

Psychology was itself a new science early in the 20th century and had to make many adjustments. Mendel's work on the units of heredity came to light in 1900. It led to a quarrel as to how far these units, the genes, determined or modified character. One argument saw them as robbing human development of other, more richly complex influences (factors) – Pearson's followers, for example, did not accept Mendelian genetics until the 1920s. Burt himself was an early convert to Mendel.

Positive certainty

Burt's main and lifelong mentor, however, was Galton. The core problem for the study of ability lay in the 'nature/nurture' question. Did ability result from heredity, or was it more a matter of environment, of a person's surroundings and upbringing? Galton had no doubt: it was heredity. He claimed a sound marriage resulted in highly gifted children in successive generations. Pearson gave this eugenics a different thrust, and pointed to mental illness, crime and depravity as the fruit of 'negative eugenics'. Galton stayed with the positive variety, claiming that his own studies showed both character and talent (key terms for Burt) to be inherited. Burt at once took this on board and by 1912 was applying it at his first academic position in Liverpool.

Cyril Burt saw that, if individual difference was now within the reach of science, then what science needed were tools of measurement. This involved pairs of twins, preferably identical twins, who have the same genetic inheritance. The idea was to study twins separated at birth, compare them with twins raised together and measure the individual differences.

After five years at Liverpool University, where his workload still left him time to devise new reasoning tests and run them at local secondary schools, Burt in 1913 took the post of psychologist to the London County Council's education department. The job was part-time and he had no assistants. He threw himself into a programme of testing the London County Council children, and on his own admission this programme cut some corners. His method and results went into a regional survey, into the classic *Mental and Scholastic Tests* (1921) and also a study of delinquency. He was very much a one-man band.

From 1932 to 1950 Burt was Professor of Psychology at University College, London. Reports speak of him as an excellent lecturer, good with the undergraduates but defensive and even hostile towards his graduate students. The British government sought his advice in the '30s and '40s when setting up the '11-plus' system of education. This applied intelligence tests at that age in order to assign children to one of three schooling levels. It was the door to meritocracy, to advancement for those who achieve. In 1940 Burt wrote *Factors of the Mind*, a book which dealt with a method of analysis pioneered by Spearman, his predecessor at University College.

A difficult man

Early in World War II the college department was moved to Wales and with it some of Burt's files (including the data on children). He continued to work at his usual relentless pace. Studies of twins appeared in the years 1943–66; he founded a new statistical journal, thus becoming a latter-day Pearsonite. But now he seems to undergo a change of character. He began a revision of *Factors* that played down Spearman in favour of himself. He faked letters to his own journal, and edited genuine papers in a manner that often outraged the authors of them. He ran a departmental colleague into the ground. Illness may account for some of this (from 1941 he suffered from Ménière's Disease, which affects the equilibrium) but not for all of it, and worse lay ahead for his reputation.

However, it was not until the late 1940s that Cyril Burt came under regular fire, and then as a result of the 11-plus system. The attack was usually on one of two fronts. It might direct itself at the intelligence test, disliked by sociologists for being culture biased and by left-wingers for being class biased. Or it might target what even his friends could see were his extremist views on the decline of academic standards and (after 1969) on race issues. There would soon be a third front for the assault on Burt, but this started only after he was dead.

Faulty figure-work

Imagine that each time you take a bus-ride you total up those passengers who are the same sex as you. To get a whole busful the same is unlikely; so is to get none the same. But the first case would show perfect correlation (written 1.0) and the second case zero correlation (0.0). You might expect the correlation to be around 0.5, and you would certainly expect this figure – as a coefficient – to differ with each separate busful of passengers.

In 1972, while reading Burt's studies of twins published over the years, a Princeton University psychologist noticed that some of the coefficients Burt gave for various separate groups of twins in the studies did not differ. They could even be identical to three decimal places. For example, in tests of intelligence one and the same coefficient 0.771 was shown for twins separated at birth, one and the same 0.994 for twins raised together. This was work that spanned more than twenty years, yet astonishingly no one had spotted the too-perfect match of these figures. It put Burt in doubt as a scientist. What it seemed to be saying was either that he had new data but did not use them to calculate fresh coefficients, or that in fact he had no new data for any calculations.

More doubts came to light. Did Burt test 'a thousand' Liverpool children, as he once claimed, or only 'over a hundred', his subsequent total for them? What happened to the follow-up tests he promised in 1954? And, with later material, why was it that Burt's methods of testing were only to be found described in obscure papers and theses?

To put the best face on this, it is possible that notes and data were left behind in files at college and lost after a wartime air raid. A recent book on the affair suggests that data were lost and later recovered, and that Burt acted as he did to save face for the person responsible. Nothing, however, can explain away the fraud of *Intelligence and Heredity* (1969), which gave test scores for a series of years ending 1955 and 1965 – impossibly, because neither Burt himself nor the London County Council ran tests at those dates.

In 1976 the *Sunday Times* declared Burt's co-authors for two of the twin studies (J. Conway and Margaret Howard) to have been invented. (Other papers appeared under J. Conway's name alone.) The recent defence of Burt suggests that here he may simply have wished to credit two pre-war assistants whom he had lost touch with, and goes on to say that he seldom gave his own role the prominence it deserved.

What effect

Judgment of Cyril Burt's guilt or innocence in all this ultimately depends on how we feel about his conclusions. He was the first psychologist to be knighted, and his immense influence shaped a whole generation. One of his former pupils, Professor Hans Eysenck, had Arthur Jensen of Harvard University as a postdoctoral student. In 1969 Jensen became a focus for America's second thoughts about 'headstart' or compensatory education. Headstart had set out to provide lower-class children with a schooling that would make good the deficiencies in home and environment which it was believed were holding them back educationally. But if ability was all about inheritance, what could such programmes hope to achieve? Jensen at once politicized the question (though he did not intend this and was widely misunderstood). Perhaps a meritocracy was always the only system?

Years ago Britain abolished the 11-plus system that Burt helped to establish. Today the world still has its share of people who would rather trust inherited intelligence as a basis for social status than anything else on offer. Against this are others who say that, even if Burt is allowed to have been right, heritability has no practical effect for teaching and education. The debate continues.

BACKHOUSE

For a century or more of modern China, the foreign business visitor has stood bewildered on Peking's dusty boulevards and wondered how to proceed. The native hosts clearly cannot be trusted. Those people at the Embassy all seem career diplomats with one eye on their next posting. Where is a true guide to be found, an all-knowing local expatriate who has real 'inside knowledge'?

Edmund Trelawny Backhouse (1873–1944), an English baronet's son, grew to be that man. Despite coming from Quaker stock he managed to run up debts of £23,000 from his wild living as a student at Oxford. He had a nervous breakdown there and did not graduate and in 1895 he was declared a bankrupt. Somewhere amid all this Backhouse learnt Russian and Japanese, so that when he reached Peking in 1898 the task of mastering the Chinese language did not seem too great. After only one year he was translating news items and documents for the Peking correspondent of *The Times* of London. Four years later, an impressively scholarly figure to the Chinese, he had been given a post to teach English at the new university and knew most people in the foreign business community of Peking.

One firm particularly anxious to work with China was John Brown & Company, shipbuilders, of Glasgow. The Chinese government had put the equivalent of £10 million towards modernizing its navy, and Brown sought a local agent who would

secure them contracts for the work. Edmund Backhouse was hired to do this. He said he knew a key Chinese politician who could help, but in 1910 this man lost the central position that would have made him of use. Undeterred, Backhouse continued to proclaim that Brown need only trust him (which included paying his large expense account) and the orders would come. This imaginary fleet was soon a joke in Peking. No ships were ever built and a contract for six coastal-defence vessels finally melted away in 1916, and with it the Brown agency.

Backhouse's greatest frauds took place during the early years of the Republic. The last effective imperial ruler of China, the Empress Dowager, died in 1908, an event that Backhouse reported for *The Times*. Thereafter he flitted between Peking and London with a variety of dodgy schemes.

Backhouse was also a knowledgeable collector of old books and manuscripts on behalf of the Bodleian Library at Oxford. but despite making valuable purchases for the library he was at fault in claiming these to be more valuable than they were. His own book, *China under the Empress Dowager*, written with J. O. P. Bland, centred on the diary of a court official that after much controversy emerged as a fake.

With the collecting, Backhouse may have been carried away by enthusiasm. No such excuse can be made for the affair of the secret China arms deal that he set up at the British Foreign Office's suggestion during World War I. Early in 1915 the Allied powers were left short of guns and ammunition following their first campaigns. Stocks of both, said the Foreign Office, might be obtained from China, where they had accumulated after the Russian–Japanese War some years ago. Backhouse went to work on his high-level Chinese contacts and on Sir John Jordan, the British ambassador. He arranged for 30,000 rifles to be shipped down the Yangtse river to the port of Shanghai and from there to British Hong Kong. By summer the quantity had swollen to 100,000, with three million rounds of ammunition. Telegrams went back and forth. The Japanese and the Russians were both involved so; in London, was Lord Kitchener at the Army Council, the Prime Minister, and the King himself. A hush-hush payment to China of £2 million was organized – everything had to be kept secret because of higher political considerations. But this shipment existed only in Backhouse's head. Eventually, after many months, a very few rifles did result from it, but no supply as ordered and no ammunition or ships. Sir John Jordan grew so exhausted and depressed that he had to take a year's leave of absence after the affair finally ended in November 1915.

Another Backhouse fraud had begun the previous year when he met George S. Hall, an official of the American Bank Note Company of New York. A deal to print 650 million Chinese treasury notes was in the offing, and Backhouse said that his closest friend, the powerful Duan Qijui, as well as the same Chinese politician who had fallen in 1910, could secure this for the company. Hall was delighted. He received a promotion on the strength of this order and by December 1916 had the contracts for the deal, which gave Backhouse £5600 as commission. Nothing more ever came of the business. Duan Qijui, by October 1917 Prime Minister, was shown the contracts and declared them forgeries. He said he had never met this man who claimed to be his closest friend, and moreover neither had the other politician whose name Backhouse used so freely.

At about the same time George Hall invested heavily in a second Backhouse scheme: a plot to steal the late Empress's most famous relic – her decorated pearl jacket – from the palace and then sell it. This scheme did at least come up with one pearl, but the jacket was ornamented with scores of pearls and where were they? Gone to London in the diplomatic bag, said Backhouse; next, he claimed they were in a bank vault for safe-keeping, or were being inspected by wealthy prospective buyers. After some months, Hall realized he had been cheated and went back to America hoping that he might forget he had ever met the man.

In later years Backhouse lived increasingly as a hermit and scholar in Peking, often on very little money. The fantasy life that had made it easy to fool gullible foreigners took him over as a 70-year-old. An example of this is his manuscript memoirs, one volume of which tells of an affair he had when he was a young man with the Empress Dowager herself.

The memoirs claim that in August 1904 he was summoned to feast and sport with the Empress, then 69 years of age, at her Summer Palace outside the city. The two days of gossip, rare foods, aphrodisiacs and sex are described in detail. This for China is indeed 'insider knowledge'.

'Doc' Brinkley:
goat-gland implanter

People whose job it is to check the qualifications which other people claim to hold do not often get thanked. This could, of course, simply prove that the system is functioning. Yet now and then, as in the case of John R. Brinkley, society might do worse than cry 'Three cheers for the Board of Registration'.

'Doc' Brinkley (1885–1942) could be the modern, all-American story. A man thinks up a great commercial idea, develops it in the free-market economy, and after working all the hours God gives is rewarded for his enterprise. That happened with Brinkley, although his idea to implant sex organs and to pump extracts into men wishing to revive or extend their capabilities was medically speaking not new. Extracts of testicle (known as the 'satyricon') were taken in classical Greece and Rome, and similar preparations continued in the Middle Ages. As the science of endocrines began, 19th-century France and Britain looked again at the possibility of rejuvenation.

What awaited Brinkley

Beginning in 1910, the Russian émigré Serge-Samuel Voronoff used testicular slice grafts in experiments on rams. The first transplant operation on human testicles was by Leo Stanley at San Quentin prison and for experimental purposes only. This got widespread attention. Others in America (notably two doctors in Chicago working on gland transplants) and a Viennese biology clinic, the 'Vivarium', did further pioneer research. Voronoff's book *Life* covered the general topic of transplants, and was seen in 1920 as contributing to a highly respectable area of medicine that could only get bigger.

Polite people spoke of 'the monkey gland' treatment, but John Brinkley by then had discovered that goats rather than monkeys made for a better operation.

Brinkley grew up in rural North Carolina. Several of his abortive attempts to become either educated or rich had an element of fraud about them (in one case he typed a letter about himself on stolen college notepaper). Even when he gained a degree in 1915 – the subjects were arts, not medicine – from a 'diploma mill' in St Louis all was not right with it. The shabby little institution could show no record of his ever studying at the place, and he bribed the registrar to backdate the award by two years. This was to help his next plan: to go to the Eclectic Medical University of Kansas (the course took one year) and persuade the authorities there that his St Louis degree could be put towards its diploma. The plan worked, and he had his diploma in three months. After this it was a matter of finding a state that recognized the Eclectic Medical's qualification (Arkansas almost alone did so), getting that state's medical licence, and seeing to it that Kansas would issue its own licence to him under the reciprocity rule.

His paper-chase completed, 'Doc' Brinkley settled in Milford, Kansas, in October 1917, where the 200 inhabitants acquired a drugstore as well as a physician. Brinkley knew country folk and what they wanted. He may well have been just the physician for them: reports agree that his medical knowledge was sound, his store kept useful drugs and that he stayed up to date on new forms of treatment. These included the gland implants at Chicago.

Billy – and beyond

Two months after his arrival in Milford, Brinkley did his own first graft, using a goat as donor. The patient had been sexually dead for sixteen years; a year later he was the proud father of a baby he and his wife named Billy. By the following summer Brinkley had built a hospital to take graft cases, and soon became in effect a full-time transplant surgeon. The choice of goats was well reasoned. Goats are less prone to transmittable diseases (where monkeys will pass on tuberculosis and VD). Their testicles are small and can be implanted whole rather than as slice grafts. They are easier and cheaper to obtain in the mid-West than monkeys, and symbolize sexual prowess there ('I'm a regular billy-goat', a Real Man will say of himself). Brinkley knew goats, and chose the Toggenberg variety as having a more tolerable odour.

Details of how operations at his Milford hospital were performed are hard to come by. Women might receive treatment too. But cases whether male or female were never written up for publication, so most of the facts only emerged later at court or other institutional hearings. As experienced by patients, the business angle was uppermost. Those who came in on a Monday were usually out by the Friday. On arriving, they had a first examination by an assistant, then were given a bed and their bill. Fees averaged $750 for the standard goat transplant, $2000 if the testis was from a human donor. Implantation was made high up, near the spermal cord, and probably went to one side only, where the duct known as the *vas deferens* left the testis. This duct would be cut, the extra gland incorporated and the *vas* then retied. Brinkley was showman enough to drop in a little mercurochrome (it added an interesting dark colour to the urine for a few days), also to attach a nearby artery and nerve to the testis which he touted as boosting its blood supply and potential. Medically the effect of this was nil, but then the whole operation (at least when the donor was an animal) lacked a genuine medical outcome except whatever psychology could provide. This is because the body's immune system ensures that, after the blood vessels grow in, any animal tissue will be rejected on being grafted, leaving only a scar.

Unqualified success

At its peak, the graft business employed everyone in Milford. Brinkley was an early example of the modern mail-order salesman. He ran his own radio station (by 1923 a thousand-watt affair with preachers, lecturers and orchestra). The broadcasts fed the mail-orders. Men seeking rejuvenation were addressed on the air, very early in the morning when they would probably be attending to their physiological problems and thus be receptive to Brinkley's message. As many as 2000 letters a day went out, each one followed up with details and chasers. Meanwhile the slaughter of goats had to keep pace with this.

Brinkley made great use of testimonials. Some of these reported good things only, but others were less friendly and he had political enemies. The local newspaper *Kansas City Star*, and later the journal of the American Medical Association, began exposing Brinkley's claims and qualifications. While on vacation in Europe in 1925 he had obtained the degree of doctor of medicine (the exam was a mere formality) from Pavia; the university decided to annul that award. Then in 1929 the Kansas State board of medical registration and examination moved against him with a lawsuit.

The case opened in July 1930 before the State Supreme Court. As well as investigating Brinkley's degrees, the court looked at what was claimed to be his lax professional conduct, his overcharging, alcoholism and felonies. In the event these additional matters were hard to prove, and the Board had a difficult time with them while Brinkley played the man of the people whose right to a livelihood was being threatened. The medical climate was on his side too: gland transplants were orthodox, and his lawyers found supportive quotations from Voronoff printed in the very best journals. However, the Board had a cast-iron case with Brinkley's bogus qualifications. These, added to the fact that surgery was involved, made it inevitable that Brinkley lost his licence.

He was not yet finished in Kansas, however. There was an election for governor that autumn and Brinkley entered belatedly as a 'write-in' candidate (a peculiarly American custom whereby the voter must add the name to the ticket by hand, written exactly as specified). His campaign was slick, and made full use of modern communications such as air travel. He only lost because 50,000 votes were spoilt.

'Doc' Brinkley continued in medicine and broadcasting, first in Texas and then at a vast new glass and chrome clinic in Arkansas. He owned three yachts and rented the biggest of them to Edward VIII and Wallis Simpson for their honeymoon. His income stayed above $1 million until in 1938 he had a bruising encounter with the American Medical Association (which he sued for calling him a quack). The case greatly damaged him; and by then human implantation and rejuvenation were anyway things of the past. He hung on for a while in Little Rock, Arkansas, always just starting or ending some legal action, until a heart attack struck.

GRAHAM

A bed is a bed is a bed. It rests you, makes you feel warm and secure, and it may help ease the odd pain. Some beds are better than others, but the basic offer remains the same. How different from the car, which sells on the promise of life enhancement and exciting personal growth. No such promise comes with a bed.

For a brief three years James Graham (1745–94) tried a new sales angle. His special bed *did* promise personal growth: those who slept in it would have children.

James Graham was born in Edinburgh, the son of a saddler. He studied medicine, apparently without qualifying; married in Yorkshire and ran a business there. Then, still probably not yet 30, he made his way to America. Benjamin Franklin's work with electricity was already known. 'Dr' Graham met the discoverer both in America and later in France, and by 1777 was using electrical treatments for his rich and eminent patients (they included Georgiana, duchess of Devonshire) in the West of England and subsequently in London. These required them to sit on a 'magnetic throne' in a bath and to take 'aetherial medicine', various balsams and dry friction. It was very much the age of electricity.

Late in 1779 Graham settled in an Adams house at the Adelphi in London which he named the Temple of Health. For a two-guinea fee visitors could wander through ten magnificent apartments hung with mirrors, sculptures and paintings, music sounding all the while. Graham's lectures with pretty girls as demonstrators could be attended in the Apollo Room. There was the elaborate 'medico-electrical apparatus' to inspect and medicines to buy. Emma, the future Lady Hamilton, might be glimpsed in the role of a glowing young Goddess of Health. But the main attraction, kept in a separate room with its own door to the street, was

the Grand Celestial Bed. Graham drew on furnishings of a Turkish harem for inspiration. His bed stood twelve feet long by nine wide (3.6m × 2.7m), supported by forty pillars of coloured glass. The domed canopy released spicy fragrance into the air; there was music from automaton players who moved their hands and instruments in time. Occupants of the bed, when they looked up, saw themselves reflected in a huge mirror. They slept between silk sheets, on mattresses 'filled with sweet new wheat or oat straw, mingled with balm, rose leaves, and lavender flowers'. Sometimes (we are not told when) the mattresses might be made from 'the strongest, most springy hair, procured at vast expense from the tails of English stallions'.

For its scientific effect the Celestial Bed relied on lode-stones, fifteen hundredweight of magnets wired up in circuit. Magnetism was all the rage, and like stallions' tails probably offered nothing more than the power of suggestion. The bed frame itself, however, was built to allow the bed to be put automatically into a tilted position, which did have some medical reasoning behind it. It was generally recommended that after coitus a woman wanting to conceive should lie still for as long as possible, to give the sperm a greater chance of impregnating the egg; holding an angle of tilt that matched the sperm's flow might indeed help with this. Certainly Dr Graham's sales promise was clear. He guaranteed 'superior ecstasy' – the barren would assuredly become fruitful. A single night in the Celestial Bed cost £50 (some clients were said to pay much more) and brought 'immediate conception to any gentleman and his lady desirous of progeny'.

If we go by one account, the Adelphi Temple grew so popular that new and larger premises had to be found. Another states that it was too costly. Whatever motive Graham may have had, by the spring of 1781 he himself, the girls and all his equipment were installed in Schomberg House, Pall Mall. A play satirizing him was on at the nearby Haymarket

Theatre. To help counter this, Graham subtly altered his style and handled the relaunch with a blaze of publicity. Prices were cheaper at the new Temple of Hymen; larger premises allowed a 'grand Elysian promenade'; and the Bed now assured its patrons that they would have not simply children but *better* children – 'beings rational and far stronger and more beautiful in mental as well as bodily endowment than the present puny, feeble and nonsensical race'.

A French visitor to Pall Mall noted something else important. The doctor lectured for two hours daily on how to avoid barrenness, 'using the plainest language in dealing with the parts concerned in generation, yet ladies as well as men crowded to hear him without a scruple'.

Eighteen months later Graham was deeply in debt, and although he continued his lectures the rest of his show was sold off. In the summer of 1783 he moved north to Edinburgh, where the magistrates banned his 'improper discussions'. Graham was tried for this, released on bail, and straightway lectured again, his audience paying the fine. His latest theory was that all life came from the earth and was dependent on the earth. By taking 'earth baths' one could live for 150 years. He and a young lady 'stripped into their first suits' and were then buried in earth up to the chin, their heads dressed and powdered, looking like 'two fine fully grown cauliflowers'. But Graham also found sensible things to say about excessive meat and alcohol, about the wisdom of cold baths, open windows and sleeping on straw and disease being caused by wearing too many clothes. James Graham practised what he preached, wearing little during a Scottish winter. This, and a bout of fevered religious mania helped on by opium, hastened his end.

Dr Graham may have been a quack and a swindler, but he understood people and their needs. Sound human judgment lay beneath the nonsense. He was far ahead of his time in seeing sexual problems as matters to be openly discussed. Sex counsellors of the 1980s were not the first to recommend pornographic pictures to partners who have lost interest in sex and a change of coital position to women who cannot get pregnant. It seems that the prolonged orgasm reported by some friends in America – who used a trial version of Graham's bed – was what made him take his invention further:

> They talked not as other men might have done of the critical moment – no, they talked of the critical hour.

The salesman in him eventually led to exaggerated claims and left him to be seen as ridiculous, but by the 20th century such matters had reached the agenda of genuine medical care.

Trofim Lysenko:
creative geneticist

Moscow, September 1965. It was fitting that he should be caught by this particular group of men. As well as scientists, they were managers and accountants. Soviet science for more than a quarter of a century had been in no position to strike back at Lysenko: now, a verdict of 'economically unsound' showed that things were changing.

Parents and offspring

Genetics is a fundamental science: it resists being told where its explanations begin and end. It teaches that a characteristic, such as the ability of one plant to come through a particularly hard winter much better than its neighbour, is due to a change (mutation) in a gene, that is to say a packet of information, on the plant's chromosome. A mutation in a germ cell (one that is responsible for reproduction) will be passed on to the plant's progeny.

Now mutations are random events, and may change the character of the plant for good or ill. There is nothing purposeful about the process. But natural selection will see to it that the

A small-sized version of the James Graham Celestial Bed which is was claimed would cure infertility.

(Above) Dr Graham giving one of his Edinburgh
lectures. When in 1783 the city magistrates banned them
as improper, his audience paid the fine and Graham
resumed them.

(Opposite) The moving spirit of genetics, Gregor
Mendel, in about 1870.

The spiritualist William Roy arranged for William
Gladstone (1809–98), above, to speak to MacKenzie
King, the Canadian prime minister, about Britain's hard
times during World War II.

MacKenzie King (right) was an ardent spiritualist. He
was also put in touch with Queen Victoria.

plants which have acquired a characteristic that is advantageous to their survival – in our example, the ability to survive a hard winter – will increase in number, compared with those that do not have their advantage. This is the Darwinian principle of the survival of the fittest. The cold-resistant survivors will breed and the mutated form of the gene will spread through the population.

This picture of nature as driven by a random, seemingly capricious process did not fit in well with the Marxist–Leninist ideology that reigned in the Stalinist Soviet Union. Nature had to be amenable to the will, and so the opposite view to Darwin's, that of the French biologist Lamarck, held great attractions. (According to Lamarck, the long-necked giraffe was that which tried harder: it stretched its neck in striving to get to the topmost leaves and then passed its acquired trait on to its offspring.) In consequence Soviet scientists were put under pressure to conform to what many saw as an outdated theory, if not as unscientific rubbish.

One man at that time was allowed to tell Soviet genetics where it began and ended. Trofim Denisovich Lysenko (1898–1976) rose to prominence at a time in the '20s when poor harvests and sub-standard farming left his country under-fed. Crops were being grown only in those areas where tradition said they grew, and agriculture needed a stronger lead from the scientists, too many of whom were seen as academics interested in theory rather than practice.

The watchword

Lysenko's first success was with 'vernalization'. This consisted of pre-soaking and pre-chilling seeds of winter wheat to allow planting in spring, not autumn, and thus to get a bigger yield. Russia knew about this method already and had researched the theory. What Lysenko did was to extend the practice not just to all varieties of wheat but also to other crops, potatoes in particular. His notion of it made vernalization the trigger of plant growth and reproduction. Hormones were unimportant.

The man was lucky with his timing. Stalin's ever firmer grip on power came just as Lysenko's own rise was taking him from an agricultural station in the Caucasus to an institute at Odessa, and soon after to the Moscow genetics laboratory. During the next four years the Communist Party moved against 'bourgeois' scientists, particularly those who had studied in the West. For a while genetics escaped: its fault-lines were unclear, people in the same lab disagreed on fundamentals, there might yet be a useful debate. After 1935, however, those scientists who followed Mendelian genetics, and orthodox Darwinism with its belief that members of the same species competed with each other, were given the label of 'class enemy'. This made them look like capitalists set against Stalin's call for a fully productive socialist agriculture. It allowed Lysenko to speak directly to the farmers.

What he told them through the two journals under his control sounded productive enough. Once beyond explaining matters to do with vernalization, he issued orders: how to develop new areas for this or that crop, what chemicals to give it, where to site a shelter-belt of trees, when to irrigate. There must be no plant and livestock breeding for true hybrids of two varieties; instead, follow a cross-fertilization within one and the same variety. In fact, such commands were meaningless because they had not been properly tested in field trials. The farmers soon discovered this, but their dilemma, although profound, could hardly be said to match that of the scientists.

Power and ignorance

Lysenko's schemes for agriculture had no real theory to call on. All he could offer (and that

ROY

The spiritualist William Roy (b. 1911), born William George Holroyd, also known as Plowright, ran the successful Hampstead Psychic Centre in London during the mid 1950s. He had gained some knowledge of electrical circuitry while working at a telephone exchange, and an assistant denounced him for putting this to use in his earlier seances. A period away in South Africa had followed. By 1955 Roy was back in London. He had had some good times during and just after World War II, when his 'Direct Voice' delivered messages to some 100,000 British supporters, but now his methods were at their best.

Clients did not just walk into the Hampstead bungalow where Roy conducted his seances – an appointment was required. Roy limited each session to twelve people, and researched his often wealthy visitors in advance via sources such as newspaper cuttings, electoral rolls and the registry of births and deaths. In his waiting room clients left their coats and handbags while chatting together before the seance. The chat was monitored by an assistant, who later went through their belongings for other personal information to pass on quickly to Roy.

This required a backroom microphone connected to the earpiece worn by Roy during the seance. He also carried a miniature loudspeaker on the end of a telescopic rod that could place sounds – recorded special effects, his own voice, that of his assistant or a ghost, or some other source as though coming from any part of the room. This operated when copper plates beneath Roy's shoe made contact with wired-up carpet nails on the floor. The voices would talk to clients individually about their interests, hopes and fears, the product of his research into them. Unshakeable faith in the spiritualist could be aroused by his hinting at some simple fact that he knew about the client. Direct messages from the departed would come via Roy through a speaking-trumpet covered with luminous paint and held aloft in the dark room so that it seemed to float. He worked in the name of a 'spirit guide', often 'Tinka the Red Indian', who took the blame for any gaps in knowledge that arose. Music and lighting were deftly blended. To suggest apparitions Roy used masks and an 'ectoplasm' of buttermuslin. Attendance at a seance cost between £10 and £12.

Roy's greatest triumph was when the Canadian prime minister MacKenzie King (an ardent spiritualist) spoke with Queen Victoria and her minister Gladstone. The conversation was banal: a watch formerly owned by Her Majesty, and Mr Gladstone on 'these grave times for Britain'. When Roy put his Canadian visitor in touch with family relatives, their more intimate talk relied on the same standard homework procedure. This never failed.

Spiritualism tends to flourish in or near a time of war. It comforts the bereaved to think they have contacted a much-missed loved one, and in the 1950s (as in the 1920s, another good time for the cult) such bereavements were recent enough. Roy earned some £50,000 from his career.

Attempts to entrap William Roy were unsuccessful. He was wired at the larynx, strapped with tape across the lips and wrists and made to hold a mouthful of coloured water throughout a seance (this he drained away via a tube into a bottle, later sucking it back up again). Eventually he started defamation proceedings against the magazine *Two Worlds*; Mrs Roy had earlier attacked its editor with a riding-crop. Suddenly, in February 1958, Roy withdrew the action, whereupon the magazine decided to risk publishing its complete file on him. A national tabloid newspaper followed up the story and Roy sold out with a full confession. He defended his trickery by emphasizing that many clients left him happier than he had found them. All he did was to give people what they wanted.

only after several years) was a bastardized 'creative Darwinism'. One of the few Westerners to encounter Lysenko said that talking to him was like explaining the calculus to someone who did not know their twelve times table. Yet the man soon won unrivalled power. He was made president of the Academy of Agricultural Sciences in February 1938 and director of the Genetics Institute in 1940.

In consequence Lysenkoism became a crisis for Soviet biology. Opportunists learnt to handle it but for the rest it was a choice between professional suicide, half-hearted compliance, or a life on the high wire juggling non-science and genuine science. Arrests, banishment, prison could be the outcome not simply for one scientist but for his or her colleagues too. Nikolai Vavilov, an international figure who had studied abroad with William Bateson, managed to compromise until 1940 and then was charged with, among other things, spying for England. In his case not all the colleagues were loyal: three of them testified against him and he died in prison during 1943. Even though the authorities did not set out to fight Mendelism or back Lysenkoism with state power, the effect was as though they did this. Whole institutes closed down. It has been shown that by 1948 there were seventy-seven geneticists and other non-Lysenkoists who had experienced some degree of repression, and 300 who had been forced into work outside their field. August of that year brought Lysenko to the pinnacle of his career. He chaired an eight-day session of the Agricultural Academy at which his address when reported took up much of successive editions of the Party newspaper *Pravda*. The proceedings were printed in a mass-edition booklet. Only a handful of geneticists (seven, by one count) dared speak against him and his sycophants.

The next decade brought a Soviet leader even more at risk with agriculture than Stalin had been. In the mid 1950s Khrushchev launched a programme (the Virgin Lands scheme) that aimed at putting whole regions under the plough for the first time in their history; the thrust of Lysenko's work had a similar purpose, so the leader's future was linked to his own.

Exposure

Khrushchev fell in October 1964, but although Lysenko had gone from the Genetics Institute by February of the following year it was hard to mount a sustained challenge against him. His placemen were still in office and many scientists wanted compromise of some kind, a show of order. The effect on biology teaching had to be considered too. At last, however, after persistent reports critical of one Lysenko research station in particular, an official inquiry team went there to investigate. The place was an experimental farm studying Jersey cattle on the Lenin Hills above Moscow. It sought to verify a typical mid-'50s Lysenkoist claim, namely that the butterfat content of milk could be raised by crossing large domestic cows with small Jersey bulls whose female offspring tended to give very rich milk. (The reasoning behind the claim was rubbish, on lines of the cow's germ cell 'choosing' to develop in the Jersey direction.) In reality the fat content of milk from cross-breeds is dependent on the inheritance of both parental lines. But the farm's reported butterfat yields did appear to have gone up, and the previous February, with Khrushchev's support, Lysenko had insisted that his scheme be adopted nationwide. Already thousands of farms were using it.

In September 1965 the inquiry found the Jersey station to be a fraud and Lysenko's herd of cows a showpiece. There had been deliberate falsification of data. The animals were specially selected and given highly intensive diets, hence the rich milk; however, even these ideal conditions could not stop their total milk yield from falling as the fat content went up. The cows also lost weight, so breeding them for beef was no answer. Management was censured for setting the farm low targets, later reduced still further to give impressive results. The scheme was mistaken and its adoption a cause of serious loss to the country.

Lysenko was furious. The inquiry had been fooled by rumours, its report was a slander on him. He did not deny the facts so much as the interpretation of them. However, none of this slowed the momentum of what was now rolling: the progress of Soviet biology toward rewritten textbooks, new programmes for the agricultural colleges, and teachers with the self-respect to face their class.

Name, date	Inventor/Company	How sold
Hostetter's Celebrated Stomach Bitters (later 'Stomachit'). From 1853.	Dr Jacob Hostetter. The Hostetter Company (Pittsburgh, PA).	Testimonials, billboard ads, journal The Almanac (15 million copies in 17 languages).
Kickapoo Cough Cure. 1881, peaking 1890–1912.	'Doc' John Healy and Charles H. Bigelow. The Kickapoo Indian Medicine Company (Worcester, then New Haven and Clintonville, MA).	Indian medicine shows in small towns. Shows and cures (cough cure one of several) then franchised via rental fee plus royalties. Kickapoo were remnant of sub-tribe of former Lake States Indians (but others used in shows).
Oxy-Tonic. 1910?	Oxy-Tonic Company (Chicago, IL).	Ads. 'The World's Greatest Pick-me-Up'.
Paine's Celery Compound. After 1872, peaking 1880–90.	Mrs Paine of Boston, MA. Wells & Richardson Company (Burlington, VA).	Pamphlet series Great Things identified Paine's with other great achievements of man, eg Discoveries, Bridges.
Pepsin Anodyne. 1900?	Dr J. C. Fahey.	Small ads.
Peruna. Peaked 1900? Restriction on contents c. 1920.	'Doc' S. B. Hartman (Columbus, OH).	Testimonials. US Number 1 in its time.
Plantoxine. After 1906.	Edward W. Crittenden. Plantoxine Company.	Small ads. Package stated 'guaranteed under the Pure Food and Drug Act 1906'.
Radam's Microbe Killer. 1905. Federal seizure 1910.	Dean, Swift & Company (Washington, DC).	Small ads. During a second vogue c. 1910 was pushed hard, especially in New York City and on Pacific coast.
Yonkerman's Tuberculo-zyne. Peaked 1905?	'Dr' D. P. Yonkerman. The Derk P. Yonkerman (Company) Ltd (London, England; Kalamazoo, MI).	Brochure, massive ads, impressive letterhead. 200-page book and sample sent free.

America's Pure Food and Drug Act became effective in 1907. It covered false and fraudulent claims made on the label, packaging and accompanying sales literature of a medicine. Not until 1938, however, was the label required to list all the active ingredients and any side effects.

SWALLOW THAT?

Effect claimed	Analysis
Anti-bilious remedy for colic, constipation, 'the intermittents' (ie fever). Drives humours out of the body, purifies the blood.	47% alcohol (reduced to 25% by Pure Food and Drug Act), cinchona bark, gentian root, orange peel, anise.
Possesses properties recognized by the medical profession as necessary to the proper treatment of diseases of the lungs. (Fined by AMA for not possessing these.)	sugar, glycerine, vegetable extractive, aromatic bodies, inorganic salts and undetermined matter, in water and alcohol.
Treats common cause of 48 distinct diseases or ailments. Tonic germicide that revitalizes all weakened cells and tissues, completely purifies the blood.	no more oxygen than is natural to common water, but sulphuric acid, a poison, in larger proportion than any other ingredient except water (0.1633% sulphuric acid, 0.1377% sulphurous acid, fixed solids (ash) 0.0191%, volatile solids 0.541%).
Permanent cure for nervous diseases. Coca found in the mountains of South America, used by aborigines and considered by them to be an incomparable nerve tonic.	21% alcohol, celery extracts, hops, coca.
Pacifies the most fretful child.	per ounce: 2.5 grains chloral hydrate, 0.1 grains sulphate of morphine.
Cures catarrh, the basis of all disease.	28% alcohol (reduced to 20%, later to 16%), herbs, senna, later formula has potassium iodide.
Corrects abnormalities of the system which create undue susceptibility to miasmatic diseases, plant pollen, *la grippe*, chronic malarial disease, hayfever, etc.	100% milk sugar.
Cures cancer, consumption, diabetes, diphtheria, yellow fever, paralysis, gonorrhoea, syphilis, leucorrhoea, falling of the womb.	99.381% water, sulphuric acid 0.59%, sulphurous acid 0.016%, inorganic matter (ash) 0.013%.
Treats consumption, catarrh, bronchitis, asthma. (UK: the only known remedy for all forms of consumption).	'No 1' treatment: 12% glycerine, 3.4% potassium bromide, tincture of capsicum 0.17%; oil of cassia 0.1%, caustic soda 0.06%, a very small quantity of alcohol, water to 100%. 'No 2' treatment: 18% glycerine, oil of almond 0.1%, burnt sugar to colour, water to 100%.

Herbert Marwitz:
one man and an eagle

An expert's opinion on the genuineness of a work of art finally comes together from a finger-tips' feeling about it. Only the daily experience of handling very similar art objects will allow this reliance on instinct to be trusted. If strong outside pressures are applied to the giving of an opinion, the instinct, not surprisingly, may falter.

Eastward

Alfred Rosenberg's massive book *The Myth of the Twentieth Century* offered Hitler what looked like historical excuses for his push eastward. This push sought to bring 'outsider Germans' back into the empire. Rosenberg believed that the supremacy of the Aryan Nordic peoples was seen less clearly in blood ties than in their disposition to be creative. The Northmen, somewhat like the ancient Greeks, were people with a genius for setting up states and civilizations. Wherever in Dark-Age Europe this activity, this culture-forming disposition, was found, there would be the Goths, the Germans. Rosenberg's main scientific prop was the elderly academic Gustav Kossinna. German prehistory for Kossinna rested on weapons finds and a love of fighting (in 1914 he was delighted by the coincidence of one of his books going to press on the day that war broke out).

Rosenberg thought that Hitler would welcome this doctrine. In fact the Führer needed no such excuses to annex the Sudetenland and other areas. He called Rosenberg's book rubbish, but nonetheless put the man in charge of the Eastern Affairs Ministry. This greatly annoyed Himmler, who saw himself as responsible for laying the racial foundations of the New Order in the east. Himmler ran the SS. Rosenberg at his Ministry ordered historical research on Germany to conform to his own beliefs. Along the power lines that ran outward from this split between the two men were two rival journals of archaeology: *Germanien*, a mouthpiece of the SS, and *Germanen-erbe*, edited by Rosenberg's ministry and its National Society for German Prehistory.

Proof of genius

In 1936 a Munich art dealer, Herbert Marwitz (1884–1954), came up with what looked to be an exciting find obtained from a source in Czechoslovakia: an eagle brooch of perhaps the 6th century AD, 24 carat gold inlaid with polished garnet-like stones, said to have been found at Königsberg in the Sudetenland. He showed it to the art historian Frederik van Scheltema. Dr Scheltema was one of the Rosenberg group of historians. The following year he wrote about the brooch enthusiastically in *Germanen-erbe*, not mentioning Marwitz. The eagle was 'one of the finest examples of early German East Gothic art'. Happy with this endorsement, in 1938 Marwitz let Scheltema handle the sale of the brooch to the German National Museum at Nuremberg for 30,000 marks.

That same year Marwitz persuaded another expert to write in the journal *Germanien* an article endorsing a large haul of Norse treasures allegedly found at Szirák in Hungary. These included a fine gold plate-disc which Scheltema also authenticated, saying that it came from Gotland in the Baltic Sea – an area that for Kossinna and his followers was the Aryan heartland. Clearly Marwitz had a use for art historians; but they were not always quite so obliging, as he soon discovered.

The National Museum began to have doubts about its eagle brooch. Walter von Stockar, a prehistory chemist at Cologne, was given it to examine. Stockar saw fresh file-marks on the gold plating, and showed by analysis that the surface crust of mineral deposits (for Scheltema best evidence of the brooch's authenticity) was a concoction of natrium silicate, whitener and sand. Aniline dye had been added to give this crust a greenish look, as though from the bronze pin after centuries in a peat bog. Also, the faker had left embedded in it a bristle from the brush he had applied it with.

Hans Zeiss, Professor of Prehistory at Munich, joined the investigation as an art historian and expert on jewellery of the brooch's Merovingian period. Despite all his objective skills in dating such work, in calling to mind items that were housed in museums possibly thousands of miles away, Zeiss would always trust his instinct. He disliked the Königsberg brooch from the start. It had been put together without understanding. Its outline was stiff, the inlay work crude, and moreover that round garnet-like stone for the eye was very unusual in the jewellery group to which the eagle belonged. Later, when a goldsmith pointed out that the bird's edges were made of drawn wire thread, Zeiss felt vindicated. Such thread was modern, and it gave modern fakes their bland look of uniformity.

Marwitz by now had fled to Italy. Fraud proceedings against 'a person unknown' were started by Stockar personally and by the police. Marwitz was brought home, a house search revealed more doubtful finds, and these went into court with the other items as exhibits for his trial. Still no one knew who his source might be; but both the Königsberg eagle and the Szirák hoard were shown to have used a respected third party as their means of sale, and Marwitz to have 'bought' these endorsements. In March 1940 Marwitz was sentenced to five years in prison and loss of privileges from his baron's title (faked too, though the court did not know) for the same period.

Genuine – by order

It might seem with this that a grubby episode was closed. However, Frederik van Scheltema, his reputation badly dented, was not of that mind. In 1941 he returned to the authenticity of the brooch. He claimed that Marwitz, a basically honest dealer, had merely sought to protect his Czech source in withholding the owner's name, and for that same reason the false surface crust had been added to conceal the brooch's priceless value on its way to Germany. That bristle had been from a toothbrush Marwitz had used to clean off some of the crust. And the modern aniline dye? Nonsense: would so perfect a fake want to risk using that? Scheltema demanded and got a commission of inquiry, Rosenberg's ministry noting ominously that 'an irreplaceable work of our Germanic art heritage' stood in danger of being lost because of 'false judgments by experts'.

The commission, packed with members of Rosenberg's German Prehistory Society, included some doubters but they were won over as the inquiry proceeded. Hidden below the brooch's large central stone was found a cross worked in gold relief. While this discovery, by suggesting an early Christian convert as the brooch's first owner, cannot have best pleased the Ministry of Eastern Affairs, it did make the eagle more authentic for the commission of inquiry. The item was genuine – indeed it ranked as 'one of the finest and most valuable pieces of gold jewellery known'.

Herbert Marwitz, sitting out the war in jail, may have chosen not to protest too loudly at this reversal of judgment. No new hearing was begun. The SS anyway had their own reasons, after the Szirák fiasco, to want Marwitz punished. In 1942, however, the reversal itself was overthrown. Stockar published his long-delayed report on the gold used to manufacture the Königsberg eagle. Chemical analysis showed it to be of far too good a quality – somewhere between 'fine gold' and 'spectrally pure' – for the brooch's stated date. In antiquity, gold always had some silver and copper added to it. To make gold of a quality such as the brooch possessed would take the best modern refining equipment. Stockar's technical expertise was unanswerable: the Königsberg eagle could never fly again.

Hero

With the coming of peace in 1945 German prehistory was able to adjust to a genuinely scientific course once more. Two of the characters most involved with the eagle, however, carried on as though they had done nothing wrong. Marwitz retrieved most of the treasures faked for his Szirák hoard and attempted to sell them for $350,000. Both he and Scheltema claimed they had been victimized by the Nazis in 1940 at a show trial. There was at least a grain of truth in this. The Munich chief public attorney revealed that his court had been pressurized both by Rosenberg and by Himmler officials during the eagle hearing, though he added that the SS were less interested in Marwitz and more in having some of the exhibits declared to be genuine.

In 1949 the missing piece of the jigsaw turned up almost accidentally. A goldsmith named Luitpold Pirzl, trying for a job in conservation, announced himself as Marwitz's supplier. He had drawings and photographs to prove it, among them one of the Königsberg eagle taken before the stones had been inserted. Not even this evidence could finish off Scheltema. The brooch he had written about was a different piece, he said, just as the gold plate-disc as illustrated in his *Germanen-erbe* article of 1939 was not the same as Pirzl's. ('But if I faked my brooch without seeing his genuine one, how could I have matched it so exactly?' asked Pirzl disarmingly.) Pirzl revealed that he had also made a twenty-eight-piece treasure hoard deliberately aimed at the leaders' Nordic tastes. The Nazis paid no attention to style comparisons; only hard-science data concerned them. They had been sure the eagle was genuine.

Hans Zeiss, the Merovingian expert, was killed in World War II and so missed this turn of events. In holding out against Marwitz's finds he ran greater risks than Stockar, who at least had hard science behind him as well as a powerful journal. Zeiss had been more outspoken, both in attacking Scheltema point by point during 1940–42 and in defending his own working methods, than any other specialist involved. This might make him dangerously unpopular in high places, but no matter. For Zeiss, either you allowed an opinion to be compromised, or you expected to be asked for complete professional integrity. He leaves behind him a feeling that while the Königsberg eagle story may not deserve a hero, to tell it without one would not be telling it right.

The Königsberg eagle-brooch was faked in Nazi Germany to support the view that an early German culture had shaped the region of Czechoslovakia known as the Sudetenland. Two years later, in 1938, Hitler would annex that region.

Alfred Rosenberg (right) ran Hitler's eastern affairs ministry, but Heinrich Himmler (below with glasses) as head of the SS believed that responsibility for the 'New Order' in the east was his. Their rivalry corrupted German historical research for ten years, and left it open to a series of fakes planned by Herbert Marwitz.

The media lay siege to Clifford Irving (above), as his fraud unravels early in 1972. What finally broke him was the coincidence of one name sounding like another.

(Left) The subject of a controversial biography: Howard Hughes in a 1947 photograph.

Two men who studied how successive generations of the same species adapt. Charles Darwin (1809–82) (above), and the Austrian Paul Kammerer (right). However, it was shown that Kammerer's published work had used fraudulent experimental results.

Elias Alsabti:
the instant scientist

On an average day, over 3000 science papers appear throughout the world, printed in journals that reach every lab and library where the topic is a relevant one.

At its best this is a service: the spread of information within a group of people sharing common needs and ideals. Seen in another light, however, it is a machine grown too large and hot for the delicate tasks set it by management. Certainly those who write can find that the publishing process, a matter of reputation and career if not also of the funding of their research, soon becomes grubby. At the end of it all, who reads the paper? The fact of being published is enough. You went through the machine and are now on record with your work.

Any system can be fooled. The rules whereby scientific papers are sent in for approval, commented on by referees and credited to their author and any co-authors are well known. They rely on the same trust that applies to lab work. Although often dented (a 1976 survey by *New Scientist* magazine showed 92% of its sample had experience of lab data being fudged) this trust is seldom broken for long. And when it does break, the perpetrator is traced.

Ticket to America

The Iraqi researcher Elias Alsabti (b. 1954) completed four years of a course at Basra Medical College. When he announced that he had devised a new test for cancer he was moved to Baghdad for his final student years and given his own lab to run (which he prudently named after the party in power). However, charging a fee to those who took his test and pocketing the proceeds soon got him into trouble. By early 1977 Alsabti was in Jordan. Here he claimed to have brought useful things with him from home: medical qualifications, more cancer expertise and (no less pleasing to his hosts) a bad name politically. All enemies of Iraq were welcome visitors. Alsabti made and exploited a contact with the Jordanian royal family. Soon, tall and white-suited, he was on his way to the USA with a government grant.

This pattern of claim then became Alsabti's style at a half-dozen or more American medical centres. While Temple University, Philadelphia, were looking into his degrees he announced that he had found a vaccine for leukaemia, but none of the detail he was asked for made scientific sense. At Jefferson Medical College in the same city he spread word that he was the victim of unfair treatment, a foreigner who happened to be related to Jordan's royalty, and won the sympathy of Dr E. F. Wheelock. Later he was caught faking experiments, and had to end what he subsequently called his postdoctoral research at Wheelock's lab.

Moving south in late 1978, still without qualifications but with a more secure visa status following his marriage to an American lab assistant, Alsabti secured for himself a six-month project at the M. D. Anderson Hospital in Houston, Texas. Shortly afterwards Jordan became alerted to the stories being told by its 'royal' protégé and stopped his grant. He remained in town, finding work at another hospital and putting the clinical data this gave him towards an MD degree (obtained from the American University of the Caribbean). Around this time, however, the magical letters 'PhD' started to head his credits: Alsabti was never one to rest on his laurels.

By mid-1980 Alsabti was a resident researcher at Virginia University, Roanoke. He owned a white Cadillac and a house. He had sixty published papers to his name. Even now, as the science world was learning that these papers were not his own, he managed get himself a few weeks on a programme at Carney, a hospital linked to Boston University. It was his final known job.

Paper output

For any scientist of ambition, the first essential is a good biography or curriculum vitae. This document touches a forelock to the powers that be. Its typed sheets, splendid with honours won at this institution and posts held at that, must be rounded off by a list of personal publications which is at least two pages in length. Alsabti's c.v. had always begun well (those brilliant degrees, the name of Jordan's surgeon-general Hanania among his sponsors). It took only a year in America to teach him how thin his list of publications was. At Houston in 1978 he started to fill it out.

First Alsabti would take a published paper by someone else, change the title-words a little, put his own name and perhaps that of an invented co-author onto the paper, and send it off to another journal for publication afresh. If the journal were out of the way, say in central Europe, that was good enough; but detection even by computer search was anyway not likely, given his change of the title. Then, with confidence, he grew more enterprising.

A researcher at Anderson (who had in fact died some years previously) was sent a paper to referee for the *European Journal of Cancer*. The manuscript of the paper sat uncollected in a mailbox until eventually Alsabti took it up, made his usual alterations, and sent it to Japan. What had earlier been 'Suppression of spleen lymphocyte mitogenesis in mice injected with platinum compounds', by Daniel Wierda and Thomas L. Pazdernik, now became 'Effect of platinum compounds on murine lymphocyte mitogenesis', by Elias A. K. Alsabti and others. The Japanese journal came out some time ahead of the European one. Daniel Wierda, then a PhD candidate at Kansas University, found that his whole thesis, his research data and their 'priority', had gone. 'I went into a depression for a week', he says of the episode.

Alsabti had an odd way of repaying favours. On leaving Philadelphia and Dr Wheelock, he stole from this man, his former ally, a copy of a grant application Wheelock had made and some other papers in draft form. These became three more c.v. items for him via Czechoslovakia, Japan and the USA. He was caught only when one of Wheelock's students noticed the Czech version and how closely it followed the American, but even to be found out did not much upset Alsabti. On this particular occasion when charged with the thefts he simply threatened a legal action of his own. Another piracy, however, was less easily carried off. It was foolish and risky: he took the name of General Hanania for one of his invented co-authors. When this came to light it contributed to his losing the Jordan grant.

Recent years have not found Dr Elias Alsabti on the science scene. He did little lasting harm there. A measure of a published paper's value to science is how often others refer to it (a Citations Index exists to count the number of times they do so). Up to the time of his world exposure in 1980 not one paper that he pirated was cited by another author. This of course suited his purpose, but it must alter the case a little for the better.

Cosy club

Only when we look further does this scandal reveal some bad loose ends in the science system itself. Had the young Daniel Wierda raised too loud an outcry, for example, he might have been charged with stealing his own research. What chance then of a PhD? Dr Wheelock was more securely placed and held all the cards, but nevertheless found it hard to go public with his experience of Alsabti. He asked one of the journals concerned to print a retraction (the effect of this is to make a paper null and void) but was refused. It was 'not policy'. Three of the four highly prestigious journals he then went to, including *Science* in America and *Nature* in Britain, declined to publish even a letter by him, considering the affair a private quarrel between two scientists. *The Lancet* alone saw things differently, in 1980, and a flood of similar horror-stories followed once the water was over the dam.

IRVING

The early 1970s were perfect timing for the idea that Howard Hughes, the American billionaire recluse, should have a biography. He was the richest man in the world, richer even than Paul Getty, yet no one had interviewed him in thirteen years and few people any longer knew what he looked like. Furthermore, one of his companies had the sole function of killing off Hughes biographies before they could appear.

What made him so topical now was another of his companies, the airline TWA. During the '60s a group of its major investors tried to bring Hughes to court. They wanted him punished for what they saw as his mismanagement of the airline. Hughes let his private lawyer do the explanations, but ended up having to pay $145 million damages and costs. The ensuing shake-up of senior Hughes' staff generated weeks of bad publicity. Hughes remained invisible – there were rumours that he was ill or dead – then suddenly left for the Bahamas. He just could not get out of the news. At the end of 1970 a handwritten letter he had sent to two survivors of the shake-up was reproduced in magazines. Among those who studied this handwritten letter was Clifford Irving (b. 1930).

Irving, a writer with several books to his name, was at home on the island of Ibiza planning his next novel for the publishers McGraw Hill when a different idea took shape in his mind. He contacted a fellow writer, Richard Suskind, who lived within reach. They met and talked and soon three letters were at the McGraw Hill offices in New York. Howard Hughes, prompted by a small kindness from Irving and by once having met his father, sounded interested – it could be said even warmly interested – in Clifford's becoming his biographer. What did they think? Irving asked his publishers. Should he take on a Hughes biography, or stick with the novel?

No questions could be more naïve. The mere thought of such a project was enough to set a fire under any publishing house. McGraw Hill told Irving to follow up at once. He had two quick meetings with Hughes, went back and forth to New York setting up research facilities, and by late March had become one party in a contract worth $750,000. As author, Irving took his share ($100,000) as an advance on royalties which when all was accounted for – paperback rights, translations, film versions, et cetera – might well come to two million dollars. The book was to be based on tape-recorded interviews with Howard Hughes that Irving would obtain and then (together with Suskind) flesh out into a full biography or autobiography. Everything was to be timed so that *Life* magazine could publish extracts starting early in 1972. Soon, security mania had set in on the project. For example, Irving was given the run of *Life*'s files on Hughes, but no one at the magazine was allowed to verify the manuscript they would so soon be handling.

Irving and Hughes met almost one hundred times between February and December 1971, generally in motels and parked cars somewhere in Latin America or the southern United States. The transcript of these talks delighted the small group allowed to read it, but obviously amid the euphoria some caution was necessary. The original three Hughes letters were given handwriting tests ('Careful study has failed to reveal any features which raise the slightest question', said the less confident of the two reports); Irving himself, on delivering his complete text, took and just survived a lie-detector test.

So there it was, the finished typescript. What convinced everyone that this was genuine, whether like the journalist Frank McCulloch they had known Hughes personally or whether like the book's publishers they were looking for a good read, was the ring of its tone and content. The text offered Hughes the man, the business secrets, the bizarre anecdotes from his days as an aviator, Hollywood director and engineer, all rattling along in the earthy arrogant style that such a narrator would use for them. McGraw Hill heaved a sigh of relief. It made the cheques they had paid out (each one now back duly countersigned 'H. R. Hughes') seem like money well spent. *Life* were so impressed they planned to begin their serialization with Irving's own story. That Hughes about now should telephone McCulloch to deny both the story and the book was taken as proof that both were genuine. Clearly Hughes's lawyers had become nervous.

Then suddenly – within twenty-three days during January and February 1972 – the project unravelled. A Swiss bank announced that 'Mr' H. R. Hughes, its new account-holder, was a woman. A reporter from *Life* went to the trouble of timing what Irving had stated were his movements during one particular busy meeting-day with Hughes: the timings were impossible, no one could move around that fast. And Jim Phelan, a freelance writer who some years previously had worked on memoirs of Hughes by a former employee that never got published, suddenly realized where Irving had found some of the best stories for his book: they were in Phelan's own draft. He flew at once to New York and confronted Irving's editor at McGraw Hill. Together the men sat down and cross-checked both versions. The fit was too close to be coincidence.

By a curious trick of fate, Irving already believed

he had been caught using this source. A fortnight earlier McCulloch and another reporter became sure that they knew the identity of Irving's link to Hughes. He was a man named Meier. The reporters called on Irving (who by now was near to getting round-the-clock legal scrutiny), were told he was unavailable, and left a verbal message saying to tell him they knew about Meier. This was a shot in the dark, and off target; but as received it was a bombshell. The previous summer Irving and Suskind had got their hands on the manuscript Phelan was trying to publish via a wheeler-dealer agent whose name was Mayer. All Irving now heard was the name spoken. Later the same day the two reporters called again, and Irving, assuming that they knew about his source, finally cracked. The woman H. R. Hughes, he said, was his wife.

By this stage people all over America were wearing T-shirts or lapel buttons sloganizing the affair. It took some weeks to run down, but by June the Irvings and Suskind had been charged, tried and sentenced, Clifford Irving to two and a half years imprisonment, the others to a few months only. What is of permanent interest about the case is that Irving himself, with no special claim to penmanship and no experience, should have done the faked letters. He found them easy. 'Once you have the mood', he said, 'you can go on forever.'

Paul Kammerer:
the fraudulent toad

A Soviet film of the 1920s, *Salamander*, tells a story of fraud and false accusation in the world of science research. The film's young hero, a biologist working in central Europe, has just proved that salamanders learn to change their colour markings to match the background of the box he keeps them in. Soon he proves something more important: this ability is heritable, it will be found in their offspring too.

Plotting with an aristocrat (who works as the hero's lab assistant), a villainous priest decides that this discovery threatens the existing power structure and must be suppressed. The two men pay a night-time visit to the lab. Later, when the hero is about to conclude his speech before a formal audience of his university by demonstrating his specimens, the assistant removes one salamander from its jar and drops it into water. All the colour runs out. A scandal then follows, the hero is declared a fraud and expelled from his post. He is seen begging on the streets with a monkey from his lab. Eventually one of his former students, a Soviet girl, finds him and at once knows what to do. She takes the train to Moscow, where a powerful commissar orders that this victim of bourgeois persecution be saved. Meanwhile, however, the hero had decided that all is over and is preparing to end his life as the girl returns. She is just in time, and together the two ride off to what a banner seen from the train proclaims is 'the land of liberty'.

Why the fittest survive

As propaganda this film had more of a message than its crude plot apparently conveyed. In the Soviet Union science was expected to take the lead, to offer truths that would support the key Marxist concept of dialectical materialism. (This concept shows the dialectic – a stalemate of two opposed interests – creating a position new to them both as the point from which to move forward.) Science obligingly supplied data that, in the eyes of some people at least, represented truths able to uphold the Marxist concept as requested. These findings indicated that what is learnt during one individual's lifetime (the acquired characteristics of that individual) may carry over to the next generation. You are a weightlifter, so your children will be born with big muscles.

This theory of transmitted characteristics was not originally Marxist. The Frenchman Lamarck devised it in the 18th century, and it went into the long debate on evolution that Darwin's *Origin of Species* added to in 1859. If indeed the weaker members of a species died out, some process must allow the fitter ones to survive. Darwinites pointed to 'variation' (the sum total of preferences guiding natural selection) as being that reason. However, for many scientists inside and outside Russia this was too much like chance. You might as well look to a supernatural cause such as religion. Lamarckism continued to have its supporters, who said that a new environment created needs that gave rise to habits, and that these habits were what was heritable. Unless you believed this, the scientist's lab was indeed just a prayer chapel. The debate became greatly confused. Each side accused the other of arguing in a circle or missing the point.

Music and animals

It was the Austrian Paul Kammerer (1880–1926), a biologist and supporter of Lamarck's theory, whom the film made into its hero. Vienna at the start of the 20th century enjoyed a remarkably rich cultural life. Art and science spoke to all classes of society and were accessible to amateurs. Kammerer, who when awarded his doctorate in 1904 had already been on the professorial staff of his university's experimental biology institute for two years, was also a gifted amateur composer. The idea that he could go with his musical ideas to so eminent a man as Gustav Mahler, then director of the Vienna Opera, and be listened to seemed perfectly natural: it was only what he himself would do for a fellow-enthusiast. Kammerer was a socialist who believed that science belonged to ordinary people. At the age of 43 he took his pension and spent much of his remaining years away on lecture tours in Europe and North America (which he visited twice). Then in 1925 came a call to Moscow, where he was to continue his research into inherited characteristics.

What prompted his belief that acquired characteristics were heritable came, as in the film, from his work with salamanders. He kept black ones and yellow-marked specimens in boxes of opposite and of self colour (for example, black in a yellow box and black in a black box) and claimed that the offspring they bred had markings that did not follow the pattern set by genetics. This was controversial enough; but his downfall came with another experimental animal, the toad.

One particular toad species known as *Alytes obstetricans* (the 'midwife toad') usually breeds on land. Its hands lack the thick dark pads of the water-breeding species, in which the male toad must grasp the female's slippery body when mating. Such pads are rough and pigmented. Kammerer found that after he had kept several generations of midwife toad away from dry land and forced them to mate in water, their hands too developed these pads. He further claimed to find pads in the midwife toad's male descendants at birth, that is, transmitted to them.

An invitation to Moscow

Similar work to this was occupying the Soviet physiologist Ivan Pavlov at the same time. With Kammerer so politically their man, it was easy for the Russian science administrators to approve Pavlov's suggestion that the Austrian should be asked to set up and run a research institute for biology. Kammerer accepted, and began putting together equipment he would need.

Sometime before then, however, his experiments, whether they involved salamanders or toads, the praying mantis or the axolotl, were beginning to raise suspicions. As early as 1913 an assistant confessed that he had not kept proper records. Another assistant (Alma Mahler, taken on as a kindness after her husband Gustav's death) would tell a more alarming tale. Some animals she removed from the lab and kept at her home for the experiments, where they would startle visitors who met them unawares. Her own notes were done very exactly, she said, in fact Kammerer would have preferred 'slightly less exact records with positive results'.

One obvious human problem for work on change down the generations is the long time that it takes to show through. Paul Kammerer was a man in a hurry. During a lecture he gave at Cambridge, England, in 1923 he spoke about the damage that World War I had done to his breeding programme, adding: 'I am no longer young enough to repeat for another fifteen years or more the experiments with the results of which I have been long familiar, before I attempt to break new ground.' As a comment on the midwife toads, this was misleading: the last male survivor had died before the war – a great loss, since it was the males that showed the transmitted characteristic of padded hands. Furthermore, although the results might be long familiar to Dr Kammerer, other scientists were still looking for solid evidence of them. A leading British geneticist, William Bateson, had been waiting for years to see adequate photographs of the toad experiments and now felt fobbed off with excuses. He criticized Kammerer from the audience at Cambridge and later in writing: the one midwife toad specimen displayed had indeed a mark on its hand, but this was in the wrong place, and also smooth, not rough as it should have been.

More than suspicious

Bateson's article in the journal *Nature* that summer sparked off a lively correspondence. Where were Kammerer's controls, for example? (A properly designed experiment also tests several subjects that fall outside its aims and purposes.) From Kammerer came words not likely to help his case:

> I willingly admit that the traditional explanation of the pads, namely that they are produced by friction with the skin of the female, may possibly be a fable. But it is by no means impossible (though of course not proved) that life in water produces the pads.

As for getting good photographs taken, well, life in post-war Austria was difficult. Although Bateson did not let him off the hook, Kammerer's work on acquired characteristics was published the following year, with a photograph taken at Cambridge, and matters rested there.

In August 1926 Dr Kingsley Noble of the American Museum of Natural History gave the affair an entirely different level of seriousness. He reported a number of tests that he and the head of the Vienna institute where Kammerer worked had run on Alytes. In that one midwife toad specimen seen at Cambridge the dark area of its hand on which so much depended was shown to have contained Indian ink, not the animal's pigment. The skin of that area was not rough, although it appeared under test lighting to have been altered to seem so.

This all pointed to a clear experimental fraud on a matter of crucial importance to the experimenter's theory. The exposure devastated Kammerer, but he did not acknowledge the deception as his own doing. As to the possibility of someone else being responsible, Kammerer would not go on record. 'Who besides myself had any interest in perpetrating such alterations can only be very dimly suspected', he wrote on 22 September to his would-be hosts in Moscow. The Russian invitation had to be turned down. For his part Kammerer hoped that, since his life's work was now wrecked, he would tomorrow summon up 'enough courage and strength to put an end to my wrecked life'. That next day, on a hill outside Vienna, he shot himself.

Whatever the truth about Kammerer's guilt or innocence, and about what seems to have been a strong flavour of the amateur in his scientific methods, the debate on acquired characteristics and heritability did not stop with him. Kammerer was given martyr status by the Soviet science establishment on his death, and echoes of his scandal could still be heard throughout the world years later. The story has a great deal of irony. As a letter he wrote to *Nature* conceded, it could be their life in water as much as their copulating that grew pads on his toads – a latent possibility, genetic in origin, needing only the right environment for it to emerge in the individual. And he did not in fact see this Alytes experiment as best proof of transmitted characteristics (sea squirts would do better).

That is one irony. Another involves Soviet science. Kammerer's theory, at the time of his invitation, attracted only one quite small group of Lamarckians in the Soviet Union. The great Pavlov himself was having second thoughts about it for his own work, and indeed 'bourgeois' Western genetics still held on as the flourishing branch of study it had been before the Revolution. Within ten years, however, distorted by ignorance and politics, the acquired characteristics theory was back. It was this theory that very nearly destroyed Soviet biology for the 20th century.

FEATS AND COUNTERFEITS
MONEY

Counterfeit money is as old as money itself, and counterfeiters today face challenges that have not altered since ancient times. Artur Alves Reis set out the tasks in planning his Portuguese bank note fraud: the forger must create a perfect product together with a flawless distribution system for it, and in so doing must stay beyond reach of the law. Reis himself achieved only the first of these. In World War II Bernhard Krüger planned to flood Britain with forged currency, failing on the count of distribution. When the war was over, José Beraha's sovereigns recorded a hundred-per-cent success.

Mankind's attempts to get round the entire monetary system appear to be more recent in origin. Tino de Angelis used receipts for a commodity stored in his warehouse to raise funds from New York loan institutions. In Paris, Thérèse Humbert did the same with the paltry contents of her bedroom safe. The Italian Carlo Ponzi enjoyed brief fame and riches from a coupon available over the counter at any post office.

Electronic transfers and credit cards still leave the conventional forger in business today, but soon his trade will be too expensive for amateurs like Charles Black or Brian Katin. Computer fraud is a new growth-area involving data systems rather than human beings, a situation that can only change.

Thérèse Humbert:
woman with a will

Four children were born to the French peasant Aurignac at Beauzelle in the Haute-Garonne. Of these, the plain elder daughter was Thérèse (?1860–1917). Her two brothers Emile and Romain separated her in age from the younger girl Marie. All three – Marie in particular – would become stooges for Thérèse in a colossal fraud.

After their father's death in 1874, mother Aurignac opened a linen shop at Toulouse. The likelihood of Thérèse ever making a good marriage was slim. Working as a laundry-maid, short and somewhat fat, the girl knew better than to look for romance. The father, a great teller of stories, had promised all of them riches and fame when on his death the family coffer could lawfully be opened and its contents revealed. When the time came the coffer was empty. So much for promises, said the girl. This episode helped form the resolute personality that many found compelling in her.

Great expectations

A windfall occurred when Thérèse was about 20. By her own telling of it, some while back when she was in a train at Nice an American passenger had been taken ill. She had saved his life by acting quickly (this had risked a fine for moving into the 1st class section) and had continued by nursing the man through to convalescence. Now news had come that would make her a rich woman. The American had died and left millions of dollars to her in his will.

Among the Toulouse households her mother supplied with linen was that of a prominent government minister, Gustave Humbert. The son Frédéric Humbert, a lawyer like his father, had already fallen under Thérèse's spell, and the windfall probably ensured their marriage.

The American Mr Crawford left not one will but two wills that interlocked. Thérèse was assured an annual income. The sum that funded this income, however, came from a legacy split three ways between Thérèse's sister Marie and two of Crawford's nephews. The entire estate was to be invested in France, and no part of the capital was to be touched until Marie's 21st birthday; even then, one of his nephews must marry an Aurignac before distribution of the estate could proceed. Meanwhile a third document, as the American lawyers read it, required all the bequeathed title-deeds and securities to be assigned to the young Monsieur and Madame Humbert and kept under seal.

Thérèse installed a fireproof safe in her bedroom at the splendid house she and her husband had bought in Paris. She hired a provincial magistrate to act as notary, showed him several outer packets in the bundles of securities that made up the 100-million-franc legacy, then got him to sign a list as the repackaged bundles together with all title-deeds and other papers went into the safe. Thérèse thereupon had wax seals applied to the outside – another item for the notary to sign to, as the American nephews insisted that she would forfeit all claim to the estate if the safe showed marks of having been opened ahead of Marie's 21st birthday or of any due time beyond that date.

Spend, spend, spend

Thanks to this legacy, the couple were now enormously rich in terms of what they could borrow against. Thérèse loved spending. She had acquired a fashionable Paris address to entertain the smart, rich and talented, and she also had the use of three country places together with a huge steam-yacht. When in town the Humberts took up their box at the Opéra and dined at the best restaurants; her annual bill for dresses and hats was in five figures. Frédéric liked to paint a bit, or fish. His heart was not in the legal profession. For Thérèse, a day that did not include some new loan to negotiate or some fresh turn in the legal complications of the wills was a day lost.

In all she borrowed on her legacy an amount in the region of fifty million francs. With reborrowings, the actual money passing through her hands was said to approach 140 million dollars. The sheer size of these loans kept her financial system going. It ensured that no one lender alone would dare to call Thérèse, for example on a promissory note she had given or on a long-overdue interest payment she owed, if by so doing he might put at risk a financial institution in which he or his associates had other interests. Money breeds money. One banker known to be willing, like M. Girand, to lend seven million would encourage another banker to go at least one million. The Humbert contacts in Parisian grand society needed only to be hinted at for the stiffest door to open. Every Deputy, every former President of France, every distinguished foreigner who once attended a shoot or a dinner, or even merely wrote to acknowledge a charity donation from the couple, was kept on record as a name worth dropping.

A few very simple tools built and maintained the system that Thérèse operated. Letterheads for companies that did not exist, faked documents of the kind that bring in other, genuine, papers took care of most problems. Thérèse's two brothers usually signed these faked items. For the legal aspects there was always Frédéric, but other lawyers in both France and America advised: not even Thérèse could deal single-handed with the complexities of inheritance law. The faked items were good enough to pass scrutiny by others.

Silencing doubters and fending off creditors might follow a certain pattern but never became a routine. The Humberts invested in property and often confidence was restored on sight of a list of their holdings, all clear of mortgage. Marie, the trigger of Crawford's estate settlement, did not live at the Paris house except during her school holidays. As she approached her 21st birthday, various snags could be offered as standing in her way and delaying distribution of the estate. Perhaps the Crawford boys were squabbling over her, or their lawyers were making trouble, or yet another will might have come to light and be rumoured to have upset the existing arrangements. Only with more money would such problems be solved. If these excuses failed and a big creditor simply refused to go away, Thérèse conveniently fell ill. Or she might pay off the troublesome person with real money and then enjoy an upsurge of her creditworthiness when the news leaked out that someone had caught her in funds.

Thérèse's final ploy, used very infrequently, was to stage-manage a private inspection of the safe. She would lock the bedroom doors, swear her visitor to silence, then open the safe by sliding a hot knife beneath its seals to allow a glimpse of a packet or two of gilt-edged securities or a quick scan of the complete and notarized list of contents. She swore the visitor to secrecy. No word of this must get out. Those who asked about the Crawford millionaire and his family were usually on the safe side of the Atlantic, except for one Lyons banker who made enquiries while in the United States that had discreetly to be silenced. If a Crawford nephew was required to come to France, one of Thérèse's brothers could act the part for a day.

The skill Thérèse showed in winning over powerful financiers commanded wide respect. However, her way with the little people – rentiers, small shopkeepers, concierges – showed another side of Thérèse Humbert. To provide a source of income for when the day of reckoning would come, she set up an insurance company named the Rente Viagère and put Frédéric and her brothers in charge of it. This funded itself from its clients' premiums and deposits, which were left unsecured. As cash-flow management this was a machine for perpetual motion. The annuity business formed Rente Viagère's largest side. Investors in tens of thousands received a brochure that skilfully appealed to old-time French virtues of piety and thrift. Annuities were paid promptly at the company's smart offices on the rue Auber. Rente Viagère used its incoming payments (they exceeding forty million francs over the ten years for which it ran) to build a name as something special and better suited to the elderly or less well-off. When the company collapsed, these clients stood in tears before its closed doors, their life savings gone.

Breaking the seals

This particular swindle, though itself without a fairy-tale ending, at least signalled the beginning of the end for La Grande Thérèse. A senior official at the Bank of France had both a public and a private reason to doubt her. Wearing his official hat he was entitled to check on what securities Rente Viagère had banked for its deposits. On discovering there were none, he let his private reason (in the shape of a father-in-law who was financially implicated in the

Madame Humbert ('La Grande Thérèse') at the height of her powers. No one dared tamper with the vast interlocking framework that supported her financial empire until the prime minister of France leaked information in a series of articles.

(Opposite) The Italian immigrant Carlo Ponzi and his wife. His fortune was made in one year, 1919–20.

(Above) Allied's salad oil tank farm at Bayonne, New Jersey. The photograph shows only one section – just how much oil was or was not stored there took the court fourteen months to establish.

(Right) 'Tino' de Angelis, president of Allied Vegetable Oil.

BANCO DE PORTUGAL

ENDEREÇO TELEGRÁFICO
BANGAL-LISBOA

CODIGOS TELEGRÁFICOS
RIBEIRO, LIEBER'S, BENTLEY'S
A. B. C. (5.ª E 6.ª EDIÇÕES)
PETERSON (2.ª EDIÇÃO)

SERVIÇO DE NOTAS*

N.° 13

E 7 ᵇ - 14

*Pede-se ao destinatário
que dirija a resposta a esta
repartição, fazendo nela
referência ao número e
data desta carta.

BANCO DE PORTUGAL

GABINETE DO GOVERNADOR

PARTICULAR

(Above) On the left is the Bank of Portugal letterhead; on the right is the forged letterhead designed by Artur Reis.

Sir William and Lady Waterlow in 1929 (right), before the second, 'Waterlow', trial that followed from Reis's 500-escudo bank note fraud.

Crawford story) hold him back from reporting this. Rather than take such a risk, he and some others who doubted Thérèse went to the prime minister, the lawyer Waldeck-Rousseau. The group decided against a direct attack. Instead, Waldeck-Rousseau leaked to *Le Matin* newspaper the details for a series of articles exposing the Humbert empire. These newspaper stories raised enormous interest, though of course Thérèse and her lawyer du Buit denied every word in them and threatened to prosecute. Having spent some years on such cases in Thérèse's defence, however, du Buit now looked to respond differently. His client had for too long been stalling her legal advisers, who were running out of loopholes. It was time to open that safe: Marie had long since had her 21st, and any more fears that by acting before due time Thérèse might forfeit the estate now lay within the power of French law to remove. Amazingly, lawyer du Buit seemed to believe the inheritance story; Thérèse was trapped by her own adviser.

Two days before the date appointed for the opening of the safe, a fire broke out at the Humbert residence. Thérèse, sister Marie, her menfolk and her daughter Eve promptly decided to take a foreign holiday. When the safe was opened on 10 May 1902 it was found to contain genuine securities: the outer packets totalled all of 5000 francs in value. The remaining contents were worthless – old papers, a coin or two, an empty jewel case. The family had left for Spain. No one knew how to contact them; meanwhile perhaps the Crawfords might be found. Du Buit had one address for them on Broadway, Thérèse another at Somerville, in Boston; legend said that the millionaire himself hailed from Chigago. No trace of the Crawfords, at these places or elsewhere in America, was ever discovered. The runaway Humberts themselves were not caught for seven months, when finally the Madrid police traced them to rented accommodation and saw to their extradition to France.

Their trial occupied half of 1903. A February hearing charged the family with libel against an Armenian money-lender. Thérèse, speaking in her southern accent with a lisp, handled this: she easily made the man look ridiculous, an extortioner. Attacks on usury always did well, the Armenian lost, and there was a wave of sympathy for Thérèse with 'her wonderful eyes which pierce and illuminate', as the *New York Times* described them. In March a committal court excused her sister Marie from all part in the trial; in the court's view she was a hysteric and incapable of answering to the charges.

When the Assize Court at the Palais de Justice opened on 8 August 1903 excursion trains ferried in spectators from all over France. The mahogany-walled courtroom held only a few hundred. Five judges presided in red silk gowns and velvet caps; many other top lawyers attended this 'trial of the century'. Famous actors, artists and authors came for the colour and the drama. They found the former – women in rich gay dresses carrying dainty lunchboxes – but as for the drama, well, for that they would have to wait.

Crawford at last

As things turned out, this first day provided all the interest there was to be. Thérèse, in contrast to her surly menfolk, looked splendid. She wore a becoming steel-blue gown, topped by a little round hat with a cut-steel ornament and a cluster of white roses. When asked where she lived she replied, 'In prison'. But apart from occasional sallies she had nothing left. The court, indeed the whole country, already knew about the inheritance, the wills, the ins and outs of her finances, the ten suicides (one of them the banker Girand) she was said to have caused. It was good to have her brothers positively identified now as stand-ins for the Crawford nephews and as signatories of most of the faked documents. But what the court

PONZI

Carlo Ponzi (1883–1949) left Italy aged 18, having broken with his working-class family. He was already a compulsive gambler with a record of petty crime. On reaching New York he found work as a waiter. We see him for a while, dapper and alert until the life began to pall. Money saved by cheating on the customers' bills covered his fare to Canada. There he took a job in a bank, where he robbed its clients by writing cheques to their accounts and this time went to prison.

On his release Carlo Ponzi, by now in his 30s, made that key discovery that shapes a career. He had been employed by a Boston import–export company as messenger, despite his prison record. Now, promoted to clerk, he found himself dealing with a Spaniard in Madrid who wanted an item to be sent to him by mail and had enclosed with his request an international reply coupon.

This piece of paper is handy when you cannot send foreign stamps or coins and want your correspondent abroad to be able to reply at no expense to themself. The foreign post office on being given the coupon will supply stamps to the amount required for a standard letter. This is done without charge (postage rates are set and the payments agreed by the Universal Postal Union); but because the coupon will first have been purchased by the sender, cash does change hands.

Spanish pesetas and US dollars and cents fluctuate with the exchange rate of the day. In Madrid, Ponzi discovered, a coupon currently cost one US cent, but that coupon redeemed in New York gave you ten cents' worth of stamps. The light snapped on in his gambler's brain. He asked the Spaniard he was dealing with if he would help try some dry runs of bulk purchase and redemption of the coupons. All went well, and so in December 1919 Ponzi opened his new business line. Henceforth he was Carlo Ponzi, investment counsellor.

What he had thought up is known as pyramid selling. This attracts clients by promising a quick return, and pays these first investors out of the money that later people invest in the scheme. There is no genuine investment to make the fund grow, and as the fraud continues the perpetrator takes more and more for himself until finally the pyramid collapses. Ponzi opened well. He offered a 50% profit on the investment inside six weeks, 100% after six months, achieving both results with ease. Soon he had solid-looking offices in Boston. Within five months the new investment money topped $1 million per week and lay in heaps on the floor. Sixteen staff worked at the Boston offices; abroad, hundreds of agents bought the coupons. It never got out how the coupons were redeemed after their arrival in America. Exchanging postage stamps for cash was not then permitted on an official basis and privately no team however large could have handled such quantities. But if that remained Ponzi's secret there was no hiding his success.

Before 1920 was over he had taken ten million dollars. He rode in a cream-coloured limo and by one account when it stopped at the lights would-be investors thrust handfuls of bank notes through the window. Ponzi was called the greatest American ever known. With his takings he bought heavily in land and property, modernizing a grand country house for himself complete with a swimming pool and a cellar stocked with fine wines. But no pyramid can last forever, and that August the Federal agents closed him down.

The end of Carlo Ponzi was particularly horrible. Sentenced to five years for fraud by a Federal court, he was rearrested by the State of Massachusetts when he came out and given a further seven years on similar charges. From prison Ponzi had written personally to his 40,000 creditors, but when finally he stepped out of jail in 1934 a crowd was waiting at the gates. A massive police guard struggled to hold back the investors who, even after fourteen years, were not ashamed to scream for their money back. The authorities felt that the wisest course of action was to deport him, so later the same year Ponzi returned to Italy, eventually dying alone and close to poverty.

wanted was Thérèse, her facts, her version of the truth. In place of this it got promises of a full disclosure 'in due course' – the phrase she had been using all year.

When the final day at last brought her statement, what she had to say was bizarre. The real Mr Crawford she announced to be the Frenchman Regnier, a shadowy figure from the Franco-Prussian War of 1870 when he acted as a go-between with the enemy, for which service he was thought to have been paid. The court fell silent in wonderment: few present had even heard of the man. Thérèse went on to say she deemed his conduct to have been so unpatriotic that she had burnt his legacy, hence the empty safe. She did not stop to detail how she and Regnier had become close or where his money had come from; the court had her statement and that was that. Jury and spectators alike were numbed by the stupidity of the case for the defence; the hearing pulled itself together, took no judicial note of her words and proceeded. Thérèse had played out twenty years of fraud with the flattest ending imaginable.

The jury needed four and a half hours to reach a verdict, and on 22 August all four members of the family in court were found guilty in the Rente Viagère business; the brothers were found not guilty on the counts of forgery, issuing forged legal papers and swindling five banks; Thérèse and Frédéric were guilty as charged on all counts. At last La Grande Thérèse could collapse. In tears that evening at the Conciergerie prison, she managed a bowl of soup and the next day lodged an appeal against the sentences.

France was hardened to scandal by the recent Dreyfus affair. But whispers of corruption, of interference both by Thérèse's father-in-law Minister Humbert and by the present Minister of Justice, would not be silenced. A parliamentary inquiry was mounted, and in February 1904 Thérèse was called to it from her prison in Rennes. The fashionable costume and jaunty manner were back: she was an unfortunate woman, they should know, not an adventuress. Don't believe those documents you have, she commanded, adding that they came from eight months at the Justice Ministry where all the good bits had been taken out.

Thérèse served three and a half years of her five-year sentence as a model prisoner. She continued to proclaim her innocence, saying that she would sue the guilty and repay every franc she owed. No one bothered with Thérèse Humbert any more, and when she died in 1917, ten years after her release, she was already a forgotten figure.

Antonio de Angelis:
the salad oil king

Soybeans are a recent crop for America, dating in any quantity only from the 1940s. Like cottonseed, when crushed the beans yield a vegetable oil that goes into products ranging from butter substitute and tinned fish to industrial resins and soap. The oil may also be processed to become salad oil. In that form any beans grown in excess of America's own requirements can be stored for export.

One Saturday in 1960 a surprise inspection began of salad oil stored at a warehouse site in Bayonne, New Jersey. The procedure involved opening the hatch of selected tanks and lowering a device into it until the bottom was reached. A sample of the contents was then drawn up. Each tank would normally hold a certain amount of water, the result of natural condensation or of leaky steam-pipes. What puzzled the warehousing firm's inspectors on duty that day, however, was that ten tanks contained water in amounts reaching many feet. The team came back again the following week, and the site manager Leo Bracconeri directed them to a tank bigger than the rest. He showed them to its one useable hatch – explaining that the others had been closed off from within during repairs – and a sample of pure salad oil came up through it. The inspectors passed the tanks as holding what was stated. But the oil company's president de Angelis took the surprise inspection and its implied criticism personally. Furious with his warehousing firm, he threatened to end their contract.

From lard to oil

That Antonio de Angelis (b.1915) should pull this stunt was in character. A pudgy Italian proud of his humble origins, 'Tino' let slip no opportunity for dramatic self-promotion. His warehousing firm were a subsidiary of American Express, the biggest of the big. In effect he had got furious with God.

De Angelis grew up in the Bronx, one of five children in a railworker's few tenement rooms. Family counted for much: Leo Bracconeri at the warehouse was a brother-in-law, and a cousin also worked there. De Angelis began at 16 in the meat trade and became renowned for his skill with a cleaver. He had a good war and by 1947 knew something about exports (a sale of sub-standard lard to Yugoslavia cost him heavy settlement charges). Two years later he won control of a publicly quoted company, but was soon caught up in another scandal. This concerned his supply of lunch meat for schools; de Angelis tried to shift the blame to the government's specifications but still had to pay a $100,000 settlement. In 1953, after an understated loss and subsequent suspension, the company was placed into bankruptcy. A long investigation showed de Angelis again involved with lard for Yugoslavia, only this time the lard did not exist. Difficulty with income tax arrears completed a patchy record for de Angelis at this stage in his career, although in one-to-one dealings he aimed to be fair and gave conspicuously to local charities.

In 1955 Tino de Angelis founded Allied Vegetable Oil: the little man from the Bronx was on his way. To begin with, for all their success, Allied were somewhat amateurish in their methods (cans of oil sent to hot countries sprang leaks) and the company was under-capitalized. Now, however, in the 1960s, its president aimed to be America's Number One 'irregardless of obstacles'.

Trading in a commodity ties up cash as goods that await their customers and payment. The goods are excellent security for loans: the practice of regarding warehouse receipts as collateral goes back to 15th-century Italy. With the loans thus raised, a trader can make further purchases when the market is right rather than only at such times as income from his customers allows him to. His lending bank will want the commodity to be placed in an independent warehouse, sometimes a shared public warehouse, that will assume full responsibility for it. A 'field warehouse' arrangement is also common. Under this the storage firm operates at its client's site, very likely as a section physically within the client's own warehouse. It is for the field warehouse company to ensure that goods remain secured and undamaged, also that they tally with what is recorded on the storage documents – the negotiable warehouse receipts.

Route to the top

Such receipts formed a key item in de Angelis's strategy. He wanted his Bayonne warehouse to become an international distribution centre taking in oil from the Midwest by rail, processing it with the latest equipment and loading it onto ships at adjacent deep-water wharves. Allied already challenged the giant Midwestern crusher companies by paying over the odds for oil. It also had to carry the overland freight costs, where the crushers could themselves ship oil abroad via the Mississippi. To be Number One, de Angelis needed to work with the large export companies in nearby Manhattan, who would buy from him at a tiny markup and

James Macpherson's 'ancient' bard Ossian was an inspired creation for its time. The 18th century wanted something to give literature and art a new direction. Ossian, faked to seem Scottish in origin, has travelled far. Here is a painter in Hungary, Kysfaludy Kaaroly, taking up his message.

Above: Munchausen's stories were not told by the Baron whose name they bear. A man on the run from the law put them together in 1786. This scene from the 1989 film *The Adventures of Baron Munchausen* gives an idea of their enduring appeal.

Right: Anton Mesmer inspired his medical colleagues to follow this hypnotic form of treatment, until King Louis XVI of France banned the cult.

Left: Louis-Philippe, King of the French. Was he in fact the son of an Italian policeman, exchanged at birth for a girl? Stella Chiappini believed so.

Below: Edward and Richard, the little princes in the Tower. Lambert Simnel passed for Edward, the older of the two, at one time. Another impostor, Warbeck, went to his death claiming to be the younger prince Richard, duke of York.

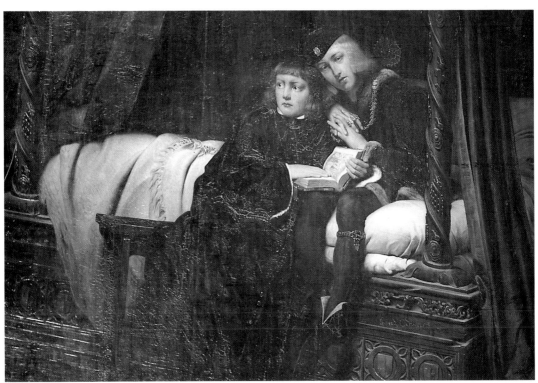

Above: Part of the Ashley Library of rare editions collected by T. J. Wise and bought for the British nation after 1937. Later it was discovered that Wise, in order to prepare a number of these volumes, had raided another national heritage: the British Library itself. He removed pages that he was short of from books that it owned.

Left: A testoon (12 pence piece) showing the head of King Henry VII (Henry Tudor). The impostors Simnel and Warbeck faced a shrewd opponent in Henry VII, who knew that once caught the lad Simnel would be harmless but that the other would be safer dead.

Han van Meegeren's *Disciples at Emmaus*. Acceptance of this painting as a work by Vermeer led to a series of similar fakes by van Meegeren in the 1940s. He spent four years researching materials and techniques before he dared bring his work to the attention of experts, but ended up having to prove that he had faked it all.

We do wrong to see the very greatest artists as unlikely ever to try their hand at faking. Michelangelo was not above passing off as antique a sculpture of Cupid that he once did.

Tom Keating at work. Helped by the publicity of his televised painting classes, he made the faker into a popular hero.

The Chevalier d'Eon. King Louis XV made use of his strange habit of dressing as a woman. The King was then used in turn by d'Eon. But just which of them came out the winner depended on what sex d'Eon really was.

The Tichborne Claimant, as seen by *Vanity Fair*. Arthur Orton's perjury trial in 1871–2 ran for longer than any case in British legal history. Even today, some lawyers believe its outcome may have been wrong.

Right: Ivan 'the Terrible', Tsar of Muscovy 1534–84. Was it his dead son Dimitry who returned to claim the throne?

Below: *Monet's Houseboat, Vetheuil in Winter*, painted by Tom Keating in the style of Monet – one of what the faker said were probably two thousand such frauds that he did.

in the massive quantities their client countries required. These companies in turn welcomed him as heading off the Midwesterners from contact with overseas markets that had always been their own turf.

De Angelis and American Express was a second example of this symbiosis. He was amazingly fortunate in his field warehouser – the company's world name and standing would ensure a loan against any warehouse receipt it might issue. For the AmEx parent company, however, the activities of its warehousing subsidiary were under a cloud. In theory they looked fine: the parent's large funds deposited with the banks to redeem its travellers' cheques would exert pressure on these banks to accept warehouse receipts. But the subsidiary's earnings were poor. Donald K. Miller, its head, faced the possibility of his warehousing company being sold off or closed down at the time of his first meeting with Allied in 1957. He knew nothing about salad oil then. De Angelis's cousin showed him round the Bayonne tank farm. Miller saw five men in white coats, was told 'this is our laboratory', and assumed that all five men were chemists. Dun & Bradstreet, the credit rating agency, said that Tino's earlier bankruptcy meant that no bank would lend to him, but de Angelis explained that the export companies would take his warehouse receipts if a reputable company like Miller's issued them. Allied's bank confirmed the facts and Miller recommended AmEx to accept the new client. He needed the Allied yearly payments as much as de Angelis needed AmEx's name. At the end of their first year together Allied was seven times larger than any other account.

The day before AmEx's snap inspection in 1960 de Angelis concluded a deal with a second field warehouser to give him twenty-four (later forty-one) more tanks. In fact the tanks did not belong to Allied, and the warehouser only existed on paper, but stock records were kept and the prescribed checks regularly run. Most of the tanks held petroleum, others were unusable, in all Allied commanded just ten, yet the weight of salad oil stored in them rose from 14.4 million to 411.8 million pounds over four years. De Angelis was expanding. Among the export companies he dealt with was Bunge, a long-standing firm in New York. Three brokerage houses handled his trading. By the end of 1962 his annual payment to AmEx came to $210,000. That company had issued receipts worth 45 million dollars against 480 million pounds weight of stored oil. 'Room for plenty more', said Miller.

Salad oil orders were filled by the export companies under the 'Food for Peace' programme whereby the US government supported American farm prices without at the same time seeming to give the food away (payment was left unconverted in the foreign country and an elaborate shuffling of papers eventually brought the exporter his dollars). On the day, the oil had to be ready. In 1962 the Bunge company experienced a nervous moment over this with Allied. Their inspectors arrived to check on delivery into the company's designated tanks at Bayonne of 32 million pounds of oil. They were kept waiting by Bracconeri, asked to come at another time, then given stock figures taken just that very morning. Finally de Angelis offered one inspector a $25,000 bribe. The man reported it and soon some top Bunge officials were at the tank farm. De Angelis oozed reassurance: there had been 'a mixup', Bunge's oil had somehow got into an AmEx tank. One official clambered along the top and peered down through a hatch inside; he saw oil shining. A colleague meanwhile had been allowed to glance over the AmEx guard's shoulder at his company stock book; he glimpsed as much as he could. De Angelis apologized for the bribe, and cordial dealings were resumed.

Need to buy

Allied's growth had become unstoppable. To get his loans de Angelis had to keep buying oil for his tanks, even though the nature of commodity futures is such that buying contracts may be sold, exchanged or deferred before physical delivery falls due. But a futures buying contract only makes sense when an order for the commodity in excess of current stocks has come in or is expected soon. De Angelis relied on government forecasts and was misled (deliberately so, he claimed) for two years in a row. A large order from Spain in 1961 never materialized. Self-glorying as ever, he decided to tough it out by more buying. In 1963 this reached manic levels as Spain again, along with Indonesia and India, withdrew custom. De Angelis would get warehouse receipts from Bunge free of charge by 'kiting' two cheques for $1 million each drawn on a different Allied bank and cancelling both cheques the moment his messenger had Bunge's warehouse receipt. By the end of September de Angelis owned almost four-fifths of New York's cottonseed futures contracts and one-fifth of Chicago's for soybeans. His 'friends all over the world' would help (they were rumoured to be the Russians). AmEx, after a top-level inspection only weeks before had cleared his tank farm, suddenly found 'a mess' at Allied. The parent company was in fact planning to dispose of its warehousing business, but by now de Angelis did not care: he had a pad of blank AmEx receipts and simply drew them up himself.

To sustain his buying at this time, de Angelis acquired a fourth broker, the reputable old firm of Ira Haupt who were eager for commodities work. Haupt gladly took his forged warehouse receipts when de Angelis was obliged to meet margin calls (the deposits that are payable immediately there is a price-fall in a commodity held as a futures buying contract). De Angelis had to maintain the price, cost what it might. A fall of only one cent per pound weight would involve him in paying millions of dollars within twenty-four hours. Almost alone on the market he was a buyer.

There were no Russians, but even had there been some this could not continue. On 15 November Allied were unable to buy when trading opened. The Exchange authority announced an investigation, and that weekend the company went into bankruptcy. Haupt at first were undismayed – after all, they held de Angelis's warehouse receipt for over $13 million (they even took another one to meet his margin calls the following week). Bunge however were less confident of their man. They checked the oil said to be held in their name. It was not there: 160 million pounds, they were told, had been pumped out to someplace else in just four hours. Haupt, borrowing in their own name to meet Allied's calls, reached the end on 20 November and were suspended from trading.

Here, there, nowhere

By the close of the month a picture of the true state of the tank farm began to emerge. Many tanks held seawater – AmEx's giant on being opened ran with brine for twelve days. Others were filled with an almost worthless vegetable oil residue, others again with petroleum. In some a solid layer topped water which in turn topped a nameless sludge. Set immediately beneath the one useable hatch of the AmEx giant was a container tube of pure salad oil: the sampling device went straight to it. The entire farm was laced with tubing that allowed one tank to be siphoned into another; exactly how much genuine salad oil had shifted to and fro at a nod from Bracconeri was never established, but it did not amount to ten per cent of any declared total quantity held at the farm. Allied were short of 1.8 billion pounds of salad oil valued at $175 million.

Tino de Angelis's fraud comes close to being management's worst nightmare. What did Miller do wrong? He may have been sloppy and over-trustful, but de Angelis represented hope for his own subsidiary. No bank would quarrel with AmEx. Bunge, too, had a welcome for this enterprising middle-man who would keep their overseas market intact. Ira Haupt wanted to build a new line of brokerage business, and here came the big spender. The commodity exchanges were a cosy club: their low margin requirements made for a healthy volume of trading, it was the American way. And the banks could draw on bad-debt reserves (held free of tax) to cover for the loans that Tino's warehouse receipts had obtained. An appalling outcome thus showed everyone acting for the best.

Among the undoubted losers were AmEx's receipt holders, soon embroiled in legal fights with the company, its insurers and each other. Haupt's customers were rescued by the Exchange. Tino himself, as the hearings dragged on during 1964–6, kept up a show of bravado outside the court. There had been a conspiracy against him in Washington at the Agricultural Department, another in Spain. Only once did he admit to swindling, which he excused as 'the hope born of ambition and determination that a setback is only temporary'. In January 1965 he pleaded guilty, and in August was sentenced to twenty years imprisonment.

BROCKWAY

William Brockway (1822–1920) is the earliest counterfeiter to have used recognizably modern methods. These were so good that for much of his long career the US Treasury firmly believed him to have acquired duplicates made from its original printing plates. Only right at the beginning, though, did something like this happen.

Brockway's name at birth was Spencer. He grew up an adopted child without formal education, but sat in on classes at Yale in electro-chemistry and law. At that time bank notes were run off by local printers while an official stood guard over the plates and paper. Brockway began his career by distracting the official of a New Haven bank during the printing of its $5 note and slipping through the press a sheet of soft, thin lead. The front and back impressions that this produced were his one approach to anything like duplicates. Using them he made a thousand of the $5 notes for himself, helped by what he had learnt at Yale. This money set him up in Philadelphia, where he got married and passed as a stockbroker, craggy and tall in his sober dark suiting.

From 1860 he employed a British engraver, William Smith. The choice could not have been better. Smith worked by day for a New York bank and by night and at weekends for Brockway. His ability guaranteed flawless counterfeits; even his 50-cent bill (a 'fractional currency' Civil War note too small for most forgers) proved to be a useful earner. Brockway also chose well in taking James

B. Doyle as his business partner. Both men had numerous bank accounts in different sectors (Doyle's were in ranching and land) through which the notes could be passed.

One of Smith's finest productions, a Union government $1000 interest-bearing bill, came to the attention of the chief of America's newly formed Secret Service, William P. Wood, in 1865. Brockway was caught with counterfeited items but made a deal with Wood and escaped sentencing, after which the two men traded secrets for some time. The Treasury, positive that a forged $1000 bill of such quality could only be a duplicate and that one of its staff had smuggled out the original, offered a large reward for information. Wood checked that he was eligible, then put pressure on Brockway to hand over what all were sure would be the duplicated plates. A banking house badly hit by the swindle did likewise with him so that it could sue the Treasury for negligence over the plates and recover its loss. Brockway however held out. Luck was on his side – Chief Wood had arrived at the Secret Service with a bad name that his performance in office did nothing to improve. After four years he was gone and the pressure was lifted from Brockway.

This run of luck came to an end in 1880. William Smith had on his drawing board a $1000 coupon bond due for redemption in 1881 and thus a valuable item. He had worked on the actual issue almost twenty years previously, so knew the plates; a paper mill at Media, Pennsylvania had been raided to give him the silk-thread fibre paper on which they would print. At that time Brockway's marriage was going through a bad patch. His wife contacted a lawyer, who one morning in court happened to be chatting with a friend at the Secret Service, agent Drummond, and suggested, maybe jokingly, they arrest old man Brockway. Sure, said Drummond, noting down where the forger might be found and put on surveillance.

Brockway enjoyed fishing. Over the next weeks several agents tailed him along the south shore of Brooklyn, where he now lived. Occasionally a stranger would join him in the boat and the two would talk together. This man was Doyle. The agents followed him away to a house owned by Smith; enquiries showed Smith to be a note engraver. After a while Doyle emerged carrying a small package; he later boarded a train for Chicago. There the local Secret Service agent detained him, and found him to be carrying 204 coupon bonds.

Just as previously with the Union note, however, expert opinion doubted that the bonds were in fact forgeries. Neither the Treasury nor the Agency wanted more embarrassment – Doyle, after all, was a respectable ranch owner. Chicago waited. Then at last came the wire that Drummond's fellow agent in that city required: 'Arrest him – a big counterfeiter'.

Brockway's arrest soon followed and he made yet another deal with the Secret Service. He took Drummond out to a copse at Richmond Hill in Queen's, and pointed to the spot where twenty-three sets of plates for notes, together with special paper and $50,000 in already printed counterfeit, were buried along with materials for the coupon bond. Again, as in the Union note trial, he walked free; but that still left Doyle facing charges. Brockway alone could speak for him, but needed some time to find the integrity in himself to do so. Finally, in May 1882, Brockway went to Chicago where, standing tall in his clerical black, he told the court lie after lie on behalf of his partner. The man, he said, did not know Smith, had no idea the bonds were counterfeit, had simply wanted someone to come in on a cattle ranching scheme. Brockway's reputation preceded this testimony, however, and Doyle was sentenced to twelve years in prison.

Alone but undaunted, Brockway then took up railway bonds. These could be a labour – one particular company president liked to sign each bond in person. The ink bottle stayed open on Brockway's desk. Eventually he was caught by Drummond in 1883 and given five years in Sing Sing, of which he served three. Yet again Brockway's famous luck returned: the man sharing a cell with him became his confederate for yet more forgeries on their release. Eventually an engraver who had been 'turned' by the Secret Service betrayed Brockway. He served a full term of ten years on this occasion – America had had enough.

When in 1905 William Brockway was seen to buy tracing paper at a store and was taken in for questioning, the magistrate next day released him. The man's age, he said, should be some protection.

Artur Alves Reis:
printer of money

In the 1920s Angola, at that time Portugal's West African colony, was in deep financial trouble. Her resources included gold, diamonds and oil, but without energy to mine them and roads to transport them the economy did not benefit. Few investors gave the country a second glance. The Angolan escudo, an inconvertible currency, was hopelessly inflated. Portugal seemed prepared to let matters drift.

For one young man this meant opportunity. Artur Alves Reis (1896–1955) arrived from Lisbon with his wife in 1916. He had forged a university engineering diploma and easily found employment. By day he was at the Public Works department; each dawn he supervised a maintenance shift on the railway. After sixteen months he held high posts in both organizations. In 1919 Alves Reis turned to a business career. A short, thick set and balding man, Reis took every chance and before long had over-reached himself. He used the reserve capital of a moribund railway company to cover his purchase of its shares and then bought into mines with what that left over. While on a visit home in 1924 he was arrested. Friends arranged for the charges to be reduced, but the two months Reis spent in prison gave him time to devise a plan.

Making money

Everything wrong with his career, he decided, came down to the lack of money. Yet what in essence was this missing substance? Bank notes were simply paper promises, therefore the bank (or he himself) must make some more. Reis reasoned that for success three things had to be perfect: the notes themselves, their distribution and a means of personal immunity. While in prison he read every word his office clerk could find written about the Bank of Portugal. Although the Bank was allowed to issue notes only up to three times its paid-up capital, this rule had often been broken recently. He calculated a sum that while not ruining the banking system would be large enough to float his scheme. A substantial loan was to be offered to Angola. In return Reis on behalf of his as yet unknown backers was to receive permission to issue bank notes to that amount. There would in fact be no loan: he would let his investors understand that the relevant officials had been bribed.

Reis worked with a small team to develop this plan. Not one of these accomplices was told the complete plan, yet each made his contribution. José Bandeira had embassy contacts in the Netherlands and himself travelled on a diplomatic passport. He knew two men representing financiers interested in Angola's oil. These were Karel Marang, a suave businessman from The Hague, and Gustav Hennies, a German with experience of deals involving backward countries. Both men were recruited by Bandeira. Reis's next task was to prove to all three that the authorities had said 'yes' to the Angola loan.

In everyone's interest

Reis drew up a paper between the government of Angola, himself and others, showing that against a loan of £1 million he would be allowed to issue Portuguese notes to the same value (one hundred million escudos). A friendly notary was happy to witness this, after which it was a matter of having three foreign consulates attest that such a notary existed and then affix their seals to the paper. With his team now comfortable – that there was no loan must have answered the question of interest on it – Reis now left Marang to find them a security printer for the bank notes. The Dutchman went first to a firm he knew in Holland: they passed a friendly word along; and soon with an embassy introduction obtained via Bandeira he reached London and the offices of Waterlow & Sons.

The plan required Sir William Waterlow, the company's chairman, to act as an innocent co-conspirator. Two items needed his connivance. Once aware of the loan, he had to be persuaded to keep it secret. He would, Marang said, be dealing solely with the Bank of Portugal's governor and then only by courier. The political consequences would be disastrous if word leaked out. Secondly, since the team had no way of knowing the numbers and letters that would appear on a new series of notes from the Bank, there would be no new series – duplicate notes, numbered and lettered precisely as before, were wanted. Waterlow fell in with both requirements. He did think to write a confirming letter to Portugal by the ordinary mail

KRÜGER

Early in World War II a Nazi project was approved to flood the enemy's banking system with counterfeit notes. These would be dropped over England, and would cause inflation and acute shortages in the shops.

Major Bernhard Krüger (b. 1904), then in charge of an SS security department in Berlin, headed the team. He was later given two key staff for it: a Russian Jewish counterfeiter, Solly Smolianoff, transferred from Mauthausen concentration camp, and a German financier and Gestapo officer, Friedrich Schwend, to handle his distribution. To make the notes Krüger chose some thirty inmates of camps throughout central Europe. These scientists and technicians lived in a fenced-off section (Barracks 19) at Sachsenhausen camp. All received special food and privileges.

Paper for authentic English bank notes had been manufactured by the firm of Portal since 1725. The counterfeiters needed over 120 attempts to match it now. Finally, one of the team discovered that for the chemistry to be right the linen rags among its ingredients had first to be washed. The SS took over a paper mill, and by May 1943 the team was getting results. It produced notes of denominations from £1 to £1000, but the large £5 formed almost half the output.

Elaborate checks were set up that aimed at attaining a perfect result. Enlargements at ×20 magnification showed the flaws (both unintended and deliberate) in a genuine note; more than one pair of eyes viewed each printed counterfeit on a lightbox against its original. Not even Smolianoff's expertise, however, could be infallible. The curlicues in the words 'Bank of England' on that £5 note showed faults. Serial numbers, dates and cashiers' signatures were another problem. The issues covered a period of over twenty years, so interchangeable litho strips (over 350 of them) giving the desired permutations had to be engraved.

What the Germans failed to anticipate was the poor response from the British to their windfall bounty. This led to new arrangements for putting the money about. Walter Funk, the Nazi economics minister, banned it from all German-occupied countries, and thus much of the counterfeit went to the neutral countries Portugal, Spain, Sweden and Switzerland for financing espionage. Schwend's hefty one-third cut of the gross take helped him to dispose of more notes against gold and dollars. Some of the Allied arms parachuted to Yugoslav and Italian partisans were bought up, and the counterfeit money also arrived in Egypt after the Allied invasion. In all, however, only some £10 to £13 million is thought to have been circulated, out of almost nine million notes with a total estimated value of over £134 million.

Two famous incidents were funded by Krüger's pounds. One was the freeing of the Italian leader Mussolini from his mountain captivity in 1943. The other episode involved the valet of the British ambassador to Turkey, who received £300,000 for his part in the spy case known as 'Operation Cicero'.

As a means of subversion Krüger's scheme had limited success (by one account it became too big for what it achieved). The Bank of England soon stopped issuing high-denomination notes. Krüger belatedly went over to dollars; Solly again did brilliant work; but air raids hit the paper mill and the team, scenting an Allied victory, dragged its feet. Krüger's Jews, transferred to an extermination camp at Ebensee, narrowly escaped with their lives. At the end of the war several truckloads of counterfeit were sunk in the waters of Austrian rivers and lakes, and the printing equipment was destroyed.

(it never arrived). Beyond that he kept all details to himself, not even telling his fellow Waterlow directors about the transaction. As to the duplicated serials, he accepted that once the new notes reached the colony they would be surcharged 'Angola' and so made distinct from notes already circulating in Portugal.

Order confirmed

Waterlow did not of course omit to ask for the Bank's formal authority to proceed. Reis was equal to this challenge. He prepared a second Angola government contract, this one bringing in the Bank of Portugal. There had also to be a letter from the Bank to Waterlow in London ordering the notes. Guessing that a Portuguese crest would figure on it. Reis asked a Lisbon printer to engrave the coat of arms as part of a letterhead for a sports club. After a few days he called and said that the club's name and address would go on the stationery later; he just wanted the engraving. Then Reis went to another printer with the crest. Here his story was that while abroad he had forgotten his promise to his friend the Bank's governor to have some letterheads made up. He was sure this little job would not be beyond a Portuguese firm; he had the crest with him ready and waiting. Within the month Sir William got his formal order – strictly confidential and with the instruction to deal with Marang direct. Once again Waterlow obliged. He might have asked a question or two: the letter was in English, not in the usual Portuguese, and it had an elaborate heading never seen before. But the governor's signature was faultless (Reis had traced it from a bank note, enlarged by a pantograph).

The order for 200,000 of the 'Vasco da Gama' 500 escudo notes was filled early in 1925. They cost the team £1500. Bandeira's diplomatic luggage spirited the cache across to Holland, where the notes were taken out of their sequence and rebatched. Then Bandeira travelled with them to Lisbon.

Total immunity

Just as there had never been any intention of releasing the money in Angola, so the prospect of distributing it at home via high-risk operators formed no part of Reis's plan. Instead he opened a bank to shift his new notes: the Banco Angola & Metropole, with branches in Lisbon and Oporto. By the sumer his bank was running well. At a time of tight money, people welcomed its easier loans and better foreign exchange terms. The bank survived rumours that something was wrong with 500 escudo notes – they were of course only rumours – and in July the bank ordered a further 380,000 from Waterlow.

Reis calculated that duplicate notes in that quantity might go undetected for a year. Meanwhile the team took their profit each in his own way. Reis liked buying things for his wife– Paris dresses and Steinway grand pianos. Bandeira spent his share on a new mistress. Marang and Hennies both transferred the money abroad. The third of Reis's conditions for success, personal immunity, was very much in their minds when they transferred the money. Reis himself had a far grander idea. Only the Bank of Portugal could bring a legal action against counterfeiting. Most of its stock was owned by private investors. If the team were to become majority shareholders of the Bank, then only an official determined to commit suicide would think of proceeding against them. Accordingly Reis bought Bank of Portugal shares throughout the spring and summer. That December, however, he was returning with Hennies from a visit to Angola where he had invested in oil and minerals. As the boat docked he was arrested; Hennies stayed on board and escaped.

The notes had gone a full twelve months, a year to the day since Marang's first call on Waterlow. Reis soon learnt what had happened. A bank teller moonlighting with the Banco de Angola noticed how the foreign exchange work he handled with 500 escudo notes was given no ledger records, and reported this to his daytime employer. Jealousy of success did the rest. This other bank reported Reis's bank. An inquiry found that new notes at the Banco de Angola were always batched out of sequence; it then found that some notes carried serial numbers and letters already used. The Bank of Portugal's directors met through the night. On the point of being arrested, Reis had put his forged Bank stationery to work again, which caused the governor and vice-governor to be briefly held. The allegations spread. There were

FRAUDWARE –

Name and position: Eldon Royce, computer bureau owner and accountant for the victim company (a California, USA, fruit and vegetable wholesaler buying many different types of produce from hundreds of growers and selling to numerous dealer customers)

Name and position: L. Benjamin Lewis, operations manager at a branch of Wells Fargo National Bank, Los Angeles, California

Period: mid 1960s

Period: 1979–81

Scope of fraud: Royce embezzled over $1 million by inflating costs of produce bought and crediting 17 dummy companies with the difference between inflated costs and those entered in the ledger.

Scope of fraud: Lewis and two co-conspirators embezzled $21.3 million via a method of covering credits paid out from accounts in Los Angeles, Santa Monica and Beverly Hills.

Computer element: False/real data simulation. Royce's program simulated the effects of various different transactions and showed him how much could be embezzled from which files without being detected by audit. A certain percentage of stock was known to shrink, so false orders and payments within that percentage would probably go unnoticed. Again, the program monitored the company's supplier accounts to show Royce which were best placed to have their purchasing and stock figures enlarged with false input. He then credited the difference to a dummy company.

Computer element: Electronic kiting. Lewis pretended to make a deposit at one branch of his bank, then credited it to another account at a different branch. The electronic inter-branch settlement system operated with a check that would throw this up after five working days. From a terminal Lewis therefore performed another transaction to cover the first one (the terminal also issued the necessary documentation). As his pyramid grew, he had to transfer increasingly large credits. The EIBSS program, however, triggered an automatic review of any transaction involving a sum above six figures. Lewis thus had to create 25 new accounts and increase the number of his smaller transactions, a requirement that gave him more and more work until finally he was unable to spend even one day away.

Detection and outcome: Royce wrote a cheque each week to one or another of the 17 dummy companies. He was unable to miss even one such inpayment, lest a sudden jump in net profits would be noticed and arouse suspicion. After six years he grew careless, wrote an unusually large cheque payable to a labour organization, and was detected when the bank became suspicious. Royce was tried in 1968 and given a five-year sentence.

Detection and outcome: Lewis was caught when he made a clerical error in one deposit. Reports tell of his leaving the bank for lunch on 23 January 1981 and never returning. Sixteen months of complex investigations finally led to trial. Lewis's testimony was crucial in the case against his co-conspirators, who were in the sports' promotion business.

Lewis himself was given a five-year sentence.

FOUR CASES

Name and position: Andrew Topp, accountant and systems analyst, and Christine Hill, bought ledger manager, of Crossfield Electronics, Peterborough, England.

Period: mid-1980s.

Period: 1987.

Scope of fraud: Atkinson and Allsop conspired to defraud Customs and Excise of £100,000 due as VAT (tax) payments on video rentals.

Scope of fraud: Topp and Hill (they were lovers planning to elope, both married to another) embezzled £1,125,655 in cheques against bogus credit invoices they issued for the company's customer accounts.

Computer element: Sales/debtor system, using a software package with a patch (suppression feature). Sold under the name 'Movieman' to video shops, this allowed the shopkeeper to reduce his daily earnings from the rented films and thus the VAT payable. The menu carried the suppression feature: one password showed a true record of the day's earnings, another brought the suppression feature into play. Package also indicated best customers/most rented films.

Computer element: Purchasers/creditors system. Topp invented two fictitious companies and set up records for them on his employers' computer, using software developed by an outside house. Through the accounts system Topp and Hill then produced business credit invoices for existing valid customer accounts. Names and addresses of the suppliers were changed to match names on the fictitious records and cheques were produced. (Curiously, Topp had earlier alerted management to flaws in the system that he cheated. He was not qualified in electronics and had lied about this in order to get his job.)

Detection and outcome: Customs and Excise computer staff spent two weeks on the program (a task they called 'Operation Patchwork'). Nine of the twelve shopkeepers caught using it settled out of court for fines totalling £34,487. The company's salesmen, on receiving immunity from prosecution, testified that the patch facility was to be revealed if a sale of the 'Movieman' package might otherwise be lost or if a customer seemed more than usually open to persuasion. Atkinson and Allsop were tried in 1986 and each given a suspended 9-month sentence with a fine of £1000.

Detection and outcome: The couple had each cleared off their house mortgage and paid £25,000 to their partner's bank account. Mrs Topp, on opening her husband's bank statement, was astonished by the amount it was in credit. She contacted the couple's employers and later the two were arrested.

Hill was given a two-and-a-half year sentence, Topp five years.

runs on the bank throughout the country; depositors mobbed its head office, and Sir William Waterlow on his visit needed police protection. Anyone with a 500 escudo note hurried to turn it in.

What to do about the notes gave the Bank a headache. First, it greatly underestimated the scale of the fraud. No one knew how many bad notes were circulating (Reis had kept back 90,000 wrongly numbered ones). Secondly, because no note was defective, none could be repudiated. There was a tiny identifying letter in the lower left corner that varied with a code, also a varying comma in the printer's name, but these did not amount to proof. So the Bank had to exchange every 'Vasco da Gama' note for one of different design, and prudently take the particulars of any customer seeking to exchange more than 200.

Finding a loser

Drudgery that might be; at least it was straightforward. The real complexities of the affair only emerged when Reis and his team came to trial over four years later. When all was considered, asked the defence, what had Reis actually done? He had paid for the notes, which were anyway duplicates, not counterfeits. At the national level, Portugal's economy had benefited from his being an inflationist – throughout Europe banks were doing what he did.

A second trial began in 1930 at London: the Bank versus Waterlow & Sons. Because damages were sought that, when put with the proceeds from Reis's liquidation, would match the amount by which the Bank thought it was out, the issues led to yet more debate. The Bank had lost nothing, argued Waterlow. When Portugal had been on the gold standard, paper money had a measurable worth; but that was forty years ago. The Bank had taken in bad notes and exchanged them. There was no outlay, no drop in profits. To this the Bank's lawyers replied that the whole principle of money made such logic absurd. A bank received value when it exchanged notes, otherwise the governor might just as well scatter money from the top of Lisbon cathedral. Eventually the case went to the House of Lords on appeal, and in 1932 by a decision split three to two the Lords awarded the Bank all it had claimed (about sixty million escudos) as damages.

Alves Reis left many questions behind him. He wanted to be the Cecil Rhodes of Angola. Some of his money was invested there – would more have followed? And then his character in the bank note affair: a large-spirited fraud, but while awaiting trial for it he attempted to pin the blame on others, so what kind of man was he? Reis could not point to a 'bigger plot' without belittling himself, and his judges matched him at pettiness. Their sentence of twenty years also covered the forged university diploma of 1916.

HARKINS

With some 3000 banks to draw on, the American cheque forger enjoys a wide field of action. Not surprisingly, the banks devise obstacles to deter the forger and most will have their own strict rules for authorizing over-the-counter payments (to take one obvious target of the forger).

Writing of William Hagen Harkins (1890–1960)

the *New York Times* described his career as 'so fantastic as to seem the creation of some errant imagination'. For much of that career Harkins used the cashier's check, and his skill with that method of payment could make other forgers look like amateurs. William Harkins, at one time himself a bank employee, well understood how the cashier's check procedure worked. Imagine you are a stranger in town wanting cash and unable to use your various credit cards. The answer may be a cashier's check bought on the spot. This will be given endorsement by an officer of the bank you are visiting (usually his or her initials) before it can be passed to a teller at the payment window where you get the cash.

Late in 1953 Harkins walked into a Boston bank and offered a large cheque to one of the tellers. She saw attached to it a note written by her cashier colleague across the hall: 'O.K. – my Uncle Jimmy. Thanks.' Her colleague seemed at that moment to be tied up with another customer, but all had been done correctly and so the quiet distinguished-looking uncle got his payment. By the time the bank found out that both the cashier's check and the attached note were forgeries, Uncle Jimmy had gone south. The fraud squad of the Bankers' Association informed Boston that it had been visited by William Harkins, who was probably better known to the squad than any other swindler of the day.

Harkins grew up in Hamilton, Washington, one of a deeply religious family that had a preacher in his younger brother Hershel. Alongside the job at the bank William studied law at night school. He was commissioned in the Air Corps during World War I and got married at that time. Then all at once the key event for Harkins's later career threw its shadow across both husband and wife. They had put their modest savings into a bank; the bank failed, and they lost their money. Harkins had such a sunny outlook that this might be thought a small, easily overcome misfortune, but the event took the joy out of life for him. The bank, he said, had cheated them. This obsession grew too much for his wife and she walked out. There would be other women for Harkins, as long as they dutifully took the part assigned to them by his new life-script. That script was everything for him now – everything that is except for the racetrack, where money could still mean fun.

Over the next thirty-five years William Harkins roamed America and Canada. He often used Hershel, his preacher brother, as an alibi when in trouble with the law. In all, Harkins was arrested seventeen times. When given a sentence he displayed a mastery of the prison parole system as applied by the various different US States. Another of his tricks was to plead insanity. During much of the 1920s, when sentenced to a long term in San Quentin prison, he hopped back and forth between that institution and a California mental home, playing off each against the other. He also seduced a nurse at the home, who later became his accom-

plice. The two went 'paper-hanging' together. When their cheques failed to stick and Harkins was given another jail sentence, the girl would visit him in prison, carrying saw blades to help with his escape – and he managed to escape three times. The police admired this for the style it certainly had; moreover William Harkins acted toward them as a real gentleman, said one, and they put him away with reluctance.

The paper-hanging skills were a matter of personal pride. Harkins would make a business call on a company office, find its drawer with the cancelled cheques, steal these and later transfer the issuing officer's initials onto the company's supply of blank cheques, which he had also stolen. His memory for signatures was photographic. This enabled him to write his own endorsements on cheques that, when presented, got past the teller as easily as did those of colleagues in the bank. The whole system – his object of revenge – stood in danger.

One memorable cheque presentation took place in New York during September 1943. It was as beautifully rehearsed and executed as a play. At a branch of the Manufacturers Trust bank Harkins purchased a cashier's check, to the amount of a few dollars only, and took it to the officer on duty. 'I just bought this and then remembered I won't be needing it', he said. 'I'd like to get my money back.' The officer initialled the cheque and motioned him along to the teller's window, but Harkins walked out. His next act was to make two identical cheques drawn on the National Shawmut Bank of Boston, each for a large amount of money and signed with a name not his own. Onto one cheque he copied the bank officer's initials given him at Manufacturers Trust. A few days later he returned there with the uninitialled cheque in his hand.

'I'm sorry, sir', said the teller. 'This needs to be initialled before I can pay you.'

'Oh yes, of course – I should know that', replied Harkins. The teller watched him cross to the officer and hand over a cheque. Harkins passed the original low-value cashier's check to this man.

'You OK'd this for me the other day', he told the officer. 'I was busy then and didn't cash it – will it still be good?'

The officer assured him it was still valid and Harkins strolled back to the teller, switching the uninitialled Boston cheque as he went and arriving at the window with its initialled twin. The teller paid out; Harkins the obsessive also made sure he received back the few dollars outstanding on the original cashier's check that was used to begin the whole swindle.

By 1954 William Harkins had been given a total of six custodial sentences. On his release that year at Richmond, Virginia, several states wanted to be next with him. Louisiana won ahead of Florida. In October for the first time in his life he entered a 'guilty' plea, and the court at Baton Rouge sentenced him to ten years in the State Penitentiary.

BERAHA

We seldom think of money itself, the coin or note, as being worth anything. Face value is what counts, and the idea that someone might want to pay more than that amount for a particular coin would seem odd unless it were a rare item no longer in circulation, and then its price would be dictated by supply and demand. The story of José Beraha (b. 1907) shows a man thinking this through.

Beraha was born in the Turkish city which later as Skoplje became part of Yugoslavia (hence his other, Serbian, surname of Zdravko). That he should further have a Spanish given-name reveals something more about the Beraha family. They were wealthy Sephardic Jews who came originally from Spain, and when the Nazis took Yugoslavia in 1943 this put them at risk. At the time Beraha was with a company in the export trade and he tried to arrange for his relatives to leave Yugoslavia, but on returning home one day was met by just the two young nephews: all others of his family had vanished and he never saw them again.

The three survivors walked seventy miles into Albania, where they found other fugitives also planning escape. Their route was to be across the Adriatic Sea to Italy. Buying a boat for this journey required payment in the form of British sovereigns. Beraha raised the necessary sum, settled his score of passengers into the leaky craft and took the tiller himself. Thirty-six hours later they made a pinpoint landing near Bari on the Italian east coast.

Resourcefulness of this kind helped Beraha to tackle the problems that awaited him and his nephews in this new country. He learnt the language, began again in trade, arranged for his neph-

ews' schooling. In 1946 he moved to Milan, north Italy's bustling business centre, where he got married. His export ventures were pushing ahead; but like everyone else in post-war Europe Beraha was held back by the complex rules and policies that controlled money. He struggled to find a means of freeing himself. At some date in 1947, remembering how useful the British sovereigns had been, Beraha sat down to work out his plan in detail.

Britain had come off the gold standard in 1931 and its gold sovereign continued to be minted only as a trading coin. The last issue as a coin for legal tender was thirty years ago, when the value had been par, with the sovereign worth £1. Now, amid post-war inflation and anxiety over exchange rates, the British gold sovereign was regarded as safer than all other forms of currency. It was excellent for trade purposes (the Saudis for example insisted that one major oil company pay them in sovereigns). Some countries used the gold coin to stabilize their own money – the Bank of England released sovereigns to the central bank of Greece with that aim. Thus by 1947 and the time of Beraha's plan the sovereign was enjoying a seller's market. Customers for it paid a large premium on the face value.

Beraha turned to the specifics of manufacturing and pricing the coin. He found that the official world price of gold in ingot form was $36 per ounce (28g). The gold content of a sovereign weighed 123.27447 grains, or just over one-quarter of an ounce, which put its metal value at about $9.00. What customers were currently paying for it however could be $20 or more, depending on the premium mark-up added by the seller. Quick to see his advantage, Beraha researched his plan's business aspects (in particular where he stood legally with it) and then set to work.

He chose a Milanese engineer, Giuseppe Bernardi, to be in charge of production. Everything was kept simple. The one-floor factory on the via Andrea Doria housed a furnace, a stamping machine, moulds, roll bars and polishers; the master dies were made locally. Beraha paid his manager on a flat-fee basis: $68 for each kilo of gold made into sovereigns (the daily output used about fifteen pounds). This gave Beraha space and helped to create mutual feelings of trust. It also left him free to concentrate on the sales side. He handled a network of agents throughout the world who were to be reached only via his high-level contacts.

People later asked why the Bank of England did not pick up the premium and itself issue sovereigns on the open market. Had it done so, any knowledgeable customers would have preferred Beraha's sovereigns because they were better than the coin they counterfeited. Beraha gave each sovereign 124.64 grains of gold instead of the 123.27 grains specified. In other words manager Bernardi made only 135 sovereigns from each kilo, whereas the Bank made 136½ on average. This still left the business with a handsome profit margin; at the same time it silenced any accusations that what was produced was a cheap forgery.

The authorities were well aware of Beraha's business as it grew, covering Africa, the Middle East, India and China, with Italy prominent in Europe. However, Beraha had thought ahead as to his position in law. The sovereign was no longer legal tender in the United Kingdom – everyone he had consulted was sure about that. So by producing a coin which created no debt on the UK Treasury, and which kept to, indeed exceeded, the gold content of a genuine sovereign, he was doing no harm to any person. That being so, he reasoned, how could he be prosecuted?

After several years of success, in 1951 the Berahas, now a family of four with a couple of young sons, decided to move away from Milan. They were rich; José was a millionaire from the sovereign trade which still did well, but competitors had arrived and some of these rivals, already wanted for activities on a smaller scale such as counterfeiting notes, were in breach of the law and thus certain to attract unwanted attention. Beraha's sense of timing once again was perfect. He arranged to sell out his business to Giuseppe Bernardi and others at the factory, then disposed of his Milan house and went to live in Switzerland. Before the year was over, under pressure from Britain, the Italian police raided Bernardi's mint and arrested its new management team. The Swiss were asked to extradite Beraha, the reason for this being that he faced charges of counterfeiting.

Beraha was ready with an idea for his defence lawyers. He wanted them to prove once and for all that in Britain a sovereign was worthless, that it could no longer buy goods or services, and that no one would even give change for it. One lawyer was therefore sent to London with only sovereigns for his out-of-pocket expenses. He offered them everywhere he went and kept an exact note (confirmed by his embassy) of how they were received. Still with the sovereigns he started with, the lawyer ended up at the Treasury, where they advised him to try a coin shop: such a place might buy them for

the metal content, and with the rise in gold's official price he would come out ahead.

The Swiss judges at Beraha's hearing were impressed by this practical demonstration. Legal tender must mean a legal means of payment, they said, and the gold sovereign clearly was not that. In 1952 they dismissed the case, much to Britain's annoyance. The following year an Italian court also dropped the proceedings against Bernardi's team, returning the equipment and ingot gold that had been seized by the Milan police at the time of their arrest.

BLACK

In his office at New Scotland Yard that morning what the Detective Chief Inspector in charge of 'funny money' most wanted to talk about were recent events. His team had just netted $4.9 million in dollar forgeries in one swoop, nearly half the entire UK total for a year.

Counterfeiters seemed to be locked in to the one-dollar bill, said the Chief Inspector. This note had no watermark or metal strip to trouble them, yet since each one fetched only fourteen cents the return on sales did not make them rich. Charles Black surely would not bother with such low denominations? The Chief Inspector grinned: oh yes, they remembered Mr Black. 'He's in public relations now – his own.' (A ghost-written autobiography of the counterfeiter had not long been out.)

At the Old Bailey in 1979 Charles Black (b. 1928) and Brian Katin (b. 1939) were sentenced to ten years and three years respectively for some of the finest dollar forgeries ever seen – mainly $20 and $50 in the high denominations, but with some $1 bills also. The man from the US Treasury told the court that these forgeries were so good they made the hair stand up on the back of his neck. Black appealed against his sentence, which was later reduced to seven years, as he felt he was paying for the sins of everyone else involved (his distributors were then not yet caught). Katin emerged from the trial very much as Black's victim.

Brian Katin had been recruited for his part when the two met at a printing trade show in 1975. A printer's employee and currently redundant, Katin had been trying without much success to make dollar bills, an area where Black, although entirely self-taught, claimed to have good experience. By Black's account the younger man was a dim individual, surly and obsessive, who suspected others of wanting to cheat him or betray him. The Old Bailey prosecutor however painted Katin a different shade of grey. For Brian Katin the forgery became his great challenge in life. It was perfectionism that drove him on during weeks of trial-and-error tests and that left him miserable when results were not up to standard.

The forgeries were done photographically rather than by re-engraving, so most problems centred on the printing process. Working in his bathroom, Black supplied photographic plates from his home in south London. They went to Katin's bungalow on the Sussex coast near Bognor, where his redundancy money had paid for an excellent offset litho machine which he installed in a secret room built behind and within his garage. Black already knew which paper to use. The best was a document paper called Optimum, 80 grams per square metre, a 100% rag quality paper that could meet the required bank-note flexibility. Katin laboured for eight months over the colour mixtures of ink (even Charles Black had to call this patience); the final specification could be made up in quantity by their supplier. Smaller amounts of magnetic ink were wanted for the serial numbers and filigree pattern on the note face. Embossing (the raised look of print and more important still its feel) could best be done by a thermographic process in which still-wet ink is dusted with resin and then heated until the ink becomes absorbed. Here Brian Katin on his home equipment never achieved a match that satisfied him, but fortunately handpressing against an incised brass block did very well instead. That left a final texturing with glycerine to apply, and then at last the notes might pass their printer's inspection.

In his autobiography Black tells how twelve months into production he and Katin came close to breaking up. This was when a batch of $20s and $50s that Katin had made was chewed to shreds by the customer's boxer dog, who took exception to the notes being hidden under his basket blanket. In this one instance, Black had not kept to his usual rule of payment on delivery and so the partners were out by £2000. The story is told without apology on Black's part and Katin is shown sulking like a child. Readers are meant to laugh at him for being an obsessive.

After the trial in 1979 Black and Katin went their separate ways. The 'funny money' Detective Chief Inspector (correctly, he is at the National Central Office for the Suppression of Counterfeit Currency) works with the British and American Treasuries and with his office's international liaison in France to ensure that forgers like them have a hard time. This involves much state-of-the-art technology. The laser colour photocopiers that were thought unbeatable only a few years ago can now be outwitted by a pattern of concentric circles on a bank note's design: these turn blurry when copied. Across the Chief Inspector's desk pass samples of more expensive security features such as the 'latent image' (an induced picture somewhat like a hologram). The magnetic safeguards are so costly that high-value bank notes could alone recoup the investment that they would take, making the Bank of England's next £5 note unaffordable, the Bank claims.

And yet, and yet . . . the range of security features for such notes is not endless – as Charles Black said, what one man makes, another can reproduce. It may be best to settle for the fact that tomorrow's bank note forgers are going to be quite different men.

TRICK OR TREAT?
OBJECTS

There is no limit to the range of man-made objects which can be faked or forged, and the motives of those who fake them or forge them vary endlessly too. The artists Han van Meegeren and Alceo Dossena both wanted recognition, but this was for reasons as different as the men themselves. Thomas Wise in England faked his literary discoveries, and Václav Hanka in Bohemia did the same. With Wise the motives were shabby; with Hanka they were patriotic. The story of a third literary fraud – Mark Hofmann in America – is just horrifying.

What the truly authentic might be, and how to apply that concept, often gets called in question by a fake. Why did those old wall paintings restored by Lothar Malskat high up in a German church cause so much fuss, if viewers from far down below could see nothing of the detail? If people buying a 'modern master' faked by Elmyr de Hory paid what a genuine work would cost, where did that leave the art world?

Faked objects of all kinds generally succeed because they live up to expectations so well. Piltdown Man supplied the long awaited 'missing link' in evolution, Bastianini's sculptures fitted a particular idea of what was 'Renaissance'. For Moses Shapira the expectations of a biblical scroll worked against his finds and fatally trapped him.

Denis Vrain-Lucas:
prodigious penman

The case of Denis Vrain-Lucas (1818–88) came before a Paris court in February 1870. Experts showed him to have faked a huge quantity of autograph letters and documents that ranged from ancient Greece to the recent past. The choice of writers and subjects stressed France's place in history – a batch of letters showed Blaise Pascal to have formulated ideas about gravity thirty-five years ahead of Newton. This, the focus of the case, during two years and more up to the trial, had torn apart the Paris Academy. One member of that illustrious body was disgraced. Yet we today, with so much else about the fakes that is totally absurd (a Gallic doctor writing to Christ, for example, or Cleopatra to Caesar), instinctively look for a hidden agenda. No true story, we feel, can be that simple.

Faker and dupe

Lucas himself, a peasant's son from Châteaudun, came to Paris after working in a lawyer's office. He sought employment with a publisher but they wanted someone with Latin; the

Royal Library would not take him on without a university degree. Only a rare manuscript dealer spotted in the man a talent he could use. His business offered its socially ambitious clients the means to acquire status and privilege. Lucas became an expert copyist. So convincing were his pedigrees that two letters he faked as being from the 16th-century essayist Montaigne went straight into a scholarly edition of that writer. On the dealer's death Lucas acquired a number of valuable items and he found he could sell copies of them as easily as originals.

Shortly before Lucas arrived in Paris the Academy appointed a geometrician, Michel Chasles, to the post of librarian. Chasles was a good scientist (he won the British Royal Society's gold medal) and he took his new duties seriously. The previous librarian had removed many important and rare things; Chasles saw it as his task to build up the collections. A colleague, perhaps innocently, wrote a note suggesting 'the industrious Lucas', and from 1861 the two men were together. Another duty Chasles assigned himself was to clarify the obscure origins of the Paris Academy for a book on its history. He was delighted when Lucas produced a correspondence between a 17th-century poet and Cardinal Richelieu showing the poet's part in setting up that great centre of learning.

Lucas had a story to accompany his finds. During the previous century, so this went, a French count had been shipwrecked while emigrating overseas; an elderly descendant was now obliged to sell off the valuable materials that had survived. Chasles checked – there had indeed been such a count, and Lucas added detail (a second descendant opposed to selling) that increased Chasles's sense of urgency to buy. Also some of the materials fell within an area of science not far from Chasles's own.

The Pascal affair

In 1867 Chasles let it be known that he was bringing out a book on Pascal's discovery of the laws of attraction. That July he read to the Academy two letters from Pascal to Robert Boyle in England. These carried the date of 1632, which proved his point about priority (Newton's *Principia Mathematica* only appeared in 1687). A fortnight later doubts were raised about the finds. Chasles refused to have the signature verified but did agree that copies of other letters said to be written to Newton could be examined by a leading British authority. On the Academy's side, Prosper Faugère, as an expert, stated that Pascal had nothing to do with the letters, and a M. Bénard traced figures in them to a modern work on cosmology. The affair soon became tinged with patriotism. Support for Pascal grew; in April 1869 the Academy gave tentative endorsement to the documents, mentioning reverently that the 'Sun King' Louis XIV was among their authors. At its very next session, however, a speaker showed that the Pascal fakes were derived from Alexandre Savérien's modern work. Reply came back that Savérien had borrowed from the letters, not they from him – and here was his covering note returning them to source. During that summer Leverrier, a leading astronomer, lectured on the science involved. It was a convincing performance, and ended with a demand that the items be given notes on their origin and then deposited with the Academy.

Also under scrutiny were twenty letters from a total of 3000 purportedly written by Galileo. Italy rejected their signatures; Galileo was shown to have gone blind three years before the date of a letter in which he complained of eye strain. Britain's Newton expert commented no less damningly on the Pascal letters, and in September Chasles confessed.

Lucas, already a month under surveillance at his lodgings, amazed everyone with his confi-

PHILOSOPHIÆ
NATURALIS
PRINCIPIA
‛MATHEMATICA·

Autore *JS. NEWTON*, *Trin. Coll. Cantab. Soc.* Mathefeos Profeffore Lucafiano, & Societatis Regalis Sodali

IMPRIMATUR·
S. PEPYS, *Reg. Soc.* PRÆSES.
Julii 5. 1686.

L⁻ONDINI,
Juffu *Societatis Regiæ* ac Typis *Jofephi Streater.* Proftant Vena-les apud *Sam. Smith* ad infignia Principis *Walliæ* in Cœmiterio D. *Pauli,* aliofq; nonnullos Bibliopolas. *Anno* MDCLXXXVII.

This first (1687) edition of Newton's book (left) was the one that Lucas should have followed for the calculations in his Pascal–Newton fakes. Instead he took figures from a later edition and applied them to Newton's thinking of 1687, thus giving himself away.

(Below left) Newton, with his telescope on the table (portrait by J. A. Houston, R.S.A.).

(Below right) The French scientist Blaise Pascal, who was accorded scientific priority over Newton by the fakes.

N.º 9 page 82

Monsieur; Selon vos observations les espaces estans comme les forces dans des temps egaux, es les corps parcourans 15 pieds en une seconde par la force attractive de la terre, on aura 41083200.

$$1 :: 15 \quad x = \frac{15}{41083200} = \frac{1}{2738880}, \text{ et tel sera}$$

. . . .

Vos tres humbles tres obeisst
Le Viteur . Galila Galiles

pour mons.ʳ Pascal

N.º 9ᵇⁱˢ page 82 (Authentique)

aspettando ordine ß servirla conforme à quello; et in tanto à lei et al S. Franᶜᵒ suo figᶜᵒ cõ ogni affetto bacio le mani, et prego da N.S. felicità. Di Padᵃ li 4 d'Agosto 1607

Di V.S. M.I.

Servᵉ Obligᵐᵒ   Galileo Galilej

(Opposite) In support of his fraud, Lucas faked letters allegedly written to Pascal by the Italian Galileo. Here the upper handwriting is by Lucas, the lower by Galileo himself.

(Above) Cupid by Michelangelo. One of several drawings on a sheet and thought to be the original for his 'antique' sculpture of 1496.

(Above right) Isabella d'Este of Mantua (portrait attributed to Titian). Her collection acquired the faked Cupid and with it a fancy story to make Michelangelo seem modest – never one of his qualities.

(Right) Václav Hanka, who faked old manuscripts for his native Bohemia in the 19th century. Portrait by Antonín Machek.

Forged Petition of Thomas Page, Richard Burbage, John Heming, Augustine Phillips, William Shakespeare, William Kempe, William Slye, Nicholas Tooley, and others, to the Lords of the Privy Council.

(Top) The Lord Chamberlain's players ask to be allowed to renovate Blackfriars Theatre in 1596. William Shakespeare is the fifth named, making this the earliest document to carry his name. A Collier fake.

William Shakespeare (above) (a portrait in the Buckingham family). He could be faked or forged all the easier if like John Payne Collier the culprit was a trusted colleague of professional Shakespeare scholars.

dence. The police described him putting in a day at the Royal Library on some item of the moment, then going with it to Chasles. In fact, very few internal errors betrayed the Pascal–Galileo–Newton materials: anyone might misspell a name or write 'laws of abstraction' instead of 'attraction', these were slips to worry the pedant. It was left for Dr Grant from the Glasgow Observatory to detect a flaw that at once convicted the documents. Grant took the best and most recent data that Pascal could have put into his calculations, namely those for 1662, the last year of Pascal's life, and compared them with what Newton had had available at the time of his first edition of *Principia Mathematica* (1687) and of his final edition (1726). Looking at given values to find the mass, density and gravity of the Sun and three Planets, Grant showed that Newton's results in his first edition were markedly better than those in the final one. The Pascal of M. Chasles, however, not only made judgments far superior to those of the 1687 Newton but did so with figures identical to those of 1726.

Production line

The trial looked hard at the possibility that the plot went wider. In this it was encouraged by the breadth of exhibits in court: letters from Alexander the Great to Aristotle, from Mary Magdalene to the king of the Burgundians ('You will find the letter I spoke of to you which was sent me by Jesus Christ a few days before His passion'), from Shakespeare, from Charlemagne. The hearing finally proved that the two men Lucas and Chasles needed no one except each other. Lucas would feign ignorance of a particular letter-writer and shyly suggest they consult the *Biographie Universelle*. That provided his factual basis; he would go ahead with his fake, and Chasles would carry back to him any snags this led to, which the faker then cleared up in his next items. Even the slip over Galileo's blindness was answered. The absurdity was that almost every document used French, often a somewhat odd 18th-century French. Moreover the fakes used paper, which only became the writing material of Europe from the 14th century.

Lucas received a two-year prison sentence. Chasles as his client had over the years paid him some 170,000 francs for 27,320 faked items; the client refused to accept that they all were one man's work, and was never charged with deception. The faker pleaded that his client benefited from the fame and attention that the letters brought him. Academician Chasles, caught up in self-imposed tasks for the Library and on ground only bordering his own area of science, was vain rather than fraudulent. Having once backed the faker, he found no moment at which a commonsense need to cry halt could speak to him.

Moses Shapira:
a dealer in scrolls

If in some dusty corner of an engineering works there came to light an ancient and unique machine, driven by vapourized petroleum and with a transmission and four wheels, it is likely that this would be hailed as an ancestor – perhaps even the father – of today's motor car. The thought that some quite other purpose was intended for the machine might never occur. Shapira's story may well rest on a similar locked-in perception, his own and the world's.

In 1868 an inscribed stone was found at Dhiban, Palestine, east of the Dead Sea. It gave an account of how the 9th-century king of Moab rebelled against the Israelites. Elsewhere the Bible alone contained this account, and because belief in the scriptures as history had begun to be modified, the Moab Stone was a key find. The late 19th century was a time of rivalry in the Holy Land, with Britain, France and Germany vying for the lead in excavating and buying.

Five years later Moses Wilhelm Shapira (1830–84), a Christianized Slav Jew with an antiquities shop in Jerusalem, became middleman and distributor for a series of Moabite pots offered to him as originating from the same area as the earlier Stone. Shapira was a self-educated biblical scholar with strongly romantic inclinations. He had been supporting the new excavations financially; he trusted his sources, and sold the pots to the German government. In fact his diggers were the victims of 'plants', and a French diplomat-scholar, Clermont-Ganneau, exposed the pots as faked.

By far the earliest

Another five years on and Shapira was involved once more in purchases from roughly the same Dead Sea area – in this case, finds from caves along the Wadi Mujib gorge. He bought fifteen strips of parchment, averaging 3½ by 7 in. (8.9 × 17.8 cm) in size. The writing on them was in a very early script with archaic Phoenician elements in the Hebrew that had gone from it by the 6th century BC, soon after the Babylonian captivity of the Jews. This made the parchments pre-Exile in date. That their content should be biblical pushed back the earliest Old Testament scripts by something like seventeen centuries. Shapira behaved very correctly. Knowing he was out of his depth, he sent his finds to Germany for the professor of bible studies at Halle to examine. This expert had painful memories from the Moabite Pots affair and, unwilling to back Shapira a second time, he reproved him for calling the parchment contents biblical. Shapira took this hint and set them aside. As a family man with two unmarried daughters to support, he had always work to get on with for his important library and museum clients (the British Museum among them).

By the 1880s, however, biblical scholarship had changed. The scriptures were being analysed for their authorship and date. In particular the first five books were thought to be by several hands writing later than Moses, who was traditionally their author. Shapira turned again to his parchments and decided they were in substance the book of Deuteronomy: Moses's final words to his people, and the Ten Commandments. By Easter 1883 he had his own translation ready. The German consul in Beirut, Professor Schröder, was also persuaded that the finds were authentic. He took them to Germany on a fund-raising trip, and Shapira's elder daughter Elisabeth joined the family there (the Schröders had a marriageable son). If this really was Deuteronomy, then it was several hundred years older than the Septuagint, the Greek translation of the scriptures made in the 3rd century BC which all later Bibles had followed.

The either/or

Berlin's experts met that July to discuss the finds. They voted 'no' to their authenticity, but Shapira did not hear the outcome of their deliberations and went on to London with the scripts. He was looking for £1 million from them. The British Museum deputed its Palestine authority, Christian Ginsburg, to have a complete transcript made of the parchments.

We see a striking difference if we read the Ten Commandments of Shapira's discovery along-side their familiar working in King James's Bible (1611), our Authorized Version. Here are two of them:

Shapira	*Authorized Version*
Thou shalt not kill the soul of thy brother. I am God, thy God.	Thou shalt not kill.
Thou shalt not commit adultery with the wife of thy neighbour. I am God, thy God.	Neither shalt thou commit adultery.

What stands out from the comparison is that the Shapira version sounds like lines to be chanted or read aloud as in rote-learning. It has a practical, instructional ring, where the Authorized Version is more abstract. Secondly, the Shapira version has references which seem almost New-Testament Christian – 'the soul of thy brother', 'the wife of thy neigh-bour'. It touches these notes throughout the text, with a music that is more intimate than the version we know.

Dr Ginsburg saw that the parchments indeed were like Deuteronomy in content, though without that book's familiar problems for the scholar (for example, Moses no longer appeared as an author writing about his own death). Obviously this must either be an ancestor of the book known in the Bible and have a pre-Exile date, or it must be a forgery of such an ancestor.

London decides

In August 1883 – like Ginsburg, acting for his government – Clermont-Ganneau arrived in London. The Frenchman got the impression that he was being denied a chance to examine the finds, but confirmed his doubts of them from among the crowd round their glass case on a public viewing-day. External appearance told him enough: they were forgeries. Shapira, he claimed, had taken quite recent parchment (Law of Moses scrolls from some synagogue) and had trimmed off the deep lower margin, which he then had aged with chemicals and used to write on. Indeed, his copiers had written across the existing margin indicators without notic-ing them. The parchment script forms were derived from the Moabite Stone. Some parch-ment strips carried stitch-marks along their vertical edge; but the upper edge was always smooth from the trimming of a knife, the lower edge always rough.

Clermont-Ganneau published his verdict before Ginsburg was ready and anticipated him on some points. The British Museum's director, too, may have influenced Ginsburg by wonder-ing that parchment had survived for over two thousand years in a climate as rainy as Pales-tine's, and by leaving his own feelings about this in no doubt. Ginsburg spent three weeks at the centre of enormous public interest, amid every kind of press speculation. Finally, in *The Times* on 27 August he announced his verdict. Shapira had sold manuscripts to the Museum before now that had clean-cut edges. The present scripts carried copyist errors indicating that an east European or Russian Jew had dictated them (like Shapira, Ginsburg too was a Chris-tian convert). Their text was a biblical mish-mash, a conflation; their new version of the Commandments 'a spurious novelty'.

That same day's *Times* asked in a leading article why anyone should trouble to forge such manuscripts and sell them for only a few shillings. Shapira asked the same question. He wrote

MICHELANGELO

A marble sleeping figure of Cupid by Michelangelo (1475–1564) is thought to have been modelled from a sketch by him. The sculpture itself is lost, but much about it is known.

When Lorenzo de' Medici saw the cupid in Florence he said to Michelangelo: 'Make it look as if it has been buried and I will send it to Rome, where it will pass for an ancient piece and sell much better'. Either Michelangelo or a dealer did bury the sculpture, perhaps in a vineyard; or maybe one of them applied chemicals to age the stone. The cupid went to Rome and was bought by Cardinal Raffaello Riario for two hundred ducats as an antique.

That summer of 1496 a correspondent in Rome wrote two letters to Isabella d'Este, the famous collector, at Mantua. In his first letter he said that some people believe the cupid to be modern while others would have it be old. A month later he wrote that the work was definitely modern, though carved so perfectly that many have been deceived.

Angry at this deception, the Cardinal sent a man to get to the bottom of the affair. On being asked to show some of his work, Michelangelo (who happened to have nothing ready) picked up a pen and drew a hand for his visitor. The astonished man then enquired if he ever worked in stone. Yes, replied Michelangelo, he did sculptures, and among other things had recently done the cupid. This admission together with the show of skill seems to have put matters right with the Cardinal.

Later the sculpture came into the d'Este collection at Mantua. A story is told of it there by a Frenchman, Jacques-Auguste de Thou, who saw the collection in 1573. Visitors were first shown the cupid by Michelangelo. After they had duly admired it, a cloth was lifted from a second cupid nearby, which was antique. This procedure was explained as following Michelangelo's own wish: he wanted his version to be shown first and the antique version afterward because in that way the merit of the older work would be more obvious. The story however does not match what others have reported about the artist's view of himself and his abilities. De Thou is more likely showing how contemporaries wanted Michelangelo to seem.

a distraught letter to Ginsburg but seemed nonetheless ready to mount some kind of defence, even in the face of anti-Jewish comment such as came from *Punch* magazine the following month. This mood however was not to last. Shapira had been over-spending at home in the expectation of riches from his Deuteronomy. Debts were mounting; Elisabeth, unmarried, returned from Germany disgraced by his shame. In March 1884 he committed suicide in a Rotterdam hotel. His parchments were sold off at auction for a few pounds and have subsequently disappeared, by one account lost in a fire.

So similar

The famous Dead Sea scrolls that emerged sixty-three years later from the caves at Qumran can easily seem to blow away the technical objections to Shapira's finds. Manuscript fragments by the thousand survived, stored under much the same cloth and asphalt covering as his had been. Some of them, like his, are written in a development of old Phoenician and Hebrew. Few exactly match in parchment texture or clarity of ink (two points that troubled the 1883 critics). A number of the larger scrolls from Qumran had been cut off along their vertical edges.

As to the texts themselves, unusual variations of biblical themes were found at Qumran too. One in particular was very close to Shapira's text. This was a retelling of Moses's last address to the people of Israel, based mostly on Deuteronomy, but it had parallels with Leviticus and again that sense of seeking to instruct or catechize. Most striking of all, the new finds from 1947 onward included writings done by the unorthodox Essene sect who lived in the caves around the time of Christ. The Essenes practised a faith that had much in common with what would later be Christian teaching, especially its emphasis on brotherly love. A few people had noted this same feature in Shapira's text during his own day. They – and he – simply lacked the knowledge that came with Qumran of how very diverse the early biblical texts could be. The general view – and his own view – that either his text was an ancestor of Deuteronomy or it was a forgery proved impossible to escape from.

HANKA

The post-war settlement of Europe after Napoleon's defeat drew a new map in 1815. Its decisions however did not touch every country equally. Bohemia stayed just as before, locked in to the Austrian Empire and without a vote even where its own taxes were concerned. Yet here too a groundswell of nationalism began, felt most clearly in the movement to have Czech officially recognized as Bohemia's language.

Václav Hanka (1791–1861) grew up in country to the east of Prague. His mother knew every Czech folksong and story: until Václav reached the age of 16 these formed his education. At school in Königgrätz (Austria's name for the town) he was allowed to write in Czech, and Hanka picked up a smattering of three other Slav languages before he went on to study at Prague University. There he made himself useful to Josef Dobrowsky, the eminent philologist. By 1816 Hanka already had his name on a volume of Bohemian folk poems. He also brought out a Czech grammar that followed Dobrowsky's own system, then under attack from some other linguists. The two men became close colleagues.

In September 1817 Hanka heard from the priest at the village of Königinhof (Králové dvur in Czech) how relics hidden away during the time of the religious wars' four centuries ago were to be seen in a store room at the church. From among a clutter of old weapons Hanka pulled out two arrows that had been given strips of parchment where the feathers would normally be. He then found whole parchment sheets, their script still clear and beautifully ornamented in blue, green and gold. In the 17th century, Hanka knew, the only means with which to counter Austria's growing influence in Bohemia had been to hoard such items from the past, and he read the parchments eagerly.

Of the fourteen manuscripts at Králové dvur, eight told of epic historical events, in particular of the battle against Tatar invaders at Olmütz in 1241. The poet-author spoke as one who had been there

in person, and used unrhymed lines of five beats (the style for much of Slav poetry). Other events described went back even earlier, to the coming of Christianity to Bohemia. The remaining manuscripts were of lyrical folk songs.

Within a year further items of this kind emerged. Four sheets discovered at the estate of Zelená Hora went by mail to the museum at Prague with no indication of their sender, a mystery also because this happened before the Královédvorský materials were published. These poems were more daring. They offered proof that pre-Christian Bohemia already had a social culture that included written laws. *The Judgment of Libussa*, a poem in which two brothers dispute their right to rule, ended:

> Shame't were we should justice seek from
>   Germans!
> We by sacred law have right and justice
> Which our fathers brought into these regions.

The hint could not be clearer, and suddenly Bohemia had a literature. Nationalist feelings ran high. The Pan-Slavists, who wanted a single language uniting all Slavs, also took heart: now Czech could advance its claim to be the language best suited for that task. Among scholars competent to judge the authenticity of the finds, those who upheld them (such as Franz Palacký and Pavel Šavařík) were opposed by others no less aware of the hot political issues at stake. One such opponent, an Austrian who would later himself be accused of forgery, said that the Královédvorský folk poems were by someone writing today. Josef Dobrowsky called the *Libussa* a literary betrayal. He named names – one of them was Václav Hanka – and a huge public debate started up.

Hanka came to seem always close by when new finds surfaced. The Czechs had been Christianized in about the year 873, so here was a 10th-century Gospel with Bohemian text added between the lines of Latin – added, Dobrowsky said, by Hanka himself. Such an accusation would normally go to court. Hanka was never prosecuted, however, and only once himself many years later brought a legal action (in 1858 he sued a newspaper and won). For the present, more serious matters were in hand. First the legacy of Old Bohemian stories had to be reworked so that those who knew only the modern Czech language could enjoy them. Sources farther afield also needed this treatment: Hanka translated Russia's tale of Prince Igor and the Celtic legend of Tristan. On home ground again he edited church litanies and service books, wrote learnedly on coins and medals, on art and law. If space was needed for a native plant from Bohemia's fields to take root, Hanka helped clear that space.

The debate on the finds brought one immediate gain. Year after year in Bohemia there had been talk of a national museum that would be worthy of the country's cultural heritage. On a wave of public interest, money for that project now poured in: 60,000 florins even before the plan was approved, and many people enthusiastic enough to give more than just cash, searching their bookcases and attics for rare items. In 1822 with Dobrowsky as director the national museum opened. Hanka had the post

of librarian, still deeply involved in editing Dobrowsky's books on the Slav languages.

That makes him look like a saint, but what drove Václav Hanka was an eccentric nature rather than any nobility of soul. The major finds were definite fakes even though they would be proved so only after his death; and he worked with no monetary interest whatsoever. Amid that moral ambiguity his value as a stimulus to literature is beyond question.

Hanka achieved very much less for the Pan-Slavist movement – there was little anyone could have done for it. Like many another would-be reformer, he let the idea of a common unifying language run away with his common sense. To imagine one Slav nation acting as standard-bearer for all others was absurd. After 1849 Hanka became an academic, a professor of Slav languages at Prague. He won a seat in the parliament at Vienna which he did not take up; he agreed to chair a political society, The Slav Lime-tree, that survived only for a few years. Ordinary politics never really interested him.

John Payne Collier:
Shakespeare finder

Each week of the year on average, twenty or more books and articles join the tens of thousands already published on William Shakespeare. Somehow the poet survives this unrelenting attention from the professionals. The story of John Payne Collier (1789–1883) tells how the Shakespeare industry itself and those scholarly writers took a bad knock.

Collier was a newspaperman's son, and after a private education he followed his father on to *The Times* newspaper and *Morning Chronicle*. Later he went over to law studies. He married a girl with money and the couple had six children. Two events however soon cast their shadow over this happy start. While on *The Times* Collier misreported a parliamentary speech which resulted in a fine and a reprimand from the Speaker of the House. He also brought out a set of sketches attacking prominent lawyers of the day – a foolish thing to do, given his ambition for a career in law, but by then Shakespeare had taken him over. At the age of 17 Collier was already fascinated by the poet's physical existence, by the Shakespeare of ink and paper. He bought an old 'Folio' edition of the plays; encouraged by the bookseller Thomas Rodd he became expert on the literature of Tudor and Stuart England. This knowledge went into his *History of English Dramatic Poetry to the Time of Shakespeare*, which appeared in 1831.

One fake proves another

The *History* was a wide-ranging book with valuable information about Shakespeare in the form of documents. However, Collier could not resist adding invented details of his own to these finds. In one such invention he composed a ballad that mentioned *Troilus and Cressida*, and noted alongside: 'This might be Shakespeare's play acted surreptitiously; possibly it was a different play on the same subject.' That note has a master faker's touch with its appearance of scholarly hesitation. Another clever fake was a request from the Lord Chamberlain's Players in 1596 to be allowed to renovate the Blackfriars Theatre and continue acting there. Shakespeare's name was listed fifth of the actor-signatories, which made this by seven years the oldest such document to carry his name. As we shall see later, Collier took care that no one missed the point of that date.

Sociable and eager to please, John Payne Collier was liked and soon he had friends in high places including the Duke of Devonshire who found tasks for him at his library. In about 1832 Collier met Lord Francis Egerton, who gave him the run of manuscripts at his family home of Bridgewater House, in St James's, some of which had lain untouched since Queen Elizabeth's time. Collier put these treasures into his next book, *New Facts Regarding the Life of Shakespeare* (1835), again with many inventions. One forgery is a marvellous trick. It hooks back into the *History* (Shakespeare's rise in status is traced from his ranking on lists in the various Blackfriars Theatre documents: 11th place leads to 5th and then to 2nd) so that a date previously faked – the fifth place we saw just now – is 'proved' by this later discovery and leads in its turn to the next one. Collier also brought in some important people with his inventions, for example the Earl of Southampton and the actor Richard Burbage, who were respectively Shakespeare's patron and most famous stage interpreter.

Doubts

By now Collier had become a full-time Shakespeare editor. More discoveries followed – evidence that *Othello* had been performed before the Queen in 1602; a ballad that may have inspired *The Tempest.* In 1840 it seemed perfectly correct that he should head a team of four and launch a Shakespeare Society. At about this time Collier also gained access to the valuable items held at Dulwich College, where he added Shakespeare's name to a letter and once again to lists of actors on warrants and deeds. One Dulwich item, the Henslowe Diary, he removed and tampered with at home. This was the account book of the first Bankside Theatre's manager, a rich source of facts for scholars. The Shakespeare Society unknowingly lent its authority to these forgeries by publishing them. They all came together in Collier's *Life of Shakespeare* (1844), masquerading as genuine scholarship alongside the rest of his book (which was often very good).

Collier at fifty seemed secure in his reputation. The Society of Antiquaries elected him vice-president, he had a civil list pension, the volumes of his new edition of Shakespeare's plays began appearing and were praised. Yet at this very time the reasons to doubt him began gathering like storm clouds. Joseph Hunter, from the public records office, did not like the language and dates in some of Collier's Bridgewater House finds, nor the paper they were written on. A colleague with the Shakespeare Society, J. O. Halliwell, went further and declared that they had been forged: all were written by the same person. Mr Collier should have the handwriting tested by experts. Mr Collier however did not reply. A scandal developed, and in 1853 the Society decided to disband.

The Perkins affair

All at once, in fact before the Society disbanded, the forger made the momentous discovery for which today he is most remembered. The bookseller Thomas Rodd, he said, had sold to him a much-worn Shakespeare (it was a Second Folio of the plays) in which were written thousands of tiny corrections to the text. On the book's cover was the name 'Thomas Perkins'; wine and tobacco stained the pages within. An actor called Perkins was known to have worked with the playwright Marlowe's company during the lifetime of Shakespeare. Had this 'Old Corrector' perhaps known a more authentic text, one that was closer to the version that Shakespeare himself had acted from and given to his players, a better text than all others now available? Was Perkins the missing Shakespearean original?

As Collier already stood under a cloud, his Perkins immediately met with doubt among the scholars. It was 'pseudo-antique', it belonged under 'literary cookery' – and the cook's identity was known. Collier took legal action against that comment but the hearing lacked evidence and came to no conclusion. Next he came up with a provenance for Perkins, an old man who said he had once owned the book of plays. Finally, he presented the volume to the Duke of Devonshire's library, where for some time it conveniently disappeared. All three of these steps are classic defensive moves by a professional fraud and Collier played them expertly; but they did not prove to be enough.

Two scholars, Sir Frederick Madden at the British Museum and C. M. Ingleby a Shakespearean sleuth, turned on their colleague from quite different lines of attacks. In 1859 Madden put the Old Corrector through a battery of tests to show that pencil writing lay beneath the ink of his many alterations, and that the ink itself was coloured water. Somewhat later Ingleby examined all of Collier's finds from Bridgewater House onward, looking at what they said and how they said it. Together, from their different vantage-points the two men moved in on Collier and destroyed him. He did not stop writing – memoirs appeared, an autobiography, a new edition of the 1831 *History* with all its faked passages still in place – but there were no more discoveries from him. On his death-bed he went on record with 'a bitter and sincere repentence' for what he had done.

The damage that Collier inflicted was more a blow to confidence than anything else. Here was a friend and colleague using a professional's tools to work on the very areas (theatre records, city accounts, property) that most interested Shakespeareans of his day. Much of what came from that work was good: they had him to thank for new facts about Stratford-upon-Avon and the poet's family, but that only made matters worse. Tidying up after Collier might be a bothersome nuisance; the real problem was how to adjust to this betrayal from within.

WISE

After their runaway marriage the poets Elizabeth and Robert Browning settled in Italy. Their habit was to write alone, not showing their work to each other. One morning this custom was broken. Elizabeth entered the room, held her husband by the shoulders to stop him turning round, and slipped some papers into his coat pocket. Browning found himself with forty-three sonnets. They were an outpouring of his wife's love, the chronicle of her marriage. At first she was reluctant to think of them being printed, but Browning insisted and later that year a small volume was privately produced:

Sonnets.
By
E.B.B.
Reading:
[Not for Publication.]
1847.

Three years passed before the sonnets were openly published in Elizabeth's collected poems.

When an author's work is privately printed most copies go to close friends, often with an inscription added. That these sonnets were so intimate would make this even more likely. Yet not one such presentation copy has been found. In fact the pretty story from 1847 was invented and the early edition faked. The man responsible was Thomas James Wise (1859–1937).

Collecting first editions, rather than rare books valuable for other features they possess, began to take commercial shape only in about 1870. Qualities linked to this 'firstness' were sentimental, the product of increased attention given to writers as people. 'Modern firsts' could range from Milton to the latest popular essayist of the day. They were a strong selling line for libraries and private collectors alike. Their prices soared, especially in America.

The 1880s were a time of author-study groups. By 1886 Carlyle, Dickens, Ruskin, Shelley, Swinburne, Thackeray and Wordsworth each had at least one such Society devoted to them. These held discussions on their subject's life and thought. They sponsored author bibliographies (complete lists, usually with descriptive notes, of every authentic piece of writing) to help collectors. And, because a genuine 'first' was often too expensive, they began offering their members imitative reprints at affordable prices. These imitations might simply show a good likeness and no more. But they could also be 'type facsimiles', editions that mirrored every detail of that original's typography, from the particular fount (type design) and its letters – some of which were perhaps worn or broken – to the choice of layout or heading style followed by the original printer. Thomas Wise already had some experience of type facsimiles when the Shelley Society put him in charge of its reprints.

Using a single printer (Richard Clay & Sons), Wise in one year (1887–8) spent three-quarters of his Society's total funds on reprints. The reprint programme covered thirty-three books. Wise exploited it in several different ways. From the type already set, he ran off extra copies on special paper which he then sold privately on his own account. In one case at least he charged a whole extra publication to the Society. He benefited above all from the command of typography and the good standing with his printer that the job brought him. Clay & Sons, innocent of wrongdoing, were sucked in. For example, for the Society's own facsimiles Wise was instructing them to print a genuine early year on the title-page rather than what would be an incorrect (current) year. They had no way of knowing, with books he was faking, that the early year was to support a false first edition that never existed. (In fact his first entirely illegal book, a piracy of some Shelley poems in 1887, was done

for an American society that itself never existed.)

Thomas Wise did not operate alone, and the role of Harry Buxton Forman (1842–1917) certainly amounted to that of co-conspirator. Forman was the better editor of the two men, and worked with several prominent authors (among them Morris and Swinburne) on their own publications. He had what Wise lacked: a feeling for ideas and content. This intellectual depth is why some see Forman as the dominant partner; certainly Wise implicated him when the truth about Elizabeth Barrett Browning's *Sonnets* began to emerge. Against this, Wise's outlet for sales purposes over many years, the dupe Herbert Gorfin, tended to play down Forman's guilt in the affair.

How the *Sonnets* were exposed, and with them forty-six other spurious publications, is a classic piece of detective work that has still not ended. It began in 1932 when two booksellers, John Carter and Graham Pollard, noticed that from the 1920s some apparently rare works by such authors as George Eliot, the Brownings, Swinburne and Ruskin had been turning up far too often and decided to investigate. They chose the *Sonnets* as their starting-point. Browning himself was on record as not having seen the poems at all until 1849; but this clinching testimony as to their date did not show whose book the 1847 edition was.

Carter and Pollard subjected the volume to a battery of tests. These showed the paper to contain esparto grass, used only from 1861 in England, and also chemical wood made by a process introduced thirteen years later. The printed text was traced, via features such as a 'buttonhook' (or kernless) f and j, to a fount dating from 1876 at Clay's (their 'No. 3 Long Primer'). Findings like these were unanswerable, and they applied to other doubtful items too.

Wise was then in his seventies, justly renowned as a bibliographer and the owner of a collection (his Ashley Library) that would later be bought by the British nation. For the two-man detective team to expose his fakes and piracies – the accusation though unstated was clear – took considerable courage. Herbert Gorfin helped Carter and Pollard by showing how sales had been made. Wise himself, however, never once replied to the enquiry other than with a muddled account of how the *Sonnets* came his way; when a full explanation was sought from him, his wife pleaded that he was unwell.

Today much remains uncertain in the case, and the

repercussions from it continue. At least a further fifty dishonest publications are now attributed to the Wise–Forman partnership. Amid the confusion it would be a mistake to feel sad for book dealers and collectors: by encouraging the new science of print analysis the episode in fact did them a good turn.

Giovanni Bastianini:
Florentine sculptor

Giovanni Bastianini (1830–68) gave the artistic taste of his century something it particularly wanted. For this he became more popular than the originals, the Renaissance masterpieces that he took as inspiration for his own sculpture.

Bastianini was born in Fiesole, near Florence, Italy, one of several children in a peasant family and its breadwinner when the father fell ill. In his early teens a local art historian taught him about drawing, after which the sculptor Girolamo Torrini took him on as an errand boy. He then studied for a time at the Florence Academy and the city's galleries rounded out his art education. Soon he was drawing well enough to interest Giovanni Freppa, an antiquarian dealer. Freppa had a workshop in the Borgo Ognissanti. He offered the young man a small salary and gave him suggestions for projects to sculpt, also the clay and marble needed to achieve them.

All Italy looked

It is said of Bastianini that he was able to work direct onto his material as Michelangelo did, without the use of a model or cast. He echoed Florentine sculptors of the 15th century in a way that for his own time was more 'naturalistic' than the effect produced by Donatello, Desiderio da Settignano and Rossellino from four hundred years ago, and seemed more of the Renaissance than they. Bastianini's favourite item was the portrait bust. His monk 'Savonarola' immediately created a sensation in the art world. No sculpture previously had existed of the great Dominican reformer, and the work sold for 10,000 lire. All Italy looked to Florence and to what was believed must be a newly discovered 15th-century studio in that city.

What Italy found there were riches. The philosopher Marsilio Ficino came to light, a new portrait to add to the bust of him in the Cathedral. There was Lucrezia Donati, mistress of Lorenzo de'Medici, who seemed to make her own quiet space even when it was noted that features of this beautiful marble with the hooded eyes were to be seen locally in a sculpture by Mino da Fiesole. As a source of hitherto unknown religious work, too, Florence was suddenly well off.

For his contemporaries, however, Bastianini's name belonged with the Benivieni affair of 1864–8. Girolamo Benivieni, poet and philosopher, the friend of Savonarola, was judged to be an excellent portrait subject except for one detail: no one knew what he looked like, no model for him had come down from his own day. There was, however, an engraving that had been done three centuries later, and with this in hand, Freppa and Bastianini scoured the district for a sitter, eventually choosing a tobacco worker called Bonaiuti as the closest match.

Marble portrait bust of Lucrezia Donati, sculpted by Bastianini. It was bought as the work of a local master from 400 years earlier.

(Above right) Bastianini's 'Virgin and Child', and beside it the same subject done by the Renaissance sculptor Rossellino in the 15th century. Nineteenth-century artistic taste tended to prefer Bastianini's version of the Renaissance to the real thing. His fakes were immediately accepted, and continued to be bought even after they were exposed.

(Opposite) Elizabeth Barrett (above) and her husband Robert Browning. They spent their married life in Italy, the setting for the story of how her sonnets came to be written. T. J. Wise faked a rare early edition of these poems.

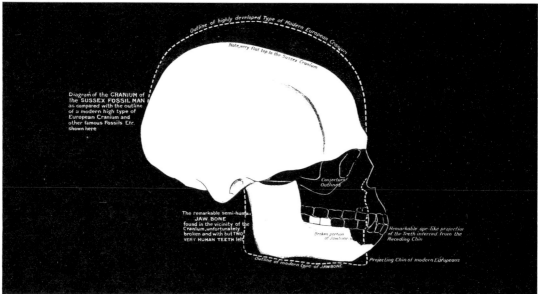

(Top) Piltdown, the group portrait (by John Cooke, RA). Sir Arthur Keith is seated centre, Dawson and Smith Woodward stand to his left.

(Above) The Piltdown skull and jawbone, drawn against typical modern European outlines.

The result was a face which had 'captivating naturalism', 'character' (a term of high praise at the time) and 'absolute truth to appearance'.

A Parisian collector by the name of de Nolivos bought the Benivieni in 1864. After two years his collection came under the hammer, and the bust was acquired for the Louvre by its director, Count de Nieuwekerke, a man close to Princess Mathilde de Bonaparte at Louis Napoleon's court. The price (14,000 francs) was a record at the museum. That fact by itself ensured that the work went on immediate display in a place of honour.

Doubts of the Benivieni's genuineness began almost at once. The gossip went that the famous Florentine dealer Alessandro Foresi had been accused by Nieuwekerke of including faked items among a recent batch of antiques he had offered to the museum. Foresi (it was said) had become angry at this, declaring that the Count would not know a fake if one were put under his nose – that indeed one had recently been put there which had cost him 14,000 francs. In December 1867 Freppa, a small fish in these waters, came out with the truth. He announced that he knew who had sat for the Benivieni bust, an order he himself had placed three years ago with Bastianini, who had received 350 francs. De Nolivos had paid twice that amount for it, 'not as an antique but on the evidence of his own eyes'.

Nonsense, retorted the Louvre. This man Freppa was some crackpot from Italy. One did best to ignore his boasting.

Embattled

The French press joined in by suggesting that no Italian today was able to turn out sculpture of such excellence. Charge led to counter-charge. Bonaparte's pillaging of Italy's art treasures, many of them now in French galleries and museums, was called to mind. Soon two sculptors went on the barricades – for France, writing in *La Patrie*, was Eugène Lequesne; for Italy and for himself, Bastianini in the *Florence Gazette*.

Lequesne opened with a statement that the bust had to be 15th-century. That much could be seen in marks left by the antique moulding process, also in traces of liquid clay on the hair which matched clay smeared inside the mould.

Bastianini replied: 'The bust was modelled freehand. The cast was taken after firing, and that is why the seams show.'
Lequesne: 'On one of the curls the clay was insufficiently bound in, and a small piece dropped off. The place still shows the original fingerprint by which it was replaced.'
Bastianini: 'Aren't fingers always used for modelling?'
Lequesne: 'The clay differs from that used in Italy today. It has become porous with age.'
Bastianini: 'I'll send you a specimen of the clay ordinarily used here. Neither chemically nor from the artistic point of view does it differ from that used in the Benivieni bust.'
Lequesne: 'Patina was applied to the surface by tobacco smoke.'
Bastianini: 'Well, as you haven't guessed my method, I'm not giving any secrets away. But I shall be happy to apply the same patina to any terracotta you like.'

Another newspaper reported Count Nieuwekerke as having offered Bastianini 15,000 francs to produce a companion-piece to the bust. On hearing this, the sculptor said in February 1868 that he would do a companion-piece for 3000, along with the twelve Roman Emperors for 1000 francs each – 'since you are a pillar of the French Second Empire'. The count did not respond. By the following June, Bastianini was dead.

Naturally genuine

The art historian Kenneth Clark, telling of his school art classes half a century later in England, gives an idea of Bastianini's influence. This lasted even after the Louvre affair had exposed him. Clark says in his autobiography:

> The drawing school contained a shelf full of casts, most of which were from the hand of the great Italian forger. On account of their academic naturalism, these 19th-century imitations were more to the taste of art teachers than genuine works by Donatello, Desiderio da Settignano or Rossellino, all of which would have had too strong an influence of style. My only instruction was to draw these unappetising objects with an HB pencil. I drew them all dozens of times from every angle. The Bastianinis were the easiest.

What the 19th century wanted in Renaissance sculpture and found in Bastianini comes over clearly from a 'Virgin and Child' he did which is in the Hermitage Museum, Leningrad (see page 128). The museum credits Rossellino with the piece. That it is not by that artist must surely be our feeling as we look at the known 15th-century copy of a true version of the 'Virgin and Child' by Rossellino also on page 128. Bastianini's cherubs and Virgin, to our taste at least, simper and smirk. They are as their own day preferred them.

It may never be proved how far this life-long sculpting was a conscious plan to deceive, formed and carried out by Bastianini and Freppa together. A tradition of copying long existed in Italy. It shades over into 're-creation', and this is what Bastianini, for his part, always claimed he was about. Several major museums, notably the Victoria & Albert in London, appeared to back that claim when they bought his work in his own day.

After his death many more pieces by Bastianini came on to the market. The Renaissance specialist John Pope-Hennessy believes that other hands may have helped with his output, sharing the Florence studio (as in another old local tradition) and producing work in common. Pope-Hennessy doubts we have heard the end of Bastianini.

Piltdown Man:
the 'missing link'

Science in the early 20th century was obsessed by thoughts of what might be 'the missing link' in human evolution. Only thirty years before, Charles Darwin had said that man along with other species co-descended from some ancient form – the common ancestor, he stated, would be as much ape-like as human. Since Darwin's day, fossil discoveries in Java (1891) and Heidelberg, Germany (1907) were of early 'hominids' that some scientists found to be not quite ape enough to bridge the evolutionary gap. This left the already known 'Neanderthal Man', whose cranial size alone, as great as or greater than that of a modern man's head, was enough to rule him out. There was no agreed picture of the human evolutionary tree – hardly surprising, since so few fossil examples were present to draw from. Each new find could alter people's ideas.

First finds

With expectations running so high, the amateur geologist Charles Dawson, of Sussex, England, became instantly alert when in 1908 road-menders digging in a flinty area of his county came up with what they called 'a coconut'. (They had in fact broken a human skull.) Dawson enjoyed remarkable collector's luck. His luck seemed to apply in particular to 'transitional' items: for primitive boat design he found an example that came between being a canoe and a coracle, for iron-work he discovered a slipper-like early horseshoe. He also had a more ordinary kind of good fortune: he made a strike of natural gas that for years lit the railway station at Heathfield in Sussex.

Dawson despite seeming a mere enthusiast was respected by Arthur Smith Woodward, head of geology at the British Museum, and when in 1911 he found more skull fragments, along with flint flakes and animal remains, Woodward was the first person in London to hear of them. The two men began excavating at Barkham Manor (the Piltdown gravel-pit site) from June of 1912. Dawson had just seen a cast of the massive jaw from Heidelberg; significantly for what now followed, he spoke of it to Woodward the month before their dig started.

Man meets ape

That summer, helped by the French priest Teilhard de Chardin (who was sojourning in a nearby retreat), Dawson and Woodward unearthed more pieces of the unusually thick skull and various other finds. Dawson, in Woodward's presence, then turned up what logically had to belong with that skull: an ape-like jawbone still carrying its molar teeth.

Dawson and Woodward showed a reconstruction of 'Piltdown Man' (as the finds became known) to a crowded Geological Society meeting in London that December. The skull, said Woodward, was essentially human. The simian jaw appeared to be that of an ape, but the regular flattening seen in its molar teeth only occurred in humans – and would be expected in a freely moving jaw articulated on to a human cranium. The two finds also belonged together for commonsense reasons: it would be stretching coincidence too far to speak of two matching fossil halves, one human, one ape, so close to each other in the same site and yet unconnected. The creature moreover belonged with what was found around him – animal remains (hippopotamus, deer and beaver) and flints ('palaeoliths' undoubtedly of human manufacture, plus older, more debatable 'eoliths') associated with the Early Ice Age. Dawson offered a date of 500,000 years for the finds. Some people at the meeting felt this was too modern; but the speakers held to it. Woodward bowed his amateur colleague forward to accept for Piltdown Man the scientific name *Eoanthropus dawsoni*: Dawn Man, Dawson's species.

Time and sequence

From that meeting onward Sir Arthur Keith of the Royal College of Surgeons became closely involved with the separate Piltdown fragments and their problems and options for reconstruction. Keith, though always loyal, was not always entirely happy with the finds. He drew attention at once to the crucial lack of a canine, or 'eyetooth', in the jaw. The following August, on what was the last dig of the 1913 season, Teilhard de Chardin picked up just such a tooth at Barkham. There was great delight all round. This canine, like the molar teeth in the jaw as found, had been been flattened in a manner compatible with the fit to a human skull. The eyetooth was somewhat like that of a chimpanzee, though it did not project above the level of the other teeth as that animal's canine would. It perfectly combined human and ape-like qualities.

BECKER

In catching out the engraver Carl Wilhelm Becker (1772–1830), the problem was to show that a coin sold as an antique was in fact made from the same die as one that he freely acknowledged to be his own work.

Becker's father, a town elder in Speyer, Germany, wanted his son to follow him into the wine trade. From his youth Carl Wilhelm had artistic talent, but nevertheless tried to meet his father's wish in a series of failed business ventures (wine among them) until his mid-thirties. He then gave up trade to study engraving at the Munich mint, and soon began making the dies of Greek, Roman and medieval coinage that specialists today still call 'dangerous' because they are flawless.

Reports speak of Becker as a genial, attractive and honest man with a sense of humour. He was fortunate in his sponsors. Prince Carl von Isenburg, a keen numismatist, appointed him a councillor. The poet Goethe twice visited Becker and inscribed to him a copy of his Life of the goldsmith Benvenuto Cellini. In Vienna the Russian ambassador Count Razumovsky admired his work.

The dealer T. E. Mionnet handled Becker's coins that were struck in gold and silver from the 331 dies, selling mainly to collectors who wanted to make up their sets. (A few instances went beyond that when Becker invented a coin of his own, such as the Greek Antipater of 1807.) Although Mionnet's prices were high Becker himself did not earn much. He had a die-cutter to pay, metal to buy, and could not work fast. A set of coins which he sold for 1350 florins carried 550 florins in direct costs; a set of genuine originals would have sold for an estimated 66,723 florins in his day. The difference gives an idea of how much profit was made by those who sold his coins as real antiques.

Certainly Becker intended some coins to seem old. A famous story tells how he would put them in a large metal box filled with iron filings that was attached to the axle of his carriage. He called that his 'Kutscherbüchse' – a box to take coins for a drive in.

That Becker knew the situation for what it was – that is, moral evasiveness on his part – is proved by a correspondence he had with a young but extremely knowledgable customer. This buyer sensed that Becker had engraved the coins, but lacked the evidence to prove it and did not want to spoil their relationship. Accordingly he wrote to Becker suggesting that a third party was perhaps trying to deceive him, and if so then how insulting to Becker that would be. Becker parried this in his reply, saying that he took no coin that could not speak for itself and advising his client to do likewise. The exchange of letters reads like a verbal fencing match.

Much of Becker's time went on trying to find a purchaser for his complete set of dies. He negotiated for over two years with Vienna, where the director of the Imperial coin cabinet wanted them (if only to prevent further Beckers from getting into museums as genuine originals) but the Emperor Francis I said no. Berlin did not take up the bidding. Nothing came of an attempt to interest the Tsar of Russia.

By 1826 Becker's eyesight had started to fade, which since he worked entirely freehand without casts or other mechanical aids made further engraving very difficult. After his death in 1830 the 331 dies were used by his widow's new husband to produce lead impressions, and these sold to amateurs for the low price of forty florins. The dies themselves later went into the Imperial Museum in Berlin.

Woodward and Keith might be powerful champions, but Eoanthropus did not meet with acceptance from every quarter. Some experts believed it to represent two creatures and two distinct periods of time: they tended to think that the jaw was older, from the Pliocene, and that the cranium was from the more recent Pleistocene (or Ice Age). At a meeting in 1913 German anthropologists ridiculed the canine tooth; even this early there were rumours of a fake. In 1915 however, two miles from Barkham Manor, a second braincase was discovered, with teeth similar to those of Piltdown I. This new find silenced most of the predominantly French and American doubts, but Charles Dawson himself had only months to go. He fell ill during that same year and died in 1916. Woodward worked steadily on at both Piltdown sites, though with almost no results, for some while after.

Important changes were soon coming for the time and sequence aspects of evolution. The

1930s began an increase in human fossil finds that still continues today. From China, Java and Africa, discoveries showed that *Pithecanthropus*, the 1891 Java hominid for example, was indeed no ape but (as Keith and others had believed) a primitive man. 'Peking Man', the new China find, was even more clearly human. In the 1940s it was learnt that *Australopithecus* from southern Africa went back earlier still, with signs of human-ness and yet two or more times older than the given date for Eoanthropus. Such finds proved something else too. Man did not begin by acquiring a large high-arched cranium and only later lose his ape-like jaw with its overlapping canine teeth. The process took a reverse direction: a human jaw and dentition came first, a lofty forehead fronting a large brain-case developed after that was in place. Evolutionarily speaking Piltdown Man had things in the wrong order.

Revealing tests

Until 1949 Eoanthropus, now something of a puzzle, at least 'could sit at the end of an evolutionary branch', to use the South African physiologist J. S. Weiner's phrase. In that year Kenneth Oakley at the British Museum obtained permission from his superiors to test samples of the finds for how much of the chemical fluorine the bone contained. (Fluorine is absorbed from soil water increasingly with age, and so can be used to determine whether bones found together are of the same or different date.) Oakley excluded any possibility that the jaw and cranium were as old as the early animal remains found alongside – indeed both had so little fluorine (0.1% compared with about 2% in the animal remains) that the 500,000-year date offered for Eoanthropus began to look like 50,000 years at most. Early Ice Age had become Late Ice Age.

This result set Joseph Weiner thinking. If the skull finds were relatively modern, they destroyed both the 'two creatures' and the 'one creature' theory of Eoanthropus. With the first case you asked 'What are these ancient eoliths doing alongside a modern man's skull?', with the second case 'Why is an ape-man living so recently?'. Weiner was Oakley's leader in this investigation, and one night in 1953 he sat into the small hours considering the possibility of a fake. The one completely reliable human feature of the jaw, he decided, was the flattened molars; but they might have been artificially ground down. The time had come for more chemistry, and for some physics.

Oakley then ran a second fluorine test on a larger sample of bone: this showed that the jaw and teeth did not belong with the skull but were younger, and that this was true also for the finds at the Piltdown II site. A whole battery of tests was then given to the fragments overall. They emerged in their true colours. The cranium had been discoloured with iron sulphate; the jaw was that of an orang-utan stained with chromium to match; the molar teeth had been filed down and the crucial canine showed traces of Vandyke brown paint. As to the other remains, an early bone tool (1914's most exciting Piltdown find) carried marks left by a metal carving instrument, and an important 'palaeolithic' flint axe had been stained to suggest age. In short, Eoanthropus no longer existed. Modern science had sawn off its evolutionary branch.

How and who

Weiner was a fair-minded man; he was also a practical scientist, who would file down and paint a chimpanzee tooth himself if it were a matter of learning how the thing might be done. To start unravelling the Piltdown fraud took someone with both these qualities. The key questions were before all else practical. Whoever initiated, made or planted the bogus objects must have been at home in the sciences of palaeontology. He would be known to everyone at the site and aware day by day of what was going on there. With each faked object, he needed to judge its value as evidence and foresee its reception by science (the jaw, the canine tooth and the Piltdown II finds came in exactly the order and time required). Weiner knew that Charles Dawson freely admitted to having put some of his first skull fragments into potassium bichromate in the belief that this would harden them. The unknown faker may have told him to do so. But all the later fragments plus the jaw had to match these earlier, now chromate-stained, ones; and by that later date Woodward was at the site, a man of unassailable reputation.

In 1955 Joseph Weiner, summing up the evidence, said that Dawson could not be shown not to have been the perpetrator. Weiner also touched on the question of who else could have played so complicated a role.

Two subsequent disclosures each added their piece to the jigsaw puzzle. The first concerned Dawson's 'coconut'. In 1959 a radio-carbon date put the Piltdown skull at 600 years, plus or minus 100 years. That date exactly coincides with the time of the Black Death (1348–50). Furthermore, behind Barkham gravel pit where the skull was found there is land known locally as Church Field – the medieval burial ground for plague victims. So Piltdown Man may well have his origin in that epidemic.

The second disclosure came in the 1980s, when two names emerged, both of them linked with each other and with Dawson, for the possible perpetrator of the fraud. One was Samuel Woodhead, Sussex public analyst at the time of the Piltdown discoveries and the other was a London University chemistry professor, John Hewitt. Woodhead (he died in 1941 – we rely on relatives for the details) had been involved in the finds and in later life became distressed about the episode, saying it was made public too quickly. We are told that he unearthed some of the finds himself and suggested the potassium bichromate treatment. Professor Hewitt for his part personally confessed to two ladies over Sunday lunch forty years after the events that he was responsible. It may be that both these men planned the affair as a joke. Both had given Dawson's natural gas at Heathfield its first test, both were Council members of the Society of Analysts. Hewitt had shared a lecture platform with Dawson, Woodhead lived near to Dawson in Sussex.

A script for this joke is easy to write. The year is 1908. One man says to the other: 'Here comes old Dawson again with his coconut. All the press ever seem to talk about is "the missing link". The poor fellow believes he has found it, so why don't we play along?' They agree to do so, and Woodhead, living locally, can visit the site as often as necessary thereafter.

Beyond these two men a dozen or more suspects have been named. Several of them have been cleared; in the rest, motive and opportunity often seem to be lacking. Teilhard de Chardin, Martin Hinton, A. S. Kennard, Sir Arthur Keith, Sir Grafton Elliot Smith, Professor W. J. Sollas and Woodward himself represent the scientists; an unidentified British Museum technician has also been put forward. Lewis Abbott and William Ruskin Butterfield were Sussex characters with the right interests. Horace de Vere Cole was a notorious hoaxer. He is on the list too, as is Sir Arthur Conan Doyle, whose novel about missing-link creatures *The Lost World* was serialized during 1912. Two of the above-named said they knew who faked Piltdown Man. One not named above promised to reveal the person's identity in memoirs to be published after his own death.

Han van Meegeren:
the Vermeer student

It is a wonderful moment in the life of a lover of art when he finds himself suddenly confronted with a hitherto unknown painting by a great master, untouched, on the original canvas and without any restoration, just as it left the painter's studio!

So wrote Dr Abraham Bredius, announcing *The Disciples at Emmaus* in 1937 as a newly discovered work by Vermeer. Few people would challenge this world authority on 17th-century Dutch painting. The faker's point had been made, and the labour of five years was over.

Han van Meegeren (1889–1947) grew up in a large and strictly orthodox Catholic family at Deventer in Holland. An adored school art teacher seems to have substituted for a father. at home the boy's obvious artistic talent was ignored. Han went away to college at Delft to study architecture. He entered a watercolour painting for his college's five-yearly gold medal, and won; whereupon he withdrew from the architecture finals, enrolled at the Hague Academy of Art simply to take their examination, and again succeeded. Such omens were too good to be dismissed. He was married with a second child on the way, but the signs encouraged him to turn down a professorship offer from the Academy and begin a career as a creative artist. Van Meegeren accepted poster and advertising commissions, painted portraits, taught drawing, and before he was 30 had held two one-man shows at which every item sold. With two rebellious friends he ran an anti-establishment magazine. It all seemed a promising start.

Art and corruption

Somewhere along the line, however, possibly in the course of putting his hostile father behind him, van Meegeren worked out for himself an alternative set of values. A number of unrelated incidents show these values developing. After his gold-medal painting had sold for an excellent price he secretly decided to paint a duplicate and earn the same money. Anna his wife found out. She listened in amazement as he told her of his plan to sell it as the original work (his customer was a foreigner about to leave Holland, who could safely be told that the first sale had been of the duplicate). As van Meegeren saw things, there was no deception about this: art was as good as the buyer believed it to be. A second incident proved to the artist that beauty would always be tainted. Van Meegeren gave a weekly drawing class to which somehow it had been arranged to bring a deer from the Royal Palace as a model. Responding to a challenge, he did a lightning sketch of the animal. It turned out very well, an ideal Christmas card, but he could only sell it by identifying the deer as Princess Juliana's. Henceforth all art was the victim of commerce in his eyes.

What happened to his friend Theo van Wijngaarden, a gifted painter and restorer, was even more revealing. Theo found what seemed without doubt to be a 17th-century painting by Frans Hals, but made the mistake of applying a cleaning solvent somewhat more generously than he had intended. The paint became softened, and because one test of a picture's age is the hardness of its oil-painted surface which can take fifty years or more to dry out, Theo decided that he should openly admit his mistake to any experts who might be shown the painting. One leading authority, despite the softness of paint, spoke for the work as by Hals and arranged a buyer. Theo next showed it to Dr Bredius, again telling him what to expect. To Theo's fury Bredius ignored his admission and threw the work out losing Theo the sale. A year later Theo went back to Bredius with a Rembrandt drawing for his opinion. Bredius confirmed it at a glance. This instant appraisal was safe enough, because both men knew that details of the work's former ownership and a full technical analysis would be required before Bredius's verdict went any further. In the event, however, matters took a rather dramatic turn leaving Bredius looking extremely foolish. Theo jubilantly cut the drawing to pieces before his eyes: he had painted it himself. The judgment of authority on which all art depended was shown to be ignorant and baseless, an empty show.

During the 1920s and early '30s van Meegeren became hypnotized by this set of values. Some critics were indeed corrupt – he had even been asked by one of them to pay for a good review. But merely because the critics disliked his work and because some critics were corrupt did not of itself make that work automatically good. Much of van Meegeren's output in truth was very poor stuff. His most rewarding commissions were 'good likeness' portraits done in a tastefully historical manner. Away from these he was sentimental, out of date and fond of mystical scenes that at times went over into soft pornography. There was no special van Meegeren voice, no distinctive personal style. Even his acknowledged technical skill belonged to the Dutch Golden Age (his prize-winning picture could have been painted in the 17th century). And yet this small talent asked much of other people. Divorce came in 1923, remarriage in 1929. His drinking and sexual adventures were too noisy for The Hague's genteel inhabitants. The city art society did not want him for chairman. At last, deprived of what he saw as due recognition, he moved to Roquebrun in the south of France in 1932, taking with him his second wife Jo and their few savings.

At Roquebrun he kept up his lucrative portrait work but the four years to 1936 were in essence one long research period. He was planning to fake 17th-century paintings, and a number of technical details needed to be mastered.

Working methods

First he had to solve the paint hardness problem. There must be a way of making paint dry thoroughly and quickly that did not also discolour it. Some early experiments with an oven led nowhere. Then, while looking at the chemistry of synthetics, he had the thought that what gave bakelite its hardness (a compound of phenol and formaldehyde) might be turned into a resin to be combined with oil and thus made useable in painting. Tests pointed to oil of lilac as the best combining fluid. This could be given the required pigment and then it could be applied as paint, or else, to avoid unwanted drying out, each brushstroke could begin with a dip in resin-oil solution and only then take up paint from the palette. An important side effect was that the drying out left behind almost no phenolformaldehyde – though of course as neither of these components was known in the 17th century no one would be looking for it.

Next came the need to produce authentic old *craquelure* (crackling) in his new painting. Here again van Meegeren made a creative discovery. It had been his plan to use an old painted canvas of the 17th century from which he would first remove all traces of underpainting to avoid its detection by X-ray analysis. With canvas three centuries old, however, he could not risk going below the original ground; but since the crackling began in that ground perhaps he could get cracks to re-emerge in the paint surfaces that he would be adding. Two delicate operations thus went hand in hand: removal downwards and renewal upwards. Van Meegeren seems to have carried out the first of these by using pumice, soap and solvent as appropriate. The exposed ground was given a coat of paint, baked, then painted and baked once more. This was his surface for the new composition, which could involve several layers

To prove himself a faker and not a wartime collaborator, Han van Meegeren paints a copy of *Jesus Teaching in the Temple* by Vermeer. Amsterdam, 1945.

(Above) The Savelli family tomb chest, by Alceo
Dossena in the style of Mino da Fiesole. Even Mino's
receipt for payment was included in the deception, yet
oddly the chest itself shows several elementary mistakes.
Caterina Savelli's sandal, for example, lacks its sole.

(Opposite) Edward Simpson, the Victorian misfit 'Flint
Jack'.

(Above) 'The dig was unsystematic and anyone could join in.' Glozel, April 1928. For France's archaeologists, was the whole affair something best forgotten about?

Dr Albert Morlet (right), with one of his many publications of the finds at Glozel. A final verdict on the story will either show modern test-methods to be faulty or else will somehow reconcile them with traditional 'dirt archaeology'.

SIMPSON

Victorian England could not cope with 'Flint Jack'. His life as a misfit poses the question of whether a fraud may be excused for being born ahead of his time.

Edward Simpson (1815–?75) – 'Flint Jack', 'Shirtless', 'Snake Billy' were among his aliases – said he had been born near Whitby, in Yorkshire. His father was a sailor. At 14 he began to go on fossil-hunting trips with a local geologist Dr George Young; later, the physician Ripley gave him a job, and he stayed as his assistant for six years. On Ripley's death Simpson began collecting fossils on his own and selling them to local dealers. By 1840 this formed his livelihood – a fair amount of which went on drink. In 1843 one dealer wanted a flint arrow copied. Jack obliged, and his entry into faking, together with his best-known nickname, dates from that time.

The years that follow are a story of wandering up and down England. Jack tried selling his wares in London for a year, but the museums were not buying. In Northampton he sold quantities of flint fakes with a few genuine fossils. He worked for a year at York on the city museum's collection of flints, then continued his roving life. The enemy drink was always at his elbow. In March 1867, needing beer money, he was caught stealing and sentenced to a year in Bedford prison. By the time he came out his exploits were common knowledge; at least one further spell of imprisonment followed.

Flint Jack faked in several different areas of find. He was a master at arrowheads, knowing exactly how to 'jump' the shell-shaped fractures away from the flat flint surface. Only a certain number could come off each stone – it was a matter of judging this from such features as the grain. In 1862 the audience at a meeting of the Geologists' Association in London found itself watching while a tramp in gipsy's clothes and navvy's boots showed how this was done. Each flint had a patina (peat bog gave a brown shiny surface, chalky soil a deep black one) where again Jack's skill came to the fore. He also made finds of primitive icons, seals and inscribed stones, wood carvings and amber ornaments, along with celts (polished flints) that needed special grinding.

The Victorian period was fascinated by the idea of completeness: the complete novels of Dickens, every Indian coinage, a full set of fossil types. The thinking here was educational – it was believed that by ordering knowledge both the memory and the appreciation would benefit. Jack at one time supplied the geology professor James Tennant, of King's College, London, with items for what today would be school sets of specimens. Tennant, an enthusiast for technical education, sold them from an office in the Strand without knowing the fossils were modern. When this faking was detected, Jack openly admitted it. Today he would get a job in a museum's educational department making reproductions.

Once they had all of something, the Victorians liked to order it by type. Their archaeologists would look at a flint find first for its external features, then at the use it might have had or at its date. How such a tool or weapon was made received little attention, hence the London audience's astonishment when Flint Jack showed that he knew this. Today with that skill he would get a job in a museum's conservation department, or as a demonstrator.

His own time found no place for Flint Jack, however, and he died a social and scientific outcast in the mid-1870s, probably in a workhouse.

of paint. When the finished work was finally baked (two hours at 105 degrees centigrade) most of the crackling reappeared, and this could be helped along by rolling the canvas or pressing with the thumbs. Ink was then added and removed to simulate centuries of dust and dirt in the cracks. Varnish did the rest.

To achieve authentic colours was an altogether simpler business. Each one had to be made from natural materials: ultramarine from lapis lazuli, indigo from plant juice, vermillion from cinnabar, gamboge from resinous gum, yellow ochre from a native earth, brown from burnt umber, red from burnt sienna, black from carbon. White was particularly important –it had to be white lead because the more stable zinc white was unknown in the 17th century. Van Meegeren found nothing out of the way in such demands; his first art teacher, disliking modern synthetic paints, had already kindled his interest in early pigments.

Such then was the technical challenge, and van Meegeren started out to meet it with some rather stodgy imitations of Terborch and Hals. He next turned to Vermeer, still experimenting, and produced two much better fakes. Both these are pastiche paintings that make use of elements from genuine Vermeers – a jug here, a floor tiling there, sometimes even a recognizable figure. The way was now clear for his supreme effort: *The Disciples at Emmaus* (see page 96/7).

Here again he was truly creative, in that no similar painting by Vermeer existed. It was not at all like the accepted idea of this artist with his gentle domestic interiors, his everyday subjects and the soft 'turning round the form' style of his human figures, all of which were elements that a faker playing safe would go for. The *Emmaus* was innovative fakery, a gamble at the highest stakes. In gambler's terms it was also a bluff, because to produce a false Vermeer that had no parallel among the painter's genuine output would seem so foolish and unlikely as to escape suspicion if all else about it were right. And van Meegeren now knew for certain that all else was going to be right.

Why Vermeer

Although an innovative choice, the *Emmaus* had its feet on the ground at several places. Here Bredius joins the story once again. In 1901 he identified a painting of *Christ with Martha and Mary* as being by Vermeer. It was the artist's one definitely biblical scene, with near life-size figures in a style that was not typical for him. Most experts saw this as an early work, perhaps of 1654; dated a couple of years later was *The Procuress*, which showed a scene that could be from the parable of the Prodigal Son. One theory was that as a young man Vermeer travelled to Italy, where like his contemporaries Terbruggen and Baburen he became influenced by Caravaggio and was inspired to produce a series of his own on religious themes. A convenient gap in what we know about his life, argued some historians, could have been taken up with that series. It only remained to find the pictures. Christ's appearance to the disciples at Emmaus was a subject that Caravaggio had painted three times. The version in Rome had certainly been inspected by van Meegeren. If (as Bredius and others believed) Vermeer had been to Italy, it was probably the one he too would have seen. There are just enough reminiscences of it in the 1937 *Emmaus* to highlight the link. And of course by echoing *Martha and Mary* and *The Procuress* the new work would belong with these known items in the Vermeer religious series that Bredius wanted to find.

Bredius's joyful announcement of the *Emmaus* now makes complete sense. To the 83-year-old, the discovery seemed to crown his life's work. Of course some people would reject the new Vermeer (two did so, one of them before Bredius had spoken) but the simple fact of his endorsement gave the painting first-rank status. By the end of the year a consortium had paid 550,000 florins to acquire it for the Boymans Foundation, where the work immediately went on show to crowds of visitors.

Van Meegeren received two-thirds of the purchase price and was a rich man. Furthermore he had made his point. Those critics he so hated, indeed art history itself, could be destroyed if the facts came out (and he had kept back enough materials from the original 17th-century canvas to show he had painted the work). He would be a celebrated artist overnight. And if the *Emmaus* were returned to him, it would still fetch a high price and leave him with a story to sell.

Why van Meegeren continued his faking, having proved himself the winner, will never be known. A kindly explanation is that once successful he needed to search out fresh challenges.

A further six Vermeers were produced between 1939 and 1942: *The Last Supper* (first version), a *Head of Christ*, *The Last Supper* (second version), *Isaac Blessing Jacob*, *Christ and the Adulteress* and *The Foot-Washing*. One of these, *The Adulteress* was bought by Hermann Goering the Nazi field-marshal, and on being discovered after the war led Dutch security police to the artist. In order to escape a charge of selling national treasure to the enemy van Meegeren had to confess to fraud, and the whole matter came out. Vexed that none of his elaborate preparations were tested scientifically, van Meegeren let his quality decline, and of his poorer later efforts he said: 'I neither conceived them nor carried them out with the same care – what was the use? They sold just as well.' At van Meegeren's trial in 1947 a prominent Dutch dealer spoke for the art world: 'We all slid downward: from the "Emmaus" to the "Isaac", from "Isaac" to the "Foot-washing".' He meant by this his fellow experts, some of whom bought the paintings purely to keep Dutch works in the country; but his remark applied also to the fall in quality of the pictures. And rising upward all the time came their prices. Goering paid 1,650,000 florins for his *Adulteress*, which during the first post-war years made van Meegeren into something of a folk hero.

There is also a less kindly explanation for his continuing to produce fakes. An artist of genuine creative ability (and van Meegeren claimed to be one) keeps his hate of the experts as something for a bad day, something to work round or to put behind him. It should not matter that much. Han van Meegeren by contrast built this hatred into his set of values. It came to dominate him and eventually he could see nothing else.

DOSSENA

A person committing fraud may have almost any motive for calling off the deception. With Alceo Dossena (1878–1937) this motive was love. Born in Cremona, Italy, to a poor family, Dossena took a night class in sculpture and became apprenticed to a well-known stonemason. This brought him repair work on the ornamental detail of old buildings, where the task was to match what he did to what was found. In 1918, after war service, he moved on. Although he never abandoned his Cremonese wife and boy, in Rome his mistress Teresa bore him a second son. He was a well-built, craggy man who liked women.

Dossena was now making sculptures full-time, installed in a succession of Roman studios (five are known). The studio on the via del Vantaggio contained a secret room. He had met the dealer Alfredo Fasoli during the war, and now worked for him and also for Romano Palesi, who had contacts in the rich art world of America. At first, to ease him into the faking of sculptures, they used the pretext that a new church was behind the orders that came back to Dossena. Payment seems to have been five or six per cent of a sculpture's selling price; this percentage fell as the price rose. Whenever he signed a work, the dealer would replace his signature with a a famous name from the past. He was never sufficiently well off to break free from this slavery.

The range of Dossena's output was wide. It included an ancient Greek Athena (so pretty that one dealer had to kiss her) which went to the Cleveland Museum of Art. His Etruscan Diana was delivered in twenty-one separate fragments and ended up at St Louis. In 1924 Helen Frick, daughter of the Fifth Avenue gallery owner, paid the largest sum then recorded for her Dossena: $225,000 for two Annunciation figures in the style of Simone Martini. Dossena could handle anything – wood, marble, terracotta, as relief or in the round. Later he would be openly commissioned, by churches, by new buildings, by rich people wanting a portrait done in Renaissance dress. He did a bust of the fascist leader Mussolini, cursing the subject as he worked.

In 1926 a dealer copied an inscription word for word from a known fake onto the Dossena wood sculpture he was selling. This brought exposure, but luckily the piece was not a major item. Boston's tomb chest, on the other hand, stated to be the work of the 15th-century artist Mino da Fiesole and accompanied by Mino's receipt, was very big indeed (see page 140). Astonishingly, the Boston Museum staff never challenged some important details of this purchase. For example, the Savelli family for whom the tomb was made had died out in the early 15th century, so how could Mino (b. 1429) have done a work showing 1430 as its date? Then too, Caterina Savelli is mistakenly portrayed wearing a sandal with no sole. And more inscription-trouble: on the tomb she is *prefata*, 'the aforementioned' or 'the above', not exactly a word one would expect to find cut in stone.

Dossena included this Boston fake in the revelations that followed his decision to call things off. Teresa, his mistress, had died, and he wanted a funeral for her that would show the great loss he felt. Fasoli owed him $7500, but when he claimed this from the dealer, he was turned away. Enraged, Dossena sued Fasoli for 1,250,000 lire in back payments, some time after which the entire story, plus Dossena's photographs of every sculpture he had made, came out (though the court dropped the case and no fraud was charged).

From 1928, writers on art began expressing doubt about several of the sculptures. Some of those who bothered at all with the now exposed artist took a generous-spirited line. There were visits to his studio, his work was exhibited in Naples and Berlin, New York staged an auction (the proceeds did not quite reach five figures). Sadly, however, next to love Dossena most wanted recognition from his peers. And on that score, *Apollo* magazine wrote of the 1930 Berlin show: 'The faker is finished, but the artist does not appear'. A leading authority of today finds him untalented and meretricious, most clearly so in the works done under his own name.

Of himself, Dossena said: 'I never copied works, I simply reconstructed them. Perfectly familiar with the various styles of the past, not as represented by any particular treatment but as manifest in the spirit, I could not assimilate them in any other way. And that was how I produced.'

Alceo Dossena died in a charity hospital.

Glozel (Auvergne, France):
the jury's still out

Archaeology, like the other human sciences, today makes use of a number of new techniques of analysis. These began with radio-carbon dating (for once living objects) and now include methods that give a time frame to inorganic objects too.

The supporters of this 'lab archaeology' have right on their side. They claim that such analysis is better than one that strays from the object itself into comparisons with what is already known about its surroundings, or about similar objects in other surroundings. 'Dirt' archaeologists however are also not wrong to believe that an isolated find looked at out of context may mislead a scientist even when the new techniques applied to it perform faultlessly – which does not always happen.

The finds

In March 1924 a young farmer ploughing at Glozel in the Auvergne region of France turned up the remains of a sunken glass kiln. These remains included bricks with odd-looking marks on them. The farmer Emile Fradin and his family were sure the site was a grave, and took everything out from it. By that summer word reached the authorities and excavations began. Fradin, just 18 and curious to learn, borrowed books on prehistory and received friendly instruction from a digger at the site. Soon more discoveries were made: inscribed tiles and pebbles (one of the books had illustrations of such things).

The year 1925 brought on stage the second main character in this story. Albert Morlet was a doctor with an amateur's interest in the history of Roman Gaul. He signed up all rights to

HULL

George Hull and his Cardiff Giant show that a fraud may enjoy several lives in succession if the conditions are right.

Early in 1868 Hull, a businessman, bought a huge block of gypsum from a quarry in Iowa and had it made into a contorted human figure 10 ft 4½ in (3.16 m) tall and weighing 2990 lbs (1356 kg). His sculptor achieved a certain realism: dark streaks in the gypsum already resembled human veins, his mallet left marks on the surface to look like skin pores, Hull himself sat for the head. Sulphuric acid gave an ageing effect to the whole piece. On its completion the creature was moved to a farm run by George's cousin William Newell at Cardiff, New York State, where it was buried three feet down in a field later seeded for clover and left a whole year to mature.

Its discovery was carefully handled to seem accidental. Newell laid out the figure, put up a tent and charged fifty cents admission to view Biblical Man. That reference was to Genesis 6:4: 'The Nephilim were on the earth in those days, the mighty men that were of old.'

The 'Cardiff Giant' drew enormous crowds. Soon the admission charge doubled and excursion parties started arriving from Syracuse, even from distant New York City itself. Had the creature really lain here thousands of years and become fossilized? Two Yale professors believed that he had. James H. Drater, the eminent palaeontologist, saw him as a statue. Dr Andrew D. White, first president of Cornell, analysed a fragment of the giant and knew him to be made of gypsum but did not announce the fact. Farmer Newell's tent receipts soared (though he only banked one-tenth as his cut, sending on the balance to cousin George).

The first public denial of the Giant came when Erastus Dow Palmer, a celebrated sculptor, declared him to be neither fossil nor statue but a fake. This announcement interested one man in particular, P. T. Barnum, then in his pre-circus days and with a museum and zoo on Broadway. Barnum made an offer for the Giant which was rejected. He then had an exact replica built of the figure. Meanwhile business initiative had begun locally. Three citizens, headed by a banker, David Hannum, bought a seventy-five per cent share in the Giant and took him to New York for the Christmas shoppers' trade. When they got there Barnum already had his replica on display.

Hannum applied for a court injunction against his rival, but the judge at the hearing considered a real fake still fake enough to be denied such restraint. Both giants went on show, at venues only two blocks apart. Barnum's advertising charged the other giant with being the fraudulent one and accusations flew back and forth. The public paid to see them both.

In January 1870 Hannum's show moved out of town. Dr Oliver Wendell Holmes, the anatomist, bored into the Giant behind one ear and found all within to be solid, lacking a fossil brain. Holmes said the Giant was a statue, probably very ancient. This caused the admission price to fall somewhat, but there were still people who wanted to see the genuine statue after all the fuss over its identity. Barnum's figure stayed on Broadway, and business held up.

The Giant was granted a fourth life when investigative journalists decided to expose him. This proved to be fairly easy. William Newell had not in fact been digging a well (the original story for the Giant's discovery). His large bank transfers of tent admission money were traced to George Hull. From there the trail led to Hull's gypsum quarry in Iowa, then on via railroad freight records to his warehousing a consignment that had weighed 2990 pounds. Cornered by the reporters, Hull told all. His stonemason, he said, had been Edward Burckhardt in Chicago. Both men were candid and good-humoured, and this redeeming feature encouraged newspapers throughout America and Europe to take up their stories. The Cardiff Giant became international news: you *had* to see him now.

excavate the Glozel site, working alongside young Fradin over the next years. Huge quantities of pots, phallic idols, animal and human bones and arrows of flint, came up, all jumbled together with no time sequence visible in them (the dig was unsystematic and anyone could join in). Dr Morlet said that the site was 10,000 years old, which because the pebbles were Old Stone Age (palaeolithic) in appearance made the accepted date for that period much more recent than was generally thought.

The most important group of finds consisted of clay tablets cut with various letters and signs. These must be New Stone Age – were they a form of writing? Salomon Reinach, director of the national museum at Saint Germain, believed so. For Reinach the tablets gave support to his theory that the invention of writing had spread south-east from Europe to the Mesopotamian valley, rather than from that valley and to the north-west. Some said that the Glozel script was ancient Phoenician. In Reinach's view it was even older. He argued that in neolithic times France already had a well developed civilization in the Auvergne.

Everything recent

Such a claim, when put with suspicions that Fradin and Morlet (probably with someone more expert helping them) had 'salted' the site with objects they wanted to be found, sparked off a huge explosion in world archaeology. A technically-minded French prehistorian ran tests on the pottery. It was too soft to have lasted for a decade, much less for several thousand years. The Battle of Glozel raged on, until in the autumn of 1927 an international commission was set up to study the site. Four Frenchmen and two foreigners reported that everything they saw there was recent. Various attempts at giving authenticity to the finds were then shown up as clumsy botching. It began to look more and more likely that steel tools had been used on the pebbles, bones and flints. The French prehistory society started fraud proceedings against 'an unknown person', which were upheld by the court but of course could not point to a culprit. The Fradins sued for libel an orientalist at the Louvre Museum.

Albert Morlet, a true obsessive, excavated on and on, writing articles and pamphlets as he went. The Fradins had opened a café with their takings from the small museum at the site, but gradually public interest fell off as France's archaeologists did their best to forget the whole affair. The last Glozel dig took place in 1942 during wartime. One by one the main actors died – Reinach in 1932, Dr Morlet in the '60s. An episode seemed closed.

New doubts for old

Emile Fradin however survived, and was not yet done with Glozel. There remained his own story to tell. In 1979 this came out in a book called *Glozel et ma vie*. Fradin had never shifted from his view that the finds were genuine, and he now sounded triumphant. A newly developed dating method known as thermoluminescence had been applied to some Glozel objects by a group of archaeologists abroad. This had indicated a date of between 700 BC and AD 100 for the finds – more modern than most of their supporters had claimed, but certainly not a date that could be called recent. Fradin rejoiced. It had all been a conspiracy, that earlier business, set up by experts jealous of his and Morlet's success.

In fact, matters were not quite so straightforward. Thermoluminescence (or TL – it measures the emission of light from electrons trapped within an object that has been exposed to ionizing radiation) requires the object to be heated as part of the test procedure. Possibly, since the Glozel site was a glass kiln where fire was used, the finds had already been heated at some earlier time which would rule out the modern TL results. And moreover the 1970s' tests were coming up with date periods for Glozel that differed greatly among themselves. By one such test the period was 350 BC to AD 100, by another it was medieval, around AD 1200. A second new technique (known as archaeomagnetism, which works by measuring the relative geomagnetic field of fired objects that have cooled in different areas of the world) said that the Glozel pottery could not have been fired within the period 1500 BC to AD 1500. Was it then recent after all? Or was there something odd about the geology at Glozel that skewed the results? Could TL itself be trusted?

DE LUNA BYRON

George Gordon de Luna Byron (d. 1882) claimed to be the poet's illegitimate son by a Spanish countess. This lifelong imposture, never disproved, meshed in with his work as a faker and forger at no extra cost of effort.

His mother (the name de Luna was hers) educated him privately in Europe. The poet Byron may have received proof of parentage on his death-bed; the mother died not long after, leaving her son some jewellery. By his own story, years of wandering brought him to India and to the army rank of major. By 1841 he was farming at Wilkes Barre, Wyoming.

The claimant's first bid came in a begging letter to John Murray, Byron's publisher. De Luna settled in London and immersed himself in literary research. An editor of the Byron correspondence had rejected a number of letters as unsuitable for publication. De Luna shared his house, and on the man's death bought these letters along with transcriptions of various others; yet more were borrowed to copy. The forgery, or perhaps at different times both the forgery and the original letter, was then put on sale.

Mary Shelley became a buyer in 1845. She was collecting her late husband's papers, and although she refused to accept de Luna's Byron claim she made an open-ended offer for any Shelley writings he might find. De Luna kept copies of everything, which led to a dispute between them as to ownership (he threatened to publish the letters). Mrs Shelley realized that these materials were at best doubtful, but she went on buying in the hope that some might be genuine.

Meanwhile the trawl for Byron memorabilia had widened with the announcement that he was to be the subject of a three-volume biography planned by de Luna. This promised to include several hundred unpublished letters, a cue for more to be sent in (their owners may or may not have got their original letters back). The work ran into trouble, however, and in 1849 de Luna sent his wife to dispose of some letters to the bookseller William White with a story that they had come to her from the poet's valet. White sold these to John Murray. A further offer of Shelley materials resulted in de Luna, as their source, being asked to the bookshop. He proved to be very persuasive: some letters from Keats, and more Byron, also went to White at this time. De Luna and his family then departed for America.

De Luna hoped to win fame for himself and publication of his father's letters in New York, but achieved neither of these things. White meanwhile had lost Mrs Shelley as a customer, so he arranged that Sotheby should auction her husband's letters. Most were bought by Edward Moxon, the most knowledgable English publisher of the day. In 1852 Moxon brought out a book of Shelley's letters with an introduction by Robert Browning. By then their real author was back.

Chance now tripped de Luna by the heels. A reader skimming through the Shelley book noticed that one passage almost exactly copied an article on Florence which his father had written some years earlier. The *Athenaeum* magazine weighed in with charges of forgery; it was found that postmarks on the letters were wrong. Moxon withdrew his entire stock of the book. In due course William White reimbursed both him and the earlier victim John Murray. De Luna left the country.

The claimant refused to stop describing himself as the son of Byron, and the fakes also continued for some time. Their grasp of the various different senses of 'authentic' is very modern. From a single genuine letter he could build up a pyramid in which each item supported or was supported by the next. This skill derived from extremely thorough research. De Luna is best seen as a compiler, an editor rather than an inventor, and some of the knots he left behind for Byron scholars may never be disentangled.

The future

In 1983 France decided to give the various different results a thorough independent study. Simultaneously a few more finds recently uncovered at some distance from the site would be analysed. At the time of writing, this study is not yet available. When released it may uphold one period or another from among those already suggested, or it may call for yet more research and testing. That does not matter here, because in terms of what marks off lab archaeology from dirt archaeology the point remains the same.

Glozel for dirt archaeology cannot be explained except as a complete freak or fraud. There are three reasons for this. First, the finds include none of the types of objects common else-where in the region from within all the date ranges suggested for them. Secondly, the finds *do* include types of object that are found nowhere else in the region. And finally there is the time sequence itself, jumping between medieval, Roman, neolithic and Old Stone Age. Objects handled by human beings never accumulate in this way except possibly on a museum tip.

The lines of approach just set out are how archaeologists have always gone about their work and viewed it as a whole. Everyone would benefit if there were a single unified view in future, rather than two archaeologies each uncomfortable with the other's perspective. The final answer from Glozel may perhaps help this adjustment to be made.

Lothar Malskat:
restorer of frescos

Singleness of purpose is a good test for creative art. It should never seem to ask itself about historical accuracy or the limits that some earlier artist worked to. An art restorer, on the other hand, faces such questions every moment. If a work has already been restored, the answers may lead back deeper and deeper like the skins of an onion. There will often be dis-agreement as to how to go about the job.

Not so pure saints

In the 1930s the elders of Schleswig cathedral, north Germany, put in hand a restoration – the second in less than fifty years – of their church's 13th-century wall paintings. The chief restorer Ernst Fey, his son Dietrich and their young assistant Lothar Malskat saw little that was medieval in the frescos. Once they had removed the upper layers of paint the original fig-ures disappeared, leaving only bare greyish plaster. Told to paint the frescos 'in their original style', the restorers decided to catch the spirit of Nazi Germany: at least that would be safe. So portraits of the saints lost their round Eastern faces, their skulls became long and narrow like the heads of Vikings, their colouring spoke of fair hair and pure Aryan blood just as the Third Reich wanted. Other figures and decorations were changed too, though some were not at once noticed. Malskat, with cover from the Feys, did most of the work. He had always been a skilful imitator.

Later, during World War II, a hundred kilometres to the south-east, the church of St Mary's, Lübeck was found to have frescos that could also be 13th century. They emerged in 1942 when flames from RAF incendiary bombs peeled away the whitewash coating from walls and pillars in the nave. Only the barest traces – outlines of figures, some patches of larger areas here and there – were visible. These were drawn and photographed. The church had been gutted by the fire and for some time stayed roofless, but thoughts were already on its restora-tion and on how to follow up the miraculous discoveries.

Together again

For an artist with Lothar Malskat's skill at imitation the first years of peace in Germany

After restoration, the 'miraculous discoveries' at Lübeck. A group of the frescos photographed in 1955.

(Opposite) A faked crucifixion scene at St Mary's, Lübeck. Mary and John are flanking Christ. One expert said of it that the *Christus patiens* style appeared to have been introduced to Lübeck by this great master.

(Right) High up amid the restorer's scaffolding, court president Dr Brammer, left, and faker Lothar Malskat, centre, examine the frescos during a break in the trial. Lübeck, December 1954.

Lord Byron the poet (below), claimed by de Luna Byron to be his father.

Mary Shelley (below right) overcame her doubts of de Luna in the hope that he might supply genuine writings by her husband.

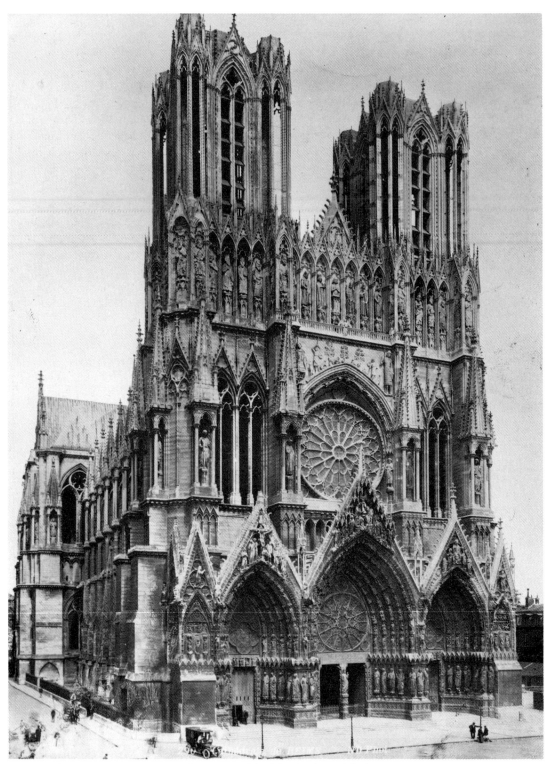

The cathedral at Rheims. Its attraction almost proved fatal for the forger 'Flag' Lagrange.

brought a living. Most galleries were closed, which meant that genuine works by the masters seldom reached the market; low-priced fakes could usually find a dealer willing to handle them. Malskat had spent the war as a soldier in Norway. Now, back home, he had some paintings to sell. He chanced to meet Dietrich Fey in Hamburg. They had a talk and decided to go into business together. Fey knew the dealers to approach. Over five years Malskat faked 600 paintings and drawings, by artists from Rembrandt to Chagall. In 1948 he tried selling on his own but was caught. Fey too narrowly escaped that same year: he was held on charges of handling faked paintings, but claimed ignorance of this – the paintings had been left him as genuine by his father. Fey's charges were dropped, and Malskat also came through his difficulties. That July Fey was commissioned to restore the Lübeck frescos and the pre-war partnership resumed.

As work progressed at Lübeck, a wave of interest spread throughout Germany. Fey's team was said to be using a 'miracle fixative' that peeled the frescos out of the mortar (admittedly no one had actually seen this happen). On-site security was tight. In September 1950 the decision was taken to examine walls of the choir for paintings, following the great success achieved in the nave. Funds poured in to Lübeck. A special postage stamp carried a 5-pfennig surcharge in aid of the restoration, and the church's reopening, timed to coincide with its 700th anniversary, took place before an audience that included Chancellor Konrad Adenauer among the distinguished worshippers.

What they saw inside St Mary's was magnificent. Rows of saints, each figure reaching 15 ft (5 m) in height, colourful ornament, bible scenes and parables, mythical beasts all shone from the walls as brightly as the first congregations would have known them. The choir held the new uncoverings, and outdid what experts had been awaiting in the nave. But there too the frescos were a revelation: their bands of zigzag border now continued unbroken, the patches and shadowy hints now formed complete paintings.

Art historians went into raptures. They wrote about French and Byzantine influence on the paintings, about their subject-matter or iconography. One expert said that the portraits could only come from models found in English book illustration. Another noted how like the frescos at Schleswig these Lübeck frescos were, but possibly done rather later.

Dietrich Fey was awarded the Federal Cross of Merit for leading the restoration team. However Lothar Malskat, the partnership's chief artist, went unacknowledged and his resentment grew.

Beauty is truth

Guiding the work had been principles of scholarly truthfulness. There was to be no continuing or adding. What was already visible, even if it was defective, was to be left alone. This applied to everything except for later interpolations, which had to be removed if that could be done without damaging the older paint or spoiling the general artistic effect. The province's head of conservation insisted that these rules were followed, but not everyone in Lübeck liked them. Why for example when a repeating pattern (say, a decorated border or a set of medallions) had once quite clearly followed on should it not do so now? New work could quite well be made distinct from original by using slightly different tones or materials for it: that also was truthfulness. Other objections were heard from the churchgoing community. St Mary's was built to witness to the living faith, not to be a museum. The age required powerful religious symbols. And since these frescos were 70 ft (20 m) above the worshippers' heads too much 'authenticity' would weaken them.

Claiming his own

What happened next should have ended the story. In May 1952, piqued at the tributes Fey alone had received, Malskat announced himself to be something more than a restorer. He had faked the paintings in the choir – nothing had been found by the search of its walls, no outlines or fragments. Fey had lent him a history of medieval painting and his models for the figures came from that book. The paintings were entirely his work. However, few people believed this announcement. Malskat was but a minor artist looking for recognition, how could he have done all this?

Three months later he provided more details, also confessing to the pre-war Schleswig fakes and to others made then and more recently in local churches. In October Fey's home was searched; a cache of modern forgeries was found, and at the same time Malskat told of the hundreds of such works he had done. At last a committee of experts reported on St Mary's. X-ray photographs showed all outlines to be modern. There was no trace of medieval fragments previously believed to have been restored, the paint nowhere touched 13th-century mortar; Malskat had spoken the truth. Still Lübeck could not accept this blow. It might be true of the choir, but surely those paintings in the nave were good? Malskat said no, they were his too, and further tests by the expert committee confirmed that he was right. The artist described how the old paint in the aisle was so decayed that it crumbled away when touched by the brush. All that could be done was to scour each surface of the vaulting and pillars, then begin again.

While awaiting arrest Lothar Malskat became a popular hero. The experts had been fooled, which always made good copy. His paintings, to the formula of an S-figure with long flowing garments, were judged to be perfectly competent and to catch the Gothic style. It did not matter that some portrayed his relatives. He had been paid no more for these frescos than for a 'correct' restoration.

Fey and Malskat, with two others of the team, stood trial from August 1954 till January 1955. Rumours ran that the whole truth did not come out; payment of fees and grant money left a smell of corruption. For art, in particular the art of restoration itself, the issues were complex. They deserved a better hearing – not for the first time, a court of law proved itself unable to handle questions of artistic morality. Some unjust sentencing underlined this fact: it had been Fey's duty to report the unworkable state of the frescos and to seek new instructions, yet his twenty months' imprisonment was only two months longer than the sentence given Malskat.

Birds of enterprise

What did emerge very clearly at the trial was just how far back a restoration can lead. When the two Feys and young Malskat had worked at Schleswig cathedral before the war, a frieze in the cloisters had below it eight medallions each painted with a turkey. As this was a bird found only in America until the 16th century, and as Fey senior declared the paintings to date from the 13th century, something was wrong. The explanation provided could not have been simpler or more appropriate: the Vikings, with typical Nordic enterprise, had voyaged to America earlier than Columbus and had returned home to Schleswig with turkeys on board for food. A few birds had survived and been painted. This tale caused great delight in Hitler's Germany – articles were written in praise of the spirit of the Vikings. But now, in 1955, it emerged that at the time no one had listened to the restorer of the cloisters in 1888, a man called August Olbers who was still alive in the 1930s. He had turned up to say that on being scoured for repainting the medallions had crumbled away leaving nothing: he, Olbers, had then thought to paint in turkeys. Mind you, only four turkeys – the other four medallions he had painted in with foxes. Of course no one bothered about a foolish old man and his doubt-less invented story; but now the turkeys were eight.

LAGRANGE

Francis Lagrange (b. 1893) claimed that the only sure route into forgery was to be the son of a picture restorer. By the age of 21 however he had quarrelled with his own Parisian father over a girlfriend in Germany. After World War I 'Flag', as Lagrange was known, found work with the French intelligence and was soon stationed in Germany and back with his girlfriend. They married, but he was deported when an informer betrayed him and he never saw his wife again. In Paris Flag learnt that meanwhile both his parents had died from influenza.

Flag survived by painting pornographic art. But in 1926 he won a prize in a competition to design a new postage stamp, which led to a call from the criminal underworld with its own offer – 20 per cent of the proceeds from the rare philatelic items he would duplicate for them. This he accepted, and later he graduated to 100-dollar bills; but faking Gauguin's paintings was more to his liking.

His underworld employer then arrived with an Amsterdam art dealer who preferred to handle genuine paintings. In the present case this would be difficult for the dealer to do: he had a rich Californian buyer determined to acquire a painting by the great 15th-century master Fra Lippo Lippi, but almost all of Lippi's known work was owned by the big national galleries. There might, though, be one possibility. The dealer showed Flag some photographs of a triptych, and explained that a cathedral museum in Rheims, northern France, owned the work. Flag saw a three-panel altar piece, the Madonna flanked by Annunciation and Nativity scenes. It was exquisite.

Installed in a hotel near the Cathedral, and with a rented studio, Flag began his copying task. The little museum was open at most times, but to escape notice he rationed the hours he spent making sketches of its triptych. There were other things to do – the panel wood to prepare, colours to make up

from chemicals supplied by Amsterdam – yet Flag in his solitary two-month assignment drifted more and more under Lippi's spell. The forger, he knew, must be able to destroy his own personality and submerge himself in another's. His own personal creativity counted for nothing.

Eventually the copy was finished and approved. The rich American, said the dealer, would be ready to pay up to five million – but for the original. Flag's copy henceforth belonged in the Cathedral museum, replacing the original which was stolen from there, smuggled through Holland and thence to America. Flag had not realized that this was the plan. He returned to Paris fearful of detection, scanning the newspapers each day but reading nothing in them about a theft at Rheims. Then payment arrived: the sale had realized four million, his own share came to 800,000 francs.

None of this stopped Flag's obsession with the Lippi. He even dreamt about the Madonna, and one day could not rest until he had gone back to Rheims in order to look once more at his work. Along with the satisfaction, the vanity and the delight of a huge joke, he felt vindicated, rewarded for his lifetime belief in his own talent. The Madonna carried no sense of guilt – indeed he tried to convince a German tourist standing next to him that the painter was himself. This act of folly must somehow have got out, because that evening one of the dealer's henchmen called and set Flag on his way home to Paris.

No one knew of the substituted painting until the 1929 Crash, when the American was obliged to sell off his collection. The Lippi triptych was included in a London auction catalogue, and the Rheims museum director noticed it – his own altarpiece – in amazement. Certain the auctioneers must have a forgery on their hands, he went to London, but on arrival was given total assurance of their item's authenticity. This sent him quickly back to Rheims. His own experts took down the piece and examined it. Soon the police were called.

Flag was only traced when the owner of the rented studio attic in Rheims chanced to gossip with a detective making enquiries. The man recalled few details of his tenants, but just as the detective was leaving he let him see a sketch fragment showing a woman's hand and some instruction for painting, which he had found unburnt near the stove. That tenant, an artist, never slept in the room, only painted there. Was this helpful? City hotel registers soon matched the handwriting and came up with the name of Francis Lagrange. By the time charges were brought, however, Flag was awaiting trial on the more serious matter of counterfeiting bank notes. He received a life sentence, to be served concurrently with ten years for the Lippi affair. Later both sentences were reduced to give him a total of fifteen years on Devil's Island.

The triptych made its slow way back to France. Flag believed that it returned to Rheims, but he was wrong: the museum was damaged in World War II and never reopened. Another account states that the original Lippi itself was a copy, and that it is now stored in a basement of the Musée des Beaux Arts in Paris.

Mark Hofmann:
a killer and an Oath

Modern print technology does not encourage historical fakes. Until about 1960 it used to be said that the pioneers Gutenberg and Caxton could visit a printer and still recognize each stage of the work in hand there. Mark Hofmann and his exposure in 1986 underlines a change. The man described as America's greatest forger knew everything about print as a product but not quite all about the printing process.

Mark Hofmann (b. 1954) grew up in a devout Mormon family. He showed youthful disbelief in the faith and never truly accepted its teaching; but at 18 he was received into the Melchizedek priesthood, duly completing a two-year mission (to England). On his return he enrolled at Utah State university, intending a medical career. He married sensibly, and then dropped out from college to pursue his boyhood obsession of Mormon memorabilia.

Gold

The Mormon Prophet Joseph Smith's vision of 1820 and the story of how an angel led him to golden plates bearing the new message put a premium on what the Church called 'faith-promoting documents'. Just as the wave of interest in Mormon history was building, Hofmann came up with a transcript that Smith claimed to have hand-copied from the golden plates themselves. Next he produced a letter from the Prophet's mother confirming exactly the account of his vision that present-day authority required. But not everything Hofmann supplied was good news. For example, he offered a document which soon after that 1820 event showed an associate of Smith describing the angel as a white salamander, a hint that the Prophet's real activities may have been money-digging with the use of folk magic, in which salamanders were known to figure. Hofmann sold his documents, good news or bad, to local Salt Lake City dealers and also directly to the Church at its headquarters on Temple Square.

By 1985 Hofmann's expensive life-style was bringing him into debt. He needed a spectacular find, and foolishly announced one – a chestful of materials taken away by a disillusioned early Mormon – before anything was ready, pledging the lot to a dealer for $185,000. However, a local financier and devout Church member called Steve Christensen, although not doubting the genuineness of what Hofmann came up with, began to involve himself directly with the faker's activities. Desperate now for cash, Hofmann returned to another line of work – literary rarities. Perhaps a coup here would help relieve his money problems.

Making the Oath

The earliest document printed in English in the Western hemisphere, the 'Freeman's Oath' of 1639, was known to exist as a broadside (single leaf) but had long been believed lost. Its text was enormously important as a statement about freedom of conscience. In mid-March 1985 Hofmann went to a New York bookstore that sold print curiosities including cheaper offerings kept in bins where the customers could browse. Mark had prepared a plant, an unimportant ballad sheet which he headed 'The Oath of a Freeman' in early-looking type and then printed off in one copy. This he proceeded to buy at the shop among some other bin-bargains, taking care to get an itemized receipt headed with the shop's name. Now the documented owner of America's most valuable piece of printing, he at once told his New York dealer of his great good luck and set about the detailed forgery.

The broadside was originally by a Massachusetts press that one year later printed the *Bay Psalm Book*, copies of which did still exist. Hofmann took a modern facsimile edition of this book, photographed a few pages and cut up the enlargements one letter or group of letters at a time. With these he built a text of the 'Oath', reduced it to the right size, and had a line block made. To give irregularity (process blocks have uniform type-height) he ground down certain letters with a drill and rounded off their corners with steel wool. Then, knowing that the ink he used might be put through a dating test, he made up ink to his own formula by burning paper of the correct date from books of the appropriate period, and adding linseed oil, beeswax and a darkening solution of tannic acid created by taking some leather from a volume of the period which he then boiled in water. His printing sheet too was of the period. He inked it, pressed it with a clamp and board, and in so doing created yet more irregularity.

By the end of March his 'Oath' was done (see page 161). The following month it was under scrutiny at the Library of Congress, Washington, with a price tag of $1.5 million. A range of searching tests satisfied all the experts (even Charles Hamilton, whose book on forgers had been a major source for Hofmann) but the Library did not buy the find.

Murderer

Time meanwhile was running out at Salt Lake City. Hofmann's earlier pledge was long due for redemption. Via Steve Christensen the Church would soon know the facts of that invented chest of materials – Hofmann was already selling items supposedly from the chest, which could only dilute its value. A trusted Mormon Elder had to be told part of the truth. Hofmann played one story off against another, and wrote cheques that came back uncleared.

On 15 October 1985 a package left overnight at Christensen's office exploded, killing him. A second bomb mistakenly killed the wife of Christensen's boss, the boss himself being its target. Their finance company was known to be in trouble. Could this be some insane creditor taking revenge? The following day a third bomb, this time in a car, wounded Mark Hofmann. His story – a package falling to the floor as he got in – matched neither his injuries nor the car's state. The police were not to be fooled. For them, in an instant, third victim became first suspect; and yet gathering enough evidence to proceed took almost half a year. Before Hofmann's eventual trial began in April 1986 his attorney plea-bargained 'guilty'. In January

1987 Hofmann was given a multiple sentence for the murders and frauds of between five years and life.

The prosecution experts already knew a Hofmann fake by the way its artificially aged ink could be seen to crack when exposed to sodium hydroxide. They found out or had confirmed a great deal more about the fakes and their defects during the long court hearing. The weakness of the 'Oath' that is most interesting, however, was shown up by a man who became involved only later and who did not need to call on the cyclotron, the microscope or the modern chemical analysis.

Everything that this man found wrong about the broadside related to old printshop practice. Lines in 17th-century printing were often out of true, but misalignments (for example in the *Bay Psalm Book* that Hofmann used) at least showed some pattern in their distortion. Here they were all over the place. There was also the drop-initial 'I'. The compositor of *Bay Psalms* did not realize that he was meant to align each such drop-initial with the top of the 'x-height' of one line and the bottom of the x-height of the line below; he set his first word always in capitals, so misalignment was automatic. Hofmann, merely copying product, aligned his drop-initial at the top of the cap height, not the x-height. Turn it how you will, his 'I' was impossible by any typesetting process.

Another 17th-century botch followed in error concerned the ornamental border placed round the 'Oath'. With the *Bay Psalm Book* the compositor had tried various different borders for the five books he set in type. One such pattern became too troublesome (it needed an ornament coming on its own in places, rather than always within a back-to-back pair) and so he gave up that pattern in favour of something easier. For Hofmann the discarded pattern looked 'the real thing', excellent authenticating detail, because using scissors and paste he didn't find it any trouble. And there was one thing more about Hofmann's border: it stood far too close to the type area of the text. Packed with hundreds of separate metal letters and spaces, a heavy forme (the type frame) would have cried out for some furniture (tightening wedges) in between border and text. Only a man who had ever dropped such a forme and then had to clear up the mess could know about that vital item of the printing process.

RUKHOMOVSKY

The people of the Greek colonial city of Olbia near the Black Sea lived at the margin of danger. It was known that in the third century BC, threatened by Scythian nomad horsemen, Olbia's inhabitants relied on the wealth of one of their number, Protogenes, to buy them security. An inscription told how he offered the Scythian king Saitapharnes 900 gold pieces to go away. Saitapharnes became angry – but there the inscription stopped. Olbia survived, however, and one possibility could be that the king was offered another, more acceptable gift. By the late 19th century overseas Greek art enriched by its contact with Scythia had become much sought after, as finds emerged from ruined settlements across the Black Sea area of southern Russia.

In 1896 the Louvre Museum in Paris purchased a gold headdress for 200,000 francs. The tiara (as the headdress became known) stood about seven inches (18 cm) tall, somewhat like a Persian fighting hat in form, with two friezes of figures in relief round the helmet and with ornamental bands to fill in its remaining areas. One frieze depicted scenes from Homer's *Iliad*; the other showed animal battles and Scythian horses being broken in. To the layman's eye the workmanship was exquisite. Moreover the piece seemed to be almost undamaged, its dents being confined to flat areas of the relief. On the tiara an inscription read: 'The senate and people of Olbia to the great invincible Saitapharnes'.

Archaeologists could not agree about the find. For

THE OATH OF A FREEMAN.

I·AB· being (by Gods providence) an Inhabitant, and Freeman, within the iurifdictiō of this Common-wealth, doe freely acknowledge my felfe to bee fubject to the governement thereof; and therefore doe heere fweare, by the great & dreadfull name of the Everliving-God, that I will be true & faithfull to the fame, & will accordingly yield affiftance & fupport therunto, with my perfon & eftate, as in equity I am bound: and will alfo truely indeavour to maintaine and preferve all the libertyes & privilidges thereof; fubmitting my felfe to the wholefome lawes, & ordres made & ftablifhed by the fame; and further, that I will not plot, nor practice any evill againft it, nor confent to any that fhall foe do, butt will timely difcover, & reveall the fame to lawefull authoritee nowe here ftablifhed, for the fpeedie preventing thereof. Moreover, I doe folemnly binde my felfe, in the fight of God, that when I fhalbe called, to give my voyce touching any fuch matter of this ftate, (in wh. ich freemen are to deale) I will give my vote & fuffrage as I fhall judge in myne owne confcience may beft conduce & tend to the publick weale of the body, without refpect of perfonnes, or favour of any man. Soe help mee God in the Lord Iefus Chrift.

Mark Hofmann's 1985 forgery of the earliest document printed in English in the Western hemisphere (1639).

(Right) The Greek-Scythian 'tiara of Saitapharnes' by
Israel Rukhomovsky, supposedly dating back to the third
century BC.

(Below) A cartoon teasing the Louvre Museum for
buying what in 1903 was revealed as Rukhomovsky's
faked tiara.

(Left) Elmyr de Hory. In six years his faked modern masters realized an estimated 60 million dollars.

(Below) A fake Matisse painting, *Lady Reclining on Chaise Longue*, done by de Hory and sold in 1977 under his own name.

(Above) The artist Tom Keating at a press conference after his arrest on fraud charges, July 1977.

(Right) *van Gogh smoking a Pipe*, a painting done by Keating in the style of van Gogh.

the Louvre's director, it had been necessary to act quickly to acquire the find as Vienna and London might reconsider their initial refusals. The head of his museum's Greco-Roman department believed the tiara was genuine, private funding fortunately was available, and within days the item went on display at the Louvre. However, doubts had already been expressed. The art historian Adolf Furtwängler of Munich, allowed to handle it for a few seconds, at once sensed it was a fake. He began with the material – gold that old would have been tinged brownish red – and went on to fault its style and content. Also, a St Petersburg professor said he knew where they made such things today. However the French stood by their convictions.

One year later the dealer who had handled the Olbia finds appeared on forgery charges and a goldsmith named Rukhomovsky was named as the forger. Still the Louvre stood by its purchase, despite a growing body of critics, until in 1903 a false confession by another forger set the story running again. Two friends of Rukhomovsky confirmed that he had made Saitapharnes' gift; the man himself was quoted in Russia as confessing to having worked on it for a client; and a French government inquiry began.

Israel Rukhomovsky (1860–1930) arrived for the inquiry amid extraordinary public interest. A Jew from Byelorussia, he had worked in Odessa since 1892, was a self-taught goldsmith and had two sons who helped. Yet this man, said Paris, had fooled the experts, two of whom had stated in defence of the tiara that not since Benvenuto Cellini in the 16th century had such ability been seen. Rukhomovsky therefore was a 'great master': crowds flocked to him, he received offers to tour, replicas of his tiara became a cult.

It soon emerged under cross-examination that the Odessa goldsmith could in no way be called a Cellini and indeed lacked both intelligence and knowledge. He had, as he said, been working to order. His client wanted a gift for an archaeologist friend's retirement and sent reference books with illustrations in them of what the tiara should depict. One such book provided the Scythian scenes, the other book some figures from 16th-century frescos in the Vatican. Rukhomovsky had also followed a late 4th-century Roman silver dish from the Bibliothéque Nationale, Paris, for the Homeric figures.

Asked to prove his own role, Rukhomovsky described how the various sections were joined together, and the methods of adding age and wear that he had used. This was still not quite enough for the inquiry: away from the tiara he was tested as to whether he could make the piece again. He succeeded, although the results and their present whereabouts are disputed. Once Paris learnt that its great master was a mere copyist all interest subsided. Rukhomovsky went back to Russia.

Adolf Furtwängler, in speaking out seven years earlier, had detected most of the fake's sources. For him, the whole tiara was a mish-mash, clumsily modern in its figures. What had most offended his historical sense, however, was the train of thought behind the neat background story read into the inscription. This story assumed that a Scythian despot in the 3rd century BC could be bought off with a stagey piece of Homer, as though Saitapharnes were a modern prince getting a commemorative mug after some visit. The Scythian had grown angry, said Furtwängler, because 900 gold pieces fell short of what he expected. He did not want a tiara – he wanted more gold pieces.

Elmyr de Hory:
the modern master

For three decades of our time there seemed to be people who could afford big-name modern art no matter what the price. The boom started in about 1961 and ended for all except a very few buyers late in the '80s. The rest of the world looked on as auctions became glamorous occasions at which the bids were headline news for a day. Everyone said it was a swindle, of course. Art dealers were profiteering from inheritance laws and tax relief that allowed the real cost of buying to be greatly reduced. Their clients, worried about inflation, simply saw paintings as a safe place to put money – they wouldn't know one artist from another. Prices climbed and climbed. By mid-1968 public opinion had decided that the dealers were con men, because many of these paintings were fakes. The dealers should be exposed and then the whole house of cards would collapse. Some people went further, asking what was so wrong about a fake anyway?

Prophet

Elmyr de Hory (1911–76) is the great faker from that period. He made two prophecies, one concerning the dealers and a second one about himself. With the first he foretold that his agent would never go on trial for what he did, because that would bring a '1929 Crash' for the dealers and they had enough influence to head off any prosecution. The second prophecy said that he, Elmyr, would kill himself rather than serve a prison sentence for faking. One prophecy came true, one didn't.

De Hory grew up in a wealthy and cosmopolitan Hungarian set where visits to Biarritz, to Karlsbad and Paris during 'the season' were still a feature of life after World War I. His parents divorced when he was 16. He went to art school in Budapest, then to Munich, finally reaching Paris where he had tuition from Fernand Léger. In the Paris of the '20s some great figures of modern art could be seen nightly at the cafés: Matisse, Vlaminck, Derain, Kees van Dongen, Picasso. For his own part Elmyr de Hory worked well, somewhat aimlessly, but with enough success to get into an important show in the company of a Vlaminck painting. His work also sold, though at the time there was no shortage of money from home for him.

World War II saw his charmed existence end. However, Elmyr proved to be a survivor, and in fact the Nazi concentration camp to which he was sent used his services as a portrait painter. Back in Paris after the war he became just another artist wanting a meal. De Hory began faking for money in 1946, perhaps unintentionally. (A friend bought one of his drawings and sold it on, thinking it was by Picasso; even if the deception was intended, de Hory did not expect it to go that far.)

All his life de Hory tried to establish a straight career of his own, but by the mid-1950s most of his time was being given to faking. North America was his base for twelve years except when he moved to Mexico in order to escape Federal charges. He sold modern works purporting to be by the Paris artists he knew when a young man, and these paintings and drawings were bought by dealers in ten US states. His elegant ways and a habit he had of name-dropping went down well.

World horizons

At some point during the late '50s de Hory was spotted by Fernand Legros, an art middle-man, and a partnership began. De Hory now lived on the island of Ibiza. Legros paid him a salary; selling the work no longer involved the artist (which was fortunate, given Legros's world horizons and Elmyr's fear of travel). Between 1961 and 1967 their partnership sold an estimated sixty million dollars' worth of oil paintings, watercolours and sketches. The biggest single customer, a Texas oilman called Algur H. Meadows, bought Dufys, Modiglianis and Bonnards (in addition to de Hory's Paris artists plus a work each by Chagall, Degas, Gauguin, Laurencin and Marquet) reaching a total quantity of thirty-two works. This is output; before long, however, stress and mutual mistrust was upsetting the team. Legros easily became violent, and would rage with Elmyr over money. Just before an auction sale near Paris was due to open, the blue sky of a 1906 Vlaminck started coming off the canvas (Elmyr had skimped the drying process). The London *Evening Standard* wrote that a stable of forgers was operating on Ibiza, though it was not known for sure who they were.

Early in 1968, helped by the French auctioneers of the still-wet Vlaminck and also by a now better informed Algur Meadows, the police were knocking at the stable door on Ibiza. Elmyr sat out two months in the town's pleasant jail; the all-purpose charges amounted to his being thought 'undesirable'. Legros received a three-month suspended sentence for travelling in Switzerland on a false passport. This might not look much punishment for their crimes, but the partnership as a going concern never sold another picture.

Elmyr de Hory's skills are impressive, even though the area of painting that saw them in use is one in which fakes are common because faking is easy there. He poured scorn on the idea that he should get inside another painter's soul. For de Hory, matters came down to a challenge for technique, and sometimes his faking highlighted an interesting technical point. He discovered for example that his own line with the brush flowed easily, but that Matisse while drawing would often look up at the model, which gave a slight 'blip' to his line. Elmyr's had to hesitate and blip too. De Hory was insistent that he never actually copied another artist; instead he produced work that the other might have done. Picasso's drawings were easy, but only if they could be his earliest ones. (Anything later was too well known and would be in the records.) Cezanne, Braque and Monet he found the most difficult to fake; all three, he said, were 'very great artists'.

Still a difference

The art world needed some time to clear up after this partnership ceased trading. No one agreed as to how much damage had been done. In New York only two legal actions were brought against a gallery (both cases concerned more faked Dufys). Some dealers said that Fernand Legros had improved the selling of art: the expert 'authentication', once made so much of, would now matter less than a dealer's personal guarantee. Pre-sale details of items would have to be given a standard form across the trade, so that they were clear to all and said what they should say.

Amid this uncertainty one thing was sure: there would be no Great Crash if Legros talked. Because some people could not tell a de Hory from a genuine work did not, after all, mean that there was no real difference between a fake and an original. Fernand Legros, extradited from Brazil in 1976, was later prosecuted by the French State and sentenced to two years imprisonment for swindling Algur Meadows. De Hory also faced extradition to France and a prison sentence there. True to his word, in December 1976 he took a fatal overdose of sleeping pills at his home on Ibiza.

Tom Keating:
the art-faker hero

Early in September 1984 almost two thousand visitors packed into a little cottage in Dedham, Suffolk, to view the former owner's paintings ahead of their sale. It was a studio clearance:

the paintings were the owner's own work. He had been dead for seven months. By all the laws of the marketplace, interest in Tom Keating should have been low, maybe a hundred pounds or so per item. But this crowd at the cottage said that something special was going on. The auctioneers mentally revised their price estimates and looked to the sale to explain it with bids and cheques.

Lessons after school

Tom Keating (1917–84) came to art entirely straightforwardly. His father, a housepainter in Forest Hill, south London, smelt of linseed oil; uncles and brothers also worked with their hands. Tom, aged 7, won a paintbox by swimming one width under water, and with this prize won a painting competition. The large family were almost destitute throughout the Depression. There was no money to stay on at school, so at 14 Tom drifted into house-painting until World War II sent him to the Far East as a ship's stoker. He was invalided out with nervous strain in 1944, married the fiancée of a comrade who had been killed, and then returned to odd jobs in south London. A serviceman's grant allowed him two years at Goldsmiths' College studying art, but Tom failed the diploma exams ('High points for painterly technique but falls down on original composition') and when the Wildenstein Gallery offered to show his paintings he could not afford frames. That seemed to leave only picture restoration as a career.

For a man fresh out of art school there was plenty to learn: relining canvases, filling cracks, judging the effect of varnish on colour, and much more. Keating paid heed when a dealer, anxious to please his client, asked him to 'uncover' attractive new elements in the composition – boating scenes, cows in an empty landscape, a pretty young girl with beribboned hair. These might be borrowed from another artist as pastiche. From there his excellent visual memory made the easy step to creating an entire new picture. Tom thought this was fun; he still had to learn that a reputable gallery would put such pictures on sale as the work of a famous artist of the '30s, at a price many times more than a Keating would fetch.

Keating's faking began in the early 1950s, but the restoration work continued for several years. As a restorer he was welcomed into a number of Scottish houses and castles, and in Marlborough House, London, he uncovered on the staircase walls a battle panorama by Louis Laguerre that had lain buried beneath multiple coats of near-black varnish. The image of the jovial Cockney, the 'cheeky chappie' able to chat with the great, is also from this time. Those who knew Tom agree that this joviality hid a sense of insecurity and came with huge swings of mood.

Avenging

His own version of why he turned to faking says a final goodbye to south London straightforwardness. By this account he saw himself as one of a painterly brotherhood that was immortal. An artist of the past whom he felt close to ('the gaffer' Rembrandt, Goya, the Englishmen Thomas Girtin and Samuel Palmer) would 'come down' to him and inspire a new work. Ideas would flow out with no effort on his part. On one occasion a picture painted itself – he awoke one morning to find what he knew must be a Degas self-portrait on his easel in place of the painting he had been working on the day before. He claimed that what happened to these works and whether or not they fooled the public was of no interest, that they simply went out into the world to have a life of their own. Nevertheless many of the earlier brotherhood (especially the French Impressionists) had died in poverty as a result of being exploited by dealers, and so he would do what he could to avenge them. It was a formula that made good his own early discouragements as much as any of theirs.

In 1964 Keating began to teach a girlfriend how to restore paintings. They moved in together and built up a business in East Anglia, the girl (Jane Kelly) handling sales. On his own for a weekend, Tom turned to a library book he had borrowed about the 19th-century visionary artist Samuel Palmer. Over the next two days Palmer came down to him with scarcely a break, and sixteen drawings were the result – some in sepia wash, others in watercolour.

Ripe for treatment

Samuel Palmer was an excellent choice – if the coming down left a choice – for the 1970s market. Fewer than 130 works by him were known to exist. His great period (that of the Shoreham paintings done near his home in Kent) spanned the years 1827 to 1837. These consisted of tiny landscapes, their sheep and wheatsheaves, bats and slumbering rounded hills painted with the magical quality of a dream. After this period Palmer became more conventional at the urging of his successful father-in-law, the artist John Linnell, and only towards his death in 1881 did his work regain some of the rapt, mystical quality of the Shoreham paintings. These Shoreham masterpieces were virtually unknown before the 1920s; high prices were uncommon until 1960. Palmer was 'discovered', he was on his way to becoming popular (his links with William Blake would ensure that), but he was still young in terms of saleroom exposure.

The first Keating Palmer to be put on the market by Jane Kelly was in 1970 at a Suffolk gallery, and it sold to Leger Galleries, London, for £9400. She sold a further three to Leger in 1970–71 and by this time had made a provenance (the record of previous ownership) for all four works – they had come to her as a bequest when her grandfather, a tea-planter in Ceylon, died in 1967. The paintings had gone out East with his father-in-law a century earlier. That ancestor's father got them from Palmer himself: it was a perfect three-step link to the artist.

In 1974 another four very similar Palmers were offered to a different London gallery for £60,000. Too many doubts meanwhile had been voiced by experts and they were declined. Five more fakes joined them, some sold, some not; tests conclusively showed the paper to be modern. Geraldine Norman, saleroom correspondent of *The Times* of London, wrote an exposé article in July 1976. She named Tom Keating a month later; characteristically he did not wait long before meeting her to tell all. Their joint book appeared just before his arrest on charges of conspiracy and criminal deception in July 1977. An old friend, the antiquarian dealer Lionel Evans, was also charged as owner of the 1974 Palmers and other works. Jane, now Jane Maurice, joined them from Canada at her own decision.

The trial covered a great many more fakes than those of Samuel Palmer. Keating estimated his output at some two thousand works in the style of as many as 121 individual artists. It was impossible to say what had become of large numbers of them, and the hearings soon turned into a free-for-all directed at the art trade itself. The press gleefully reported its 'bent' dealers, its easily-fooled experts. Readers' letters discussed money and aesthetics, the House of Lords discussed action by the Trade Department to save a national asset: the British art market itself. Then Tom Keating had a motorcycle accident; early in 1979 the trial was called off because of doubts about his health (there was bronchitis and a heart condition). Jane Maurice, who had turned Queen's evidence, and Evans, who changed his plea to guilty on a minor charge, both received suspended sentences. Keating walked free.

Although the police tried to kill his most celebrated fakes (the 1974 Palmers for example are under guarantee never to be sold as the work of Samuel Palmer), Keating's own uncertainty made tracing the others a nightmare. He often gave paintings away on impulse, or sold them for amounts too trivial to record. Evans claims to have a list that will be released only on his death; Geraldine Norman says there is more to her story too. Keating himself described his fakes as having tiny clues – the day's date, rude comments – embedded in them, but this is now generally thought to have been mere showing off. His easy-going way with materials (modern poster paints thickened with decorator's emulsion for the Impressionists, flecks of coffee for Rembrandt age-spots) ensures that science will find it easy to detect him.

You too can do it

The trial created public interest in Keating as the man who had run rings round the experts. His output picked up too. Most of the works being viewed at Dedham before the studio sell-up in September 1984 were done after the trial, and the ones signed as Keatings have a relaxed, engaging feel to them.

What made him and them so particularly hot, so attractive to customers who might never think of paying big money for a picture, was something very simple and better remembered than a trial called off five years previously. Two days after his death a television series had begun in which Tom Keating showed viewers how to paint like the Impressionist Masters. He spoke of the importance of *plein air*, demonstrating how Camille Pissarro would have brought the open air to a painting, then went on to van Gogh, Manet, Monet and Cezanne.

This de-mystifying of a highbrow subject, this promise of a shared discovery, was indeed immortal brotherhood. The auction bids and cheques from the September sell-up produced £274,000. 'Monet', 'van Gogh' and 'Sisley' were the big ones, naturally, but even a portrait of Tom with Jane went for £6000.

A QUESTION OF IDENTITY
PEOPLE

The best impostors, acting out someone else's life, seem often to want their new identity for itself alone. That is their talent. Anastasia and Tsar Dimitry are better performers than the Tichborne Claimant, who was just after the money.

In fact most if not all of the people in this section combine imposture with claim. Dr Barry's pretence was her means of becoming medically qualified; but she also claimed a right to be as difficult a person as the next man. The backers of an imposture always have a double motive. Those who funded the Pretenders Simnel and Warbeck wanted more than the royal title in return, and so did the American admirers of Sarah Wilson, the Princess Susanna.

Modern life does not favour the impostor. We are given a computerized record before we are born. Our schooling and employment, our DNA fingerprints, confirm us as ourselves. We also know exactly how we look: before about 1860 and the photograph, little notice was taken of what made one person differ from another. A false Martin Guerre passed for the true one after only a few years away. Today too there is no such place as 'abroad'. The world has shrunk since James Reavis baffled southwestern America with tales from distant Spain. Now Phoenix, Arizona would fax Madrid and check him out.

Even with these obstacles the best impostors can still get beyond the detail and relax into their role. They will never be fully understood, because when all is done they have most deceived themselves.

Martin Guerre:
a man takes a wife

In 1538 a very young couple – he was going on fourteen, she not even quite that – were married at the French village of Artigat, in the Ariège. Martin Guerre came originally from the other, Basque, side of the country near the Atlantic, and grew up in Artigat as something of a misfit. Locally his name got him teased (it meant an ass). By contrast, the beautiful Bertrande de Rols very much belonged in the district. Her dowry of a vineyard, as well as the usual cash settlement and furnishings that included a bed and a splendid coffer, showed her family to be well established.

For eight years the couple had no children. Eventually a 'wise woman' was hired to break the spell: they were given special foods to eat, and four masses at the village church. Bertrande at once became pregnant and had a son. However, Martin did not much enjoy being a rich peasant heir and a father. Sword exercises and boxing – he was tall – were the only fun to be had in Artigat. He had no schooling to admit him into one of the professions, nor could he be a shepherd and escape that way on long journeys among the mountains. So when in 1548 he quarrelled with his father (this was more than mere words: he had stolen some of the old man's grain, which for a Basque family amounted to dishonouring him) Martin decided to leave.

His still-young wife was well looked after by both the families. After some years Martin's uncle Pierre married her widowed mother, and she moved in to their house with her son Sanxi. Bertrande had always liked Martin's four sisters; they, her mother and uncle Pierre's daughters by a first marriage now made it a life among women. As well as owning a tile factory in the village, the Guerres had land in their former Basque home country. Money would not be lacking, and after Martin's parents died Uncle Pierre saw to that. A son and heir gone missing did not make much work for lawyers on Bertrande's and Sanxi's behalf. Meanwhile the old parental house in Artigat intended for Martin Guerre could be leased out.

Although safe and comfortable Bertrande was in a kind of limbo. Martin's leaving had closed the door to a second marriage no matter how long his absence. Could she perhaps fake news of his death? The bishop responsible for their church had his seat at Rieux, several hours' ride away, and took little notice of Artigat. A woman less mindful of honour might have risked a lie and claimed another man. But Bertrande was strong-willed; during the long childless time at the beginning of her marriage, she had never considered taking another husband and she wouldn't now. But suddenly in 1556 she lost the initiative.

'Martin Guerre is back!' His four sisters were the first kin to hear this joyful news. They fetched Bertrande to an inn some miles up valley where 'Martin' was resting from his long journey. She did not immediately accept that it was he, but after some affectionate words and memories (the long white stockings he liked so much – had she kept them safely in the big coffer?) Bertrande saw her husband once again.

The wanderer returned

This sequence of joy, doubt, a shared secret and recognition was followed with each member of the family in turn, then with the whole village. The man might not be as tall and agile as before. He spoke more easily, seemed brighter and more open. But anyway, after eight years it was hard to recall exactly what Martin Guerre looked like. Unless you were very wealthy, the only portrait you would see of anyone was the king's head on a coin or the Good Lord himself over the altar. If this man's own sisters could forget that earlier he had carried a scar above one eyebrow, if they chose to embrace him in delight, well, why couldn't others? And the wife beyond doubt was honourable.

'Pancette' du Thil, the newcomer, may have known Martin Guerre. They both did some soldiering, though for different kings. Du Thil came from the north west, beyond Rieux, and after a youth of petty crime had left his village for much the same reasons as Martin did. He joined the foot-soldiery of Henri II and fought in Picardy. The real Martin was there too. After entering the household of Cardinal Mendoza in Burgos as a lackey, Martin Guerre had been drafted into the army of King Philip II of Spain. But all that formed their past histories. For the near-present, Pancette was on record as being mistaken for Martin in 1553 or 1554, and as seeing the possibilities that this opened up. He soon afterwards began his study of the man he would become. Everyone liked talking to Pancette, he had a golden tongue and a wonderful memory. Rather than return to his own village after the soldiering, he turned south toward Artigat and the chance of an inheritance larger than anything he stood to get

Pancette and the judge at Toulouse. A scene with Gérard
Depardieu and Roger Planchon from *Le Retour de Martin
Guerre*, the 1982 film of the story.

Lambert Simnel (left), acclaimed at Dublin and crowned there as Edward VI; Perkin Warbeck (below left), who went as Richard IV. Both impostures were a challenge to Henry Tudor by disaffected Yorkists.

(Below right) The Pretender Dimitry, Tsar of Muscovy. 'He caught the eye with his vitality'; had his luck held and his mistakes been fewer, the course of Russian history would have been changed.

(Opposite) Boris Godunov, Tsar from 1598 to 1605. Many people supported the Pretender Dimitry only to rid themselves of the hated Godunov family.

King Louis XV, the Chevalier d'Eon's secret patron (portrait after Vanloo).

lawfully. Step by step he built up his new self. There was no hurry.

Once they were together in 1556, Pancette and Bertrande with the boy Sanxi moved into the old parental home and took up the life of a married family. They were happy (others noted this). It must have been acknowledged by Bertrande that they were counterfeiting a marriage, 'living tally' as common law still allowed but which in her case would be judged adultery under canon law. She remained serene, however, and the couple had two daughters (one, Bernarde, survived). Her husband learned more details about Martin 'in conversation day and night' with her. It was a warm, companionate life.

A storm gathers

Pancette became skilled in helping to run the Guerres' affairs, and in buying, leasing out and selling land. He had new ideas for making them rich. Even some of the ancestral property in the Basque country, it seemed, could usefully be sold. This innovation led to a row with the uncle Pierre Guerre and when asked to show the accounts he had been keeping since his brother's death, the old man refused. Somehow, perhaps because in truth Pierre was keeping back some part of the inheritance but more likely because he resented Pancette's wish to put the profits from it to work, this request and refusal found them both in court. Local law and custom were on 'Martin's' side: as heir, he had a right to see such accounts. Pierre took this as his signal to express doubts about 'Martin'. The man, he said, was an impostor. Pierre's sons-in-law agreed; so did the shoemaker (true Martin had larger feet). There was some attempted violence, and within three years of Pancette's arrival in Artigat the entire village was split over the matter.

Bertrande stayed loyal. With Pancette she worked out a carefully matched story of their presumed years together going back to 1538. As a trial judge later put it, some details made easy knowing but hard telling. The woman coached the man in places, dates and times for what had been 'the most secret acts of marriage' and in 'what went on before, during and after these'.

The couple were soon to need their story. In the autumn of 1559 a local landlord, suspecting Pancette for the loss of one of his barns in a fire, had him imprisoned; the court was told that furthermore the man was a marriage-breaker. Pierre meanwhile had made secret inquires and could produce two men who knew Pancette du Thil from earlier days. On his release from the arson charge Pancette was seized by Pierre and the sons-in-law, informed that Bertrande wished for this, and was then taken off to prison at Rieux. His wife of three years either simply could not hold out against the pressure from her mother and stepfather, or else decided to go along with the court action that Pierre had begun in her name and trust to the worked-out story to carry the day.

Two trials

At the hearing, 150 people were called to give testimony. Those who were unable to speak one way or the other about the accused's identity outnumbered those who said he was Martin Guerre added to those who said impostor; but there were more people against him than were for him. Apparently unanswerable items such as Martin's scar, the warts he had and his larger feet did not bother the accused. Bertrande kept to the agreed story except where she was forced to call Pancette an impostor, to which he retorted 'Pierre Guerre told you to say that'. When asked if she would deny him under oath, she refused. Pancette himself stayed complete

SIMNEL & WARBECK

The rival English houses of Lancaster and York, helped by a split among the Yorkists over Richard III, finally patched together a coalition in 1486. Henry Tudor was thought to be excluded from succeeding to the throne by a ruling on his mother's family. His marriage to Elizabeth of York, Edward IV's daughter, formed part of the pact and followed recognition of his claim by Parliament. For the next dozen years, however, he would be troubled with rival claimants backed by supporters abroad.

Lambert Simnel (1477–?1534), in real life a baker's son, came into the care of an Oxford priest named Richard Symonds to figure in an imposture. Rumours had begun that the two little princes in the Tower had not been murdered, and initially the plan was for Simnel to be passed off as one of them. This was replaced by a better story – the believed escape of Edward, earl of Warwick, Edward IV's nephew. Symonds took his boy to Ireland in 1487, where the local anti-coalition Yorkists flocked to him. Requests for aid went to Warwick's aunt Margaret, duchess of Burgundy, and Simnel was crowned Edward VI in Dublin Cathedral. Henry made the simplest possible reply: he paraded the real Earl of Warwick through the streets of London.

Margaret took up Simnel's case and procured two thousand soldiers. With the rebel Lord Lovell and John de la Pole, earl of Lincoln, these joined an Irish contingent that summer and crossed to England, landing in Lancashire. Near Stoke-on-Trent they met Henry's stronger forces. The ensuing battle left 4000 Yorkists dead, Lincoln among them. Symonds and Simnel were taken prisoner.

A second claimant started more promisingly. Perkin Warbeck (?1474–99) came from a rich family in Tournai, Flanders, with a background of languages and travel. An employer brought him to the notice of Irish Yorkists, who remarked on his regal good looks. After some debate his imposture settled for Richard, duke of York, the younger of the little princes. An invitation to France had to be cut short but the new duke was welcomed in Flanders by Margaret of Burgundy, who coached him in his part. Maximilian, the Habsburg regent, also acknowledged him, as did James IV of Scotland.

Warbeck mounted three sorties against England during 1495–7. The first used 1500 men supplied by Maximilian to attempt a landing in Kent. It failed disastrously: one-tenth of the force was caught and executed. Then from Scotland (where the far-sighted James arranged for him to marry but not to be given many soldiers) he invaded the north. Bad weather and strong opposition ended this attempt. Finally after a year in Ireland Warbeck took advantage of a local rebellion against taxes to attack from Cornwall. At Bodmin he proclaimed himself Richard IV and counted 15,000 men with this local support, but loyalist troops broke them up at Taunton and Warbeck left his supporters, taking refuge in a sanctuary. One week later he agreed to

master of the courtroom, alert, witty, quick to read each new turn in the proceedings. Yet for all that, the verdict was 'guilty'. And the plaintiff Pierre Guerre's wish for amends (an apology and fine) was thrown over when the King's attorney, who was also a party in the trial, requested death. Pancette, told he would be beheaded, at once appealed to the Parliament of Toulouse. His case reopened there in April 1560.

Peasants would quite often go to a rural court presided over by one judge and argue their case before him without the help of a lawyer. Toulouse however was the regional capital, and its criminal chamber impressed, as did the dozen or so judges in splendid robes who brought with them much power and experience. Pancette had been superb at Rieux but now, still alone, he did even better. The Toulouse court looked at the quality and 'manner' of those it heard testify (after the many depositions already given there could be little new evidence). Pancette came across as 'truthful in everything' – confident in manner, loving to his wife and sure that she was acting as she now was only because she had been compelled to do so.

The Toulouse judges were seeking a verdict that would keep together rather than sunder two people. In the words of one reporter, they wanted to help the marriage, its children, and the defendant's case. As for Pierre, his manner was unsatisfactory. He was ordered to be chained

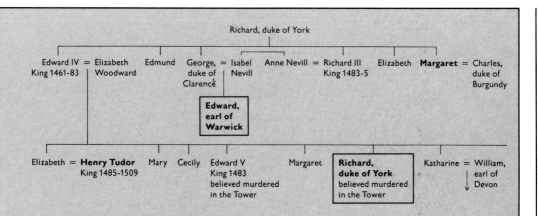

come out.

Both Simnel and Warbeck relied heavily on the Duchess Margaret. She wrote letters recommending them to other princes and saw to it that they got help. Her own reason for hating Henry Tudor was that on his accession to the throne most of the estates and money granted her by her brother Edward IV were confiscated (Warbeck undertook to return them). For us today, the interesting question is how Margaret managed to act out her belief in a second claimant after suffering such embarrassment with the first. She is said to have pretended to disown Warbeck as a test of his ability to reconvince her in the role. He passed with flying colours – indeed by some accounts he genuinely believed he was the Duke.

Henry treated both impostures with total self-assurance. Simnel he laughed at: the 10-year-old became a scullion in the royal kitchens, later promoted to falconer, while Symonds spent the rest of his days in a monastery. Warbeck was left to trip himself up. The man confessed, received a custodial sentence and in 1498 fled to sanctuary once more. The king had him removed and sent to the Tower. A fellow prisoner there was the Earl of Warwick. A letter to him from Warbeck outlining escape plans reached the governor, who informed the king of its contents. Both prisoners were tried for treason and executed in November 1499. Warbeck, a miserable figure, pleaded royal descent. Warwick died with dignity.

and kept away from both Pancette and Bertrande. False accusation spoke in his behaviour over the accounts and in the attempted violence: false accusation broke the Eighth Commandment. But just as the judges hovered around a decision, the balance of their opinion settling toward an outcome that would favour Pancette, a strange figure appeared at the court chamber. 'As ever, the Good Lord showed himself willing to aid the course of justice': Martin Guerre, hobbling on one leg, had returned from the Flanders wars.

Hers the fault

Pancette throughout both hearings could rely on support from the four sisters, but the eldest sister now fell on her brother's neck and wept, the others soon following her. Resistance crumbled away. Even though the old new Martin seemed better to recall things from the past than the new new Martin was able to do, his time was up. Bertrande knew this, and grovelled: Pancette had tricked her, she said, had tricked everyone. She had so much wanted her husband back that she had believed the sisters, yet the moment she realized the man was an impostor she had taken him to court. Martin listened impassively 'with a hard, wild face'. A wife alone knew a husband and the fault was hers alone.

The court kept to its wish that a marriage might be preserved. Pancette was sentenced to be hanged, after making 'honourable amends' in front of the church at Artigat. It was a final brilliant speech confessing his crime and his regrets, and leaving his property to Bernarde, his daughter. Martin and Bertrande Guerre were reconciled and eventually had another son.

Yuri Otrepyev:
Tsar Dimitry

Ivan IV ('the Terrible') reigned man and boy for fifty years as Tsar of Muscovy. He took wife after wife to ensure a son who would keep unbroken the male line of descent from Rurik the Viking. Of these wives only the first one and the last, his seventh, brought surviving male issue. Ivan quarrelled with and tragically killed his eldest boy. Fyodor, childless too like his elder brother, succeeded Ivan on the Tsar's death in 1584. Sixteen months before that event Ivan's third son, Dimitry, had been born.

Amid the uncertainty surrounding the new Tsar Fyodor a strong man emerged. Boris Godunov was Fyodor's brother-in-law. He took over from the council of state set up by Ivan and ruled as regent. Boris sent Dimitry's mother to live at Uglich, some eighty miles outside Moscow, giving as his reason that she had been plotting for her infant son to be Tsar.

Dimitry proved to be an epileptic. At the age of 8 he had a fit while out of doors with his play-mates, cut himself on a knife and died. The circumstances were ugly and confused. A town riot broke out, other children were blamed for the death – some were killed in their turn and the father of one of them was lynched. Four days later an inquiry team led by Prince Vassily Shuisky arrived in Uglich. Had the boy really died? Shuisky could not have known what Dimitry looked like, and the boy's mother, grief-stricken, shut herself away. The inquiry threw little light on the matter; the people blamed Boris Godunov. Rumours began that the boy had survived.

Useful rebirth

Twelve years later the new young valet of a Polish prince came tumbling out with a story that culminated in the revelation that he was in truth that boy Dimitry, the son of Ivan. For this Polish prince, the notion that Muscovy's Tsar had taken refuge under his roof supplied the answer to a problem. His estates lay close to the border with Muscovy and suffered from bandit raids. He realized too, beyond his own concerns, that Dimitry carried a message for Poland itself and indeed for its Catholic Church. The Cossacks of the nearby Don region, always a threat, detested Boris Godunov and could become this Pretender's allies against him, thus leaving the Poles alone. Moreover, Boris now ruled as Tsar. The Pope sought a defence against expansion by the Moslem Turkish Sultan: if this young man and what would mainly be his Catholic supporters could be enlisted, then after Boris was overthrown a valuable bulwark in Moscow would result. It might even be that the 1000-year split between the Roman Catholic and Russian Orthodox faiths would heal.

The young Dimitry stood broad-shouldered like his father Ivan though not so tall. Marvellous on a horse, graceful and agile, he caught the eye with his vitality. Clearly he had been

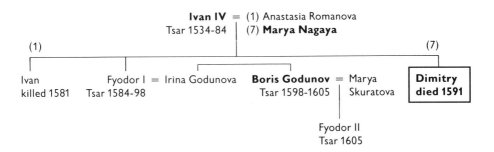

educated. From a safe base removed farther to the west the Pretender's cause took shape. It called for skilful diplomacy on all fronts. Sigismund, elective king of Poland, had only recently signed a treaty with Boris Godunov. Many members of the Polish Diet (the legislative assembly) believed Dimitry to be a fraud, and even after one of his former servants, sent as Sigismund's spy, had recognized him to be the child he had known, the Pretender still needed a majority vote. Dimitry's self-belief got him through all doubts and difficulties. He went to live with a relation of the prince whose valet he had been, a senator named Mniszech. (Mniszech faced bankruptcy: the Pretender was his last great chance.) Dimitry impressed the ice-cold King Sigismund. He worked on his own conversion to Catholicism, showing that he understood that this should be kept from his Russian Orthodox supporters. He corresponded with the Pope. He fell in love with his host's daughter, Marina, and signed a marriage agreement (effective once he was on the throne) that would make Mniszech rich for life.

Under threat of attack Dimitry and his cause prospered. Two assassins sent by Godunov to kill him were caught: they proved him genuine. Later, Tsar Boris tried to tell the Cossacks that Dimitry was an escaped Kremlin monk known as Yuri Otrepyev, or 'Grishka'. The Tsar had found a second and third monk to tell the story of their wanderings with the Pretender, and also used Otrepyev's uncle, but these exposure attempts failed too. By September of 1604 Dimitry's followers, some 2500 Polish and Russian knights, infantry and Cossacks, were ready to move.

Triumph

The march on Moscow showed a peak (victory at Novgorod Seversky), a trough (defeat at Dobrynichi) and four level months of idleness in the town of Putivl. As the year drew to a close the Polish Diet assured Boris's envoy that the Pretender would get no help from its king, but that of course no one could do anything about the Cossacks. In May 1605 news reached Putivl that Godunov was dead. One of his old favourites, now his son's general, went over to Dimitry. The advance became unstoppable. In June Dimitry and his swollen army entered Moscow, only days after the young Tsar, Boris's son, had been hacked to pieces by a mob.

Dimitry immediately began to make mistakes – as he rode up to the Kremlin gate an icon was offered him but he neglected to follow custom and kiss it. He went on into the palace accompanied by two Jesuit priests and a Lutheran official: such people were unclean in Russian eyes. He misread the strength of enemies. Prince Shuisky, the inquiry leader, had three times in the past proclaimed Dimitry's death at Uglich. Now the prince swore that the man was genuine – another boy had been substituted for him fourteen years ago – but soon changed this to whisper a rumour whereby the new Tsar was an impostor. Astonishingly, Dimitry heard him confess the earlier triple denial and let him go.

Some of his actions as Tsar came with built-in errors. The marriage to Marina Mniszech made a religious clash almost inevitable. A resplendent ceremony in the Cathedral of the Assumption was planned for the Catholic bride, and Dimitry went about preparing it with discretion. He offered the Pope a Christian crusade against the Sultan Ahmed. He saw to Marina's confirmation according to Eastern rites, a necessary preliminary to her being crowned, and overruled her protests at wearing the shapeless costume that tradition demanded for that part of the ceremony. And he rewarded good behaviour: one observer said of the procession that it flowed like a slow river of gold. But all was in vain. The Pope refused to allow Marina to take Orthodox Holy Communion after the service, and Dimitry too held back when the moment came. For the Russians it was scandalous – the Tsar no longer believed in the Holy Faith. This one moreover was a title hunter, calling himself Caesar and Invincible; only God was invincible. The aristocracy saw his ideas as foreign, just as his hated Polish courtiers were foreign too. The man had installed an orchestra in the Kremlin. He wanted more trade with the outside world, more Russians to go abroad to study. And most alarming of all, the 'little people' loved their dashing new young Tsar with his sense of justice.

Disaster

There was also Prince Shuisky. The prince, ambitious for the throne, knew that his own hour had struck and that he must move quickly. He declared Dimitry to be a Pretender chosen to be Ivan's son only to rid the land of Boris Godunov. Nine days after Marina's enthronement a mob broke into the palace. Dimitry gave battle, not once faltering or hinting at his imposture while facing death. After being stabbed repeatedly he was tied by the testicles and thrown to the courtyard seventy five feet below. His body was left for three days so that all might walk by and curse it, then it was burnt. The ashes were placed in a cannon pointing to the West – toward Poland – and fired off in that direction. By that time Prince Shuisky, a lineal descendant of Rurik the Viking, had been crowned Tsar.

The mystery of Uglich remains a mystery still. Today, historians in general believe that the real Dimitry did die as a boy, and that the Pretender was indeed a monk called Grishka or Yuri Otrepyev.

D'EON

Charles Geneviève Louis André Timothée d'Eon de Beaumont (1728–1810) was born in Tonneterre, France, and qualified to be a lawyer before starting a career in secret diplomacy, as dealings between countries often became at that time. He had always liked dressing as a woman, and his reasons may in part have been professional; it was said that while in Russia during 1755 he disguised himself as his superior's niece in order to hear gossip from the court maids of honour. In 1761, after military service, he transferred to London with the post of embassy first secretary. Louis XV dubbed him Chevalier. Henceforth d'Eon claimed to have special powers from his king to work on a secret royal plan for the invasion of England.

D'Eon was gifted for such tasks but made some important enemies at a murky time in French politics. The new ambassador, Count Guerchy, arrived in London with letters of recall for him and demanded that the Chevalier hand over his secret files. D'Eon held on to the documents, relying on a letter dated October 1763 in which (so he alleged) the king ordered him to resume female clothing and lie low, staying clear of enemies and keeping all his papers until he received further royal instructions.

One evening after an embassy dinner d'Eon suffered violent stomach pains. Believing this to be Guerchy's doing, he moved to new lodgings and ceased all contact with the embassy. Guerchy applied to King Louis for an extradition order which was granted and George III endorsed the request: the Chevalier was now without status in London. He barricaded himself indoors, counterattacking Guerchy by pamphlet and letter, also playing up the value of his secret files in negotiations for their release to the British. Guerchy brought and won a libel action against him: when officers of the court called on d'Eon to serve the verdict they found only a cousin and two women seated at the fire (one of them was d'Eon). At the Old Bailey in February 1765 d'Eon in turn brought charges. He accused Guerchy of having plotted his death; a grand jury ruled there was a case to answer, but the ambassador declined to appear and shortly afterwards was recalled to Paris. His successor liked d'Eon. Through the king's adviser, Count de Broglie, he made efforts to win him – and the papers – back to France.

Meanwhile, however, the question of what might be d'Eon's true sex had become the subject of general debate, even of bets; as a result the man was said to have a temper and to have thrashed several London bookmakers. D'Eon was offered his former job in Paris, a reward for the achievements in Russia, plus a pension of 12,000 livres. What Count de Broglie did not know, however, was that the Chevalier was deeply in debt and had given the secret papers as security for a loan. This revelation called up horrifying possibilities. The Chevalier went everywhere in society; with the papers no longer safe and their owner a public scandal, an

incident could arise at any moment to ruin King Louis diplomatically. What, in truth, was the fellow's sex? D'Eon swore an affidavit to declare himself as male. De Broglie's secretary now assured the king that 'Sieur d'Eon is a woman and nothing but a woman, of whom he has all the attributes.'

The 18th century knew nothing about hormones. Charles d'Eon, described as effeminate in appearance but with a dark beard, probably did have a rare glandular imbalance. Certainly for a while yet he made good use of it and of his secret files. In 1774, wishing to return home to France, he agreed that on settlement of his debts the documents would be sent to Paris. This was a trick: on its arrival the file chest proved to hold nothing of importance. D'Eon took the king's emissary to his lodgings in London, produced the papers that were sought and bartered himself a better deal. One condition insisted on was that he agree to dress for the rest of his life in woman's clothing and thus end the scandal. However, this did nothing to stop the bets: in all, some £120,000 may have been staked (to settle one wager a surgeon swore to d'Eon's being female).

The agreement to dress as a woman became a source of misery for d'Eon, but he could not afford to lose the money. Once he was back home all France flocked to see this 'nice problem', as the philosopher Voltaire put it. D'Eon had bartered back his old military rank in the Dragoons, and yet was arrested when he donned uniform. The French navy would not have him. It was observed that 'she shaved too obviously'. Queen Marie Antoinette, not easily discouraged in her friendships, ordered her personal milliner to make the Chevalier an outfit. At the first possible moment he fled back to England.

From 1785, in England without a pension, he gave fencing displays dressed as a woman: a popular costume was that of Joan of Arc. During one such bout on tour he was wounded; the injury did not heal and he lost even this source of income and slipped into poverty. An autopsy after his death confirmed beyond all doubt that Charles d'Eon was male.

CROSS-DRESSING

→ → → → → → → → → MALE → FEMALE → → → → → → → → → → →

BACKGROUND AND CAREER	DRESS	CONCLUSIONS
François Timoléon de Choisy, b. Paris 1644. Father: Chancellor to the Duke of Orleans (also a cross-dresser who was kept in girl's clothes by his mother). Studied for the Church from age of 18, became abbé and respected for his devoutness. Travelled to Siam in 1685 with French ambassadorial suite. Wrote *Memoirs*, and a Life of David.	Mother (aged 43 at de Choisy's birth) idolized him and dressed him as a girl to age of 18. This led to his becoming a fashion trendsetter. Acted female role in Bordeaux theatre for five months prior to taking Holy Orders. His hair was done up in large curls; he wore diamond earrings, black patches, a necklace of pearls. Had several lovers, and with one of them staged a mock marriage. Wore women's clothes privately later in life and liked to retain the patches.	Motive: vanity. 'I have many a time heard someone whisper near me, "There's a pretty woman!".' Gain: admiration and attention. 'It is an attribute of God to be loved and adored; man has the same ambition. It is beauty which creates love, and beauty is generally woman's portion.'
'Jenny de Savalette de Lange', b. ?1790. Nothing known of origins, but swore to being daughter of a count and spent entire on-record life claiming recognition from the Bourbons of father's services. Has been identified as the 'Lost Dauphin' (Louis XVII). Most likely met true count and daughter in exile from France, taking over girl's identity and claim-proofs on her death. Secured several favours, eg postmistress jobs, pensions.	Seen only wearing women's clothes, in style of Empire or Restoration (a black cap surmounted by a broad-brimmed hat). Described in 1815 as a tall gaunt woman with hair in plain bands.	Motive: financial (as postmistress of Villejuif, near Paris, received a 1200-franc salary). Gain: security, eg an apartment in the Château de Versailles from 1822. A royal bedcover of Louis XIV was found among his effects when he died.
Fred G. Thompson, b. Columbus, Ohio, 1888. Turned out of family home at age of 14 by father; went to Chicago, where worked as chambermaid, later as cabaret singer. Twice married (once, in 1912, to a man). Went as 'Mrs Frances Carrick'. Suspected of being the woman killer in Tesmer hold-up case of 1923, but released. When he sought to appear at a Chicago vaudeville theatre in women's clothes, the police intervened and he lost the case that he subsequently brought against them.	'Always desired' female clothes, and wore them from youth onward. Was in nightdress and kimono when arrested summer 1923. Next day had enough beard showing through the face powder to leave his sex in no doubt. At the trial appeared in satin trousers, silks, rouge and with hair in braids. Mrs Tesmer, the victim's widow, identified Thompson as the 'laughing, blue-eyed girl' killer (his eyes were grey).	Motive: need to earn a living, but a feminine disposition was certainly part of it. 'God gave me a double nature', he said to the police. Gain: sexual freedom. After his second marriage, to a girl, Thompson lived *à trois* with his wife and his husband Frank Carrick.

WHO GETS WHAT

← ← ← ← ← ← ← ← ← ← ← MALE ← FEMALE ← ← ← ← ← ← ← ← ← ← ←

CONCLUSIONS	DRESS	BACKGROUND AND CAREER
Dressed in man's doublet above a woman's skirt (sometimes exchanged for breeches). Tried in 1612 for wearing men's apparel, sentenced to stand for three hours at St Paul's Cross during Sunday morning sermon; arranged for those watching to have their pockets picked.	Motive: financial (possibly influenced by hormones). Gain: earned one of the largest fortunes in England. 'The world consists of the cheats and the cheated.'	**Mary Frith**, b. London, ?1589. Parents: father a shoemaker, mother a gentlewoman. Brought up as girl but always a tomboy, renowned fighter with cudgel or quarter-staff. Named 'Moll Cutpurse'. Pickpocket, fence for stolen goods then sold back to owners, highway robber. Heroine of *The Roaring Girl*, play by Middleton and Dekker.
Wore men's clothes only from start of her life as a pirate: jacket, trousers and kerchief around the head. She gave herself away, reported one female victim, by the size of her breasts.	Motive: to escape from husband James Bonny. Gain: a new identity. 'If you had fought like a man, you need not be hanged like a dog' (said to Rackham while the two were under sentence, Anne pregnant by him at the time).	**Anne Bonny**, d. ?1720. Parents: Irish lawyer father, mother his housemaid. Family emigrated to Charles-Town, S. Carolina. Bonny noted for hot temper and strength. Escaped a bad marriage to join Captain John Rackham as pirate in the Bahamas. Sentenced to death when captured; may have been freed by father's bribes.
At Middlesborough, dressed as a man to go out drinking (Baptists then withdrew fellowship from her). Wore men's uniform during Revolutionary War service, binding her breasts tightly. Retained male dress for one year after being discharged, found it 'more convenient'.	Motive: an answer to boredom. Gain: escaped into new life. 'Enlistment not the original plan, nor patriotism the original motive' (said by her biographer).	**Deborah Sampson**, b. 1760. Father a *Mayflower*-descended sailor drowned when she was aged five, mother farmed out the children. Placed with staunchly Baptist family in Middlesborough, Mass. Soon bored by farm duties, she enlisted into army at Worcester in 1782. Served 18 months (twice wounded). Later married, three children. Granted government pension.
After running away she dressed always as a man. Her sex was revealed late in life, when she had difficulty in putting on female dress at the West Ham workhouse. Hair cut short, keen eyes and a large firm mouth helped maintain her disguise.	Motive: to escape from husband Percival Coombes. Gain: a new identity as the Gentleman Painter. 'I never hesitated to show I disliked coarse and vulgar talk.'	**Catherine Coombes**, b. Axbridge, England, 1834. Father's name Tozer. At age of 16 married a first cousin. When she opened a school, husband mistreated both pupils and teacher. Ran away to train as housepainter; in London, employed as foreman. Had to enter workhouse after injury in an accident in 1897.

Karl Naundorff:
the found Dauphin

No French king was succeeded by his son in either the 18th or the 19th century. A 'Dauphin' (traditionally a title bestowed on the king's eldest son) from that fact in itself will attract mystery. Add the French Revolution, and a 'Lost Dauphin' seems inevitable.

Before their death at the guillotine, Louis XVI and Queen Marie Antoinette had four children. The eldest, Marie Thérèse (b. 1778), would live to old age in exile. One brother and the sister died very young. That left the remaining brother, Louis Charles, duke of Normandy (b. 1785) to become Dauphin at the age of 4. The same year saw the start of revolution, and the family were in effect prisoners at the Tuileries Palace in Paris.

By June of 1791 several royal relatives had fled the country. Louis tried to follow their example. The party leaving Paris included his sister Elisabeth and the Dauphin's governess. All six travellers had Russian papers showing them to be Baroness de Korff and her entourage. There was a reversal of roles: the governess played Baroness, the Queen her companion, Louis a valet and Elisabeth the childrens' nurse. Their hope was to reach the city of Metz and its loyalist troops, but they were recognized on the way and brought back to Paris with abusive insults.

Imprisonment and death

The family's next home inside the fortified tower building of The Temple was a prison indeed, but even there for as long as they stayed together some happiness was possible. Louis could give lessons to the Dauphin. They had a garden. The boy was lively, cheerful and healthy. However, in the autumn of 1792 orders came for the king to live apart and prepare for his trial. He saw the family once more on 20 January 1793, the eve of his execution; the Dauphin, he said, must dismiss all thoughts of revenge.

That July the boy was put in a separate room, to be cared for by a shoemaker family called Simon as part of a re-education process. Contrary to royalist reports, Simon was kind to his young charge: he installed an aviary stocked with birds, there was a dog to play with and a billiard table. Later, together with his sister, Louis Charles was made to sign a document accusing the queen of various crimes, among them that she had corrupted him sexually (at her trial it came out that this meant incest). Their aunt Elisabeth also signed. That occasion in October was the last time the Dauphin saw his own family: the two women were executed, and his sister Marie Thérèse eventually went to Austria as part of an exchange involving French prisoners of war. His time with the shoemaker family ended soon after, in January 1794. They were not replaced.

The boy now stayed alone. Occasionally there would be a visit by government commissioners. One such observer, De La Meuse, reported that he had grown totally silent and unresponsive, with bad swellings in his limbs and what seemed to be rickets. Closer attention was ordered: by March 1795 two warders had arrived. They became alarmed by his ill-health. Doctors were called in, the first of whom was said to have doubted the boy's identity and to have died a few days later. Two subsequent doctors noted high fever and larger swellings in the boy. He was moved to a better room, but by this time nothing could be done and Louis Charles died on 8 June. Next day the doctors, with a further two who had not even seen the

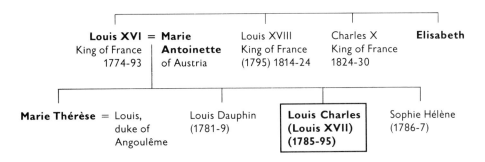

patient, established the cause of death as scrofula. The body was put in a coffin that evening and then into a common grave at St Marguerite's churchyard. Its exact resting-place was never found; and the original certificate, which showed death to have occurred on the later date of 10 June, also vanished.

Dauphin lost, Dauphin found

Doubts about doctors, faulty dates, no body or grave – these left the way open for impostors. Stories that the Prisoner of The Temple had escaped were heard almost at once. In all, more than forty 'Lost Dauphins' came forward (one of them John James Audubon, better known as the American expert on birds). By far the most durable and convincing claimant, however, was Karl Wilhelm Naundorff (1785–1845).

By Naundorff's account, the rescue had been accomplished by drugging him and substituting a wooden figure in his bed. He awoke in a fourth-floor attic of the same building. On discovering the wooden figure, the authorities hushed up the affair by imprisoning instead a deaf and dumb child – the unresponsive boy reported by commissioner De La Meuse. Rumours began that this was not the true Dauphin; an unsuccessful attempt was made to poison him; the first doctor called in detected this and was himself poisoned. Another ricketty child then became the Dauphin. He died on 8 June, and it was in the coffin intended for this child that Naundorff, once more drugged, was smuggled out to royalist sympathizers in the Vendée. The dead child was stowed in the fourth-floor attic. The surviving doctors signed what was put in front of them; and the common grave at St Marguerite's churchyard became an unmarked one.

As the 'Found Dauphin', Naundorff visited Italy and England – not greatly welcomed in either country, by his own telling. He tried unsuccessfully to enlist against the French, then in 1812 settled near Berlin as a watchmaker, pointing to this skill as inherited from King Louis his father. In 1818 he married and started a large family. Six year later he was arrested in Brandenburg on a charge of arson that grew into one of false pretences. After serving a prison sentence he moved to Saxony. By now his claims had attracted wide attention. Letters written earlier to Marie Thérèse and her cousin the Bourbon heir de Berry, and on Naundorff's release from prison to the king, Charles X, all went unanswered. But recognition came from other quarters.

On a visit to Paris in 1833 Naundorff won over three former court officials, including a governess of the Dauphin, Mme de Rambaud, as well as other more prominent figures. Pressure

SERRES

Olive, Princess Cumberland (1772–1834) won attention as a writer and artist. She exhibited work at the Royal Academy in London; she wrote several books, including one on handwriting and an account for young people of St Athanasius's creed. As an impostor she made claims that could best be called delusions of grandeur and treated as an illness. Olive's claims are of interest because of the consequences for British royalty had they continued in being.

Olive Wilmot was the daughter of a Warwick housepainter. Her bachelor uncle James, an Oxford academic and priest, opened the wider world to her. When she was 17 years old this uncle married her to John Serres, a distinguished marine painter. The couple had two daughters but separated in 1804, whereupon Olive Serres found herself free to paint and teach. After being introduced to members of the royal family she was appointed landscape painter by the Prince of Wales, with whom she began a confused correspondence that included requests from her for loans.

Her imposture began in 1807. She created a fiction that made her the daughter of the Duke of Cumberland, and her uncle's grand-daughter rather than his niece. The motives for this were clear: she was an over-imaginative woman insecure in mid-life, moving among the rich and wanting to involve herself more with her influential uncle.

Henry Frederick, duke of Cumberland, was George III's youngest brother. He was essential to Olive's fiction, and timing played a crucial part. In 1772 the Royal Marriage Act forbad the marriage of anyone in line of succession without the sovereign's approval. Olive arranged her fictional dates so that Uncle James should meet and marry 'the Princess of Poland' (the elected king of Poland's sister) early enough to have a daughter by 1750; so that this child, passed off as the housepainter's daughter, should catch the Duke of Cumberland's eye while still in her teens; and so that their secret marriage, performed by the Reverend James Wilmot, should take place in 1767. The duke soon broke with this girl, and in 1771 he married again, bigamously – just in time to be ahead of the Royal Marriage Act. The 'Princess Cumberland' (our Olive) was born the following year to his abandoned wife.

Propping up this story were some seventy documents. The key items were two marriage certificates. One showed the duke marrying James's daughter in 1767. On the reverse was a second, purporting to be a certificate of the marriage of George III himself to one Hannah Lightfoot, also performed by James Wilmot eight years earlier. This evidence carried a diabolical threat. King George had a lawful wife in Queen Charlotte. Overthrow that wife by showing King George already married to someone else, as you must do with Cumberland's second wife, and the royal succession from George IV onward is destroyed.

Olive, Princess Cumberland drove in a liveried coach until debt caught her up. In 1823 the Home Secretary denounced her claim as baseless. She had some support for it during and after her lifetime, but only in 1866 did the action of her elder daughter, Lavinia Ryves, prompt the constitutional lawyers to end Olive's threat. Mrs Ryves (who claimed the title of Duchess of Lancaster) took her mother's case to court in order to have the royal descent and a legacy of £15,000 confirmed. She met a massive counterattack led by the Lord Chief Justice, and the evidence was thrown out. Ironically, if she had won confirmation of the royal descent Mrs Ryves would have declared herself to be illegitimate – by being in line of succession her mother would come under the Royal Marriage Act, and the sovereign had not approved the marriage to John Serres.

mounted on Marie Thérèse to see him. She arranged for an inspection by Vicomte la Rochefoucauld, who met him twice and was struck by Naundorff's undoubted physical resemblance to the family. Two supporters (one of them the ex-governess) then implored Marie Thérèse to interview the claimant in person: she refused all audience to Mme de Rambaud and said to the other messenger that, since her brother was dead, an interview would serve no purpose. Naundorff himself attempted to reach her when she was in Saxony during August 1835, but arrived the day after she had left. The following summer he issued a French civil court summons to Marie Thérèse, her husband and the former king Charles. Two days after doing so he was deported from France. The legal onslaught continued from England, where he spent most of the rest of his life.

Karl Naundorff's bid to be the Lost Dauphin was more than self-proclaimed. He was said to have shared several distinctive features with the boy: a large mole on the thigh, a scar on the upper lip, protruding rabbit-teeth, triangular marks on his skin left by a vaccination. He certainly knew the layout of The Temple, as well as many details of the Bourbon family that had never been published. But often he leaves us choosing between one certainty and another. Mme Simon, the shoemaker's wife, recognized him at once. On the other hand his two warders both swore that they had been present at the Dauphin's death. All three people knew the boy intimately.

In the wider world the claimant did not lack supporters with political axes to grind. He also managed to tap a vein of mysticism. It was a time of visions and spiritual encounters on the Catholic fringe. Naundorff wrote books giving these happenings the status of religious orthodoxy, and was repaid when twice a visionary sought to warn the king that Louis XVII still lived. This was support at a price, however: his writings were banned by the Vatican and in general harmed his cause.

Into the present

Naundorff's greatest strength, aside from his personality, lay in the fact that a real identity could never be found for him – no birth certificate, no relatives other than the six children of his own. Consequently he had nothing to disprove. And that personality made him inventive and tenacious, a man with huge energies. Late in life at Camberwell in England, after accidents that included burning down his laboratory, he devised a new type of explosive. The British had no use for this, so he went to the Dutch war department with it. Holland seems thereafter to have adopted Naundorff for the few months of life he had remaining: the inscription on his gravestone at Delft begins: 'Here lies Louis XVII'.

This bold title was more than Naundorff claimed for himself while alive. He always went by the name of Duke of Normandy, and promised the newly installed Orleans royalists never to assert any political rights if he were recognized. All he wanted was the assurance of burial on French soil – and of the former royal family's civil property.

His Dutch-naturalized descendants were in fact granted the name Bourbon. They continued to battle for the claim in France, bringing lawsuits, issuing a manifesto, petitioning the Senate, and in 1950 opening their ancestor's grave to seek some clue from his anatomy when the French Court of Appeal ruled against declaring invalid the Dauphin's 1795 death certificate. The family opposing them, the Bourbon-Parma line of descent, held to a simple argument. Just as it had never been shown that the Dauphin had escaped from The Temple, so the claimant had never proved that he, Naundorff, was the Dauphin.

Kaspar Hauser:
the German conundrum

Germany's 'wild boy', the foundling Kaspar Hauser (?1812–33), may have been a fake from the start. Built round him by others, certainly, was one particular huge imposture. Yet as fraud neither story can match the truth of his treatment at the hands of real-life people.

In May 1828, bedraggled and almost speechless, the boy appeared near the Nuremberg house of a cavalry officer with a letter for him. The letter outlined his birth, his orphaned state, and announced a wish to be 'like his father'. At first he had no words to say more than that. By June, however, he was able to describe his upbringing in a room 7 ft by 4 ft (2 m × 1¼ m), with two shuttered windows, straw to sleep on and a diet of bread and water. Feeding him was a gaoler who despite the darkness taught him to repeat the words he knew and even a primitive writing.

The enigma grows

The authorities are divided on the state of the boy. Some have him walking and speaking well, with all his senses; others describe a physical, mental and emotional cripple unable to bear sounds or bright sunshine. The Nuremberg city mayor talks of his desire to learn which is reflected in the fact that by September Hauser had begun writing down his own life story.

With no clue as to his parenthood and no result from the mayor's searches, the city adopted Kaspar Hauser. (His name itself was a guess: a handkerchief, almost the boy's only possession, carried the initials 'K.H.'.) He first went into the care of a schoolteacher named Daumer, who believed in cures by homeopathy (treating disorder with a drug that induces its symptoms). Kaspar was visited by the country's leading criminologist, Anselm von Feuerbach, who favoured hypnotism. Both men had their ideas from Mesmer. It is clear that they and the many other visitors asked too much of the boy and abused his 'desire to learn'. He complained of headaches, brought on by over-stimulation; would they please return him to his kindly gaoler? After a while the peepshow stopped. In its place Daumer supplied religion, Latin and Greek – all of them unimaginable cruelties, the boy being what he was. For Daumer, though, as for most observers, the boy was an angel.

What Kaspar did like was horse-riding. He also worked well with his hands and made little boxes out of cardboard which were much sought after. He had exceptional ability to see in the dark; his hearing and touch, especially the touch of metals, were unusually distinct. Any moral instruction failed to take root. The youth seemed sexually dormant, yet at the same time contemptuous of girls: he preferred his first experience of a snowfall. By November, as he grew less sensitive so he became less lovable to Daumer. The angelic innocent learnt to lie: he discovered he could escape both blame and hard work by being untruthful. This, the discovery of every small child, was not permitted to a teenage learner.

Into private care

One day in October 1829 Kaspar was found in the cellar with a bloodstained forehead. He had been attacked, he said, while returning from an outside lavatory. His assailant had worn black: it was the third fearful occurrence of the year. Although several independent witnesses confirmed seeing such a man, whom Feuerbach believed must be Kaspar's original gaoler come to claim him, Daumer was sceptical. Lying had become second nature to the boy, he said.

The authorities moved Kaspar to other care and sent him to school, which he hated. Soon another violent incident (a pistol explosion following a quarrel with his landlady) warned them to move him again. The next surrogate parent, a Baron von Tucher, found him truthful and reliable; but in the spring of 1831 an outside source of disruption arrived. Philip, 4th earl of Stanhope, had heard of the assassination attempt on Hauser while previously in Nuremberg. The Earl of Stanhope was a German-educated English peer who admired Rousseau's notion of the Noble Savage. The 'wild boy' made a perfect subject of study and the earl had money enough to indulge his curiosity.

Other versions of what interested Lord Stanhope in the boy were less kindly (Tucher spoke of 'monkey love'). But neither the mayor nor the baron objected to the idea of being rid of their burden – Tucher had additionally been making house room for two police guards. Lord Stanhope, after flinging money at the boy, decided that the first few words Kaspar had been found with were Hungarian. He despatched Baron Tucher with him to Hungary that summer; nothing resulted. In September the baron spoke out: Stanhope must either stop interfering or take full charge officially. Meanwhile another home was chosen for Kaspar and a new bodyguard, at a pastor's house twenty-fives miles away in Ansbach, and at the end of 1831 Lord Stanhope formally adopted him.

More quarrelling occurred at this latest refuge. After another twelve months Stanhope's interest had evaporated: he said the boy should earn a living. Kaspar was found a clerk's job at the local law courts. He saw his Nuremberg friends occasionally; there were more attempts in both Germany and Hungary to trace his parentage; he was presented to the King of Bavaria, who had shown friendly concern. But by now Stanhope had dropped him. In December 1833 Kaspar again reported an attack, this time in a public park by a man who left some scribbles in mirror-writing that said Kaspar would identify him. Like the earlier attacks, it may have been a bid to gain attention. The wound, possibly self-inflicted, was from a knife; fever set in and three days later Kaspar died.

Motherly ambition

Kaspar Hauser's true origins never came to light, but from the first a rumour linked him with the royal house of Baden, south Germany. This is the huge imposture. By the time he would have been aged five (that is, years before he first appeared outside the officer's house in Nuremberg) it was already a story without motivation: a potential Grand Duke's mother had come into her own with a Baden title she could pass on. And well before Kaspar's death that potential duke was Grand Duke in fact.

Nevertheless for over forty years the legend persisted that Louise Geyer, morganatically married as second wife to the old Grand Duke and ambitious for her son, in 1812 had substituted an unknown child for the great-grandson infant who alone stood between her and her plans. The real heir spirited from the palace that night had been Kaspar; the child put in his place had died days later. (This much at least was true – a death did occur.) But where was Louise's gain there? What could she have achieved with Kaspar that would not implicate her in the deception? It was a tale made even more absurd by the dead Baden infant's parents. The mother (Napoleon's adopted daughter, Stephanie Beauharnais) was aged only 23 and there were to be three more children born to her, one a second boy. And then 1817 brought Louise Geyer's creation as Princess of Baden, which opened the succession to her own son (children

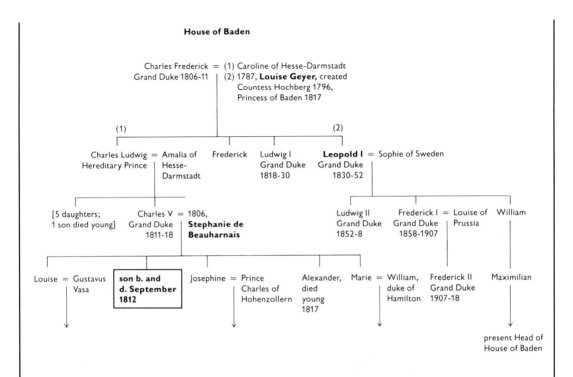

House of Baden

of a morganatic marriage inherit only the mother's title: before that date she had been merely the Countess Hochberg). 1830 saw her son enthroned.

All the trappings of romantic legend, even down to a 'White Lady' (Louise, of course) regularly glimpsed before a Baden death, are encrusted round this royal imposture. Despite its many supporters it holds no core of truth or human interest. The enduring mystery is of Kaspar Hauser at odds against the real world. This youth, seen as mankind before the Fall, whose mind was 'a sheet of white paper', who was not permitted lies or laziness but once he had learnt them was shunted from this caretaker to that, has inspired twenty plays, three films and two full-length novels. Verlaine wrote a poem about him. A Society for Kaspar Research started up over a century ago. None of this makes amends for the way his time treated Kaspar Hauser, but it is better than yet more imposture.

WILSON

Sarah Wilson (?1754–?1824), a quick dark girl, left home in Staffordshire, England, at the age of 17 to find work in London. A good position soon came: she was taken on by Miss Caroline Vernon, the queen's lady-in-waiting, as her own maid.

Queen Charlotte occupied private apartments at Buckingham House. Some of the staff came with her from Germany at the time of her marriage and included a strict elderly woman, Frau von Schwellenberg. The plentiful gossip must

(Left) The foundling Kaspar Hauser in a modern portrayal (1970) that refers to the royal claim put forward for him. (Below) Kaspar's coat, kept in the museum at Ansbach, Germany.

The royal claim of Karl Naundorff has been one of the longest on record. His son seen here (1811–99) styled himself King Charles XI of France, and later descendants have continued to seek their rights as Bourbons.

Dr James Barry, Inspector General of army hospitals, was not what he seemed.

Stella Newborough (right), Princess of Orleans. She claimed to be 'a victim of greed' and that another sat on the throne in her place.

Maria Stella

NÉE DE JOINVILLE.

Née à Modigliana (Italie), le 9 Avril 1773.

Victime de la Cupidité.

(Below) Prince William of Hohenzollern and his wife Dorothea. (Below right) Harry Domela, reading the book about his impersonation of the Prince that he wrote while in jail awaiting trial in 1927.

occasionally have been in English, however, because Sarah learnt a lot. She heard all the scandal, for instance that her employer's sister had just been divorced for adultery with the Duke of Cumberland, and she discovered who was getting the best appointments. This closet-knowledge she filed away for later use.

By early 1771 Sarah believed it safe to remove some of the queen's jewellery: the items were not checked regularly, it seemed, and a ring, some brooches and a portrait miniature of Her Majesty would not be missed. She also took a dress, it was so easy. A night or two later she went to the closet again – as Frau von Schwellenberg thought she might do.

During the reign of George III all theft of royal property carried a death sentence. Sarah's employer pleaded with the queen, and transportation was ordered for the girl instead. Sarah boarded a prison ship that July. That autumn she landed in Baltimore, America, where she was put up for sale.

Frederick county, Maryland, where her purchaser William Devall lived, was still under King George's jurisdiction. Sarah quickly escaped the Devall home and went south. Virginia and the Carolinas were among 'the Thirteen' states that would soon declare independence, so would seem not the best place for her now. For Sarah had become Princess Susanna Caroline Matilda, the queen's sister.

What she found, however, was total friendliness and acceptance. Indeed, not to have Princess Susanna to stay marked down a family socially. Many of the older settlers had emigrated to America and were hungry for her warm, intimate details of English life. She was kind and gracious to them. Her linen was embroidered with a crown and monogram, her case carried the queen's miniature. The months at court lent just that touch of royal condescension expected from such a person. To this host she spoke of a position in the Treasury, to that one she offered his own ship-command. Despite her cover story (some disagreement obliging her to leave court), the princess's influence there went unquestioned. She herself knew what she could do for people. The offers of course were in exchange for money, and these payments continued even after it came to light that the queen's sister was almost 40 and lived as a recluse.

Meanwhile, William Devall had at once announced Sarah's escape, together with a reward of five pistoles for her return. An attorney searched

Philadelphia, then Charles-Town, 'raising there a loud hue-and-cry for her Serene Highness'. Princess Susanna's reign lasted for about eighteen months. She was found on a Carolina plantation, graciously allowing the gentlemen to kiss her hand. Arrest followed at pistol point.

Sarah was returned to the Devall household where she stayed as a servant for the next two years, but war was near and brought some confused comings and goings. A second English slave-girl named Sarah Wilson arrived in Maryland and this new girl seems to have been switched with Susanna, who again escaped, on this occasion to the north. Devall had meanwhile become Lieutenant Devall, of the Maryland Militia. This was no time to pursue a runaway servant.

The war did Sarah another kindness. William Talbot, a young English officer of good family, was posted to America with his regiment of dragoons. Sarah married him and followed the regiment through its campaigns. When the fighting stopped Talbot realized (or was told) that there could be no return to England with a wife liable to instant arrest. He decided on a business career in New York; the start-up money for this venture drew on Sarah's takings as Princess Susanna, which she had carefully put by. They settled in the pleasant Bowery district, later with a large family of children, to whom Sarah made an excellent wife and mother.

BARRY

James Barry (?1799–1865) came from Ireland to London as a six-year-old girl with no father and no given name. She may have been a niece of the artist James Barry, RA. These mysteries (she added to them by writing of her mother as 'my aunt') were partly deliberate. She wanted to study, but since a girl could not enter higher education at that time she left London and enrolled at Edinburgh University as a boy.

The artist Barry's orbit brought in important people, among them Lord Buchan and the Beaufort family (who were dukes of Somerset). Buchan took charge of the girl from her second year in Edinburgh's medical school. A brilliant student, Barry graduated at the age of 12. Back in London she walked the wards and worked as a pupil dresser to a top surgeon of the day. At this time military medicine aimed at becoming professional where before it relied on barber surgeons; in 1813 Barry joined the army.

Her posting to South Africa in 1816 almost certainly involved the Beaufort connexion. Lord Charles Somerset was Governor of the Cape, and the young army assistant surgeon at once became the duke's personal doctor. Away from medicine the two had a curious relationship as patron and protégé, with a strong emotional colouring to it. Rumour linked them, and speculated about Barry's true sex, from the first. She faced this with style. Strutting on specially built-up heels, her dog Psyche at her side and a sword almost bigger than herself, James Barry became a celebrity.

In social medicine the new arrival broke many barriers. She fought for a leper colony to be built, and for lunatics to be regarded as sick people. She plunged herself into reforming the hospitals, poked into their drains, opened their windows, and set up regular changes of bed-linen. Her ideas on diet were progressive; she saw to it that fruit and vegetables got onto the menus. Later she demanded decent married quarters for the soldiers' wives.

Barry's promotion to Medical Inspector in 1822 put her in charge of licensing the Cape's practitioners. Here, her concern for standards soon blew up a storm over one unqualified but well-liked apothecary. Much the same principles along with more outspokenness landed her in serious trouble when in 1825 she refused to allow a drunken sailor on a prison charge to be declared mad. She had already made an enemy of the Governor's Secretary, and her report to Lord Charles attacking the top legal officer at the Cape for mishandling the affair was maliciously shown to the man himself. Dr Barry was summoned, refused to speak, and was then given a civil sentence. By this time a poster linking her and Somerset had appeared on the street. Lord Charles annulled her sentence, but still Barry had not done and threatened to bring the case to the attention of an inquiry team who were there on other business. When later that year a medical board did away with what had been her unique powers, she resigned as Inspector and took a demotion. Typically she bounced back with a brilliant solo performance when one of her patients, Mrs Munnik, looked to be dying in labour. Barry had only read about the Caesarian operation, but went to work and saved both mother and child, a feat commemorated to this day by the South African family, in which the first son is always named James Barry.

The tendency to be her own worst enemy with the authorities ran through Barry's whole career. A fake man, she wanted the right to be a genuinely difficult person. In Mauritius she blazed away at the use of army doctors for private services; on St Helena she attacked a Treasury official who refused to buy wholesale for the civil hospital as he did for the military one. In Corfu during the Crimean War she grew angry with the commanding general for putting her just-recovered patients on fatigues (the general reported this to Lord Raglan as 'injudicious interference'). Florence Nightingale, crossing her hospital square in the hot sun one day, found herself berated by Barry on horseback. She wrote of this some time later: 'She kept me standing in the midst of a crowd. I should say she was the most hardened creature I ever met throughout the army.' The two women worked at opposite ends of the sexist scale: where Nightingale traded on her femininity, Barry denied it all her life.

Despite the gossip – by one story she went to Mauritius to have Somerset's child – Barry's true sex seems to have been detected only once. During the 1840s she fell ill and went to sleep uncovered. When she awoke, two brother officers were at the bedside who had to be sworn to secrecy. For the most part she deliberately tried to call attention to her slight, small figure, high colour and dyed hair. On her final posting in Canada, now Inspector General of Hospitals, she wore a silk bow on the breast of her uniform frock coat, long white gloves and a pair of dandified boots in patent leather when travelling long miles on visits in her horse-drawn sleigh.

The spring of 1859 brought her down with flu. Back in London she wrote a final memorandum begging to be allowed to finish her time of service (she stood to lose financially without this) but no action resulted. When the top job in army medicine became vacant, Barry did not get it and Miss Nightingale commented that there was 'not one man in the department whom one wished to see as director-general'.

Barry's last months went on travel and visiting friends. She died in London: an army surgeon-major (he had known her for years) certified her death without comment. It was Sophia Bishop, an Irish cleaning woman laying out the body, who declared: 'The devil a General – it's a woman.' Pointing to stretch-marks on the corpse, she added

'And a woman that has had a child'.

Sophia went to the army agents to collect money owed to her by Barry's landlady, along with a bribe for her own silence. There was no bribe, and the story appeared in a Dublin newspaper. When the registrar of births and deaths wrote to the surgeon-major inquiring politely why his certificate had failed to remark on Dr Barry's sex, he was told that that officer did not consider it his business whether the doctor were male or female.

Stella Newborough:
Princess of Orleans

For the writer Alexandre Dumas, who would later open up mystery after mystery from his country's murky past, the story of Stella, Princess of Orleans, had all the required ingredients. One thing alone disqualified her. From 1822 Dumas had been employed in the household of Louis-Philippe, then Duke of Orleans and later King of the French. To be seen savagely attacking that house's legitimacy did not form part of his plans. So he listened, astonished, to what the lady said and let her go.

The changeling

In May 1824 Lady Stella Newborough, a naturalized Englishwoman born in north Italy, occupied an unusual position on the fringe of Europe's aristocracy. With money, three sons and a home on estates in Estonia and Wales as well as in London, she could, at the age of 52, have settled for a secure middle age. But Stella had just reached the end of an intensive search that left her restless and only partly fulfilled. At stake was her whole identity. She had found one half of it.

Stella Chiappini (1773–1843) grew up in the little village of Modigliana, Tuscany. Among seven children she was not her mother's favourite. The father, a local policeman, gained a promotion when Stella was 4 years old and the family moved to Florence. Life was better; Stella had a good education but decided to make her career on the stage. In 1786 she caught the eye of an English widower, a man who had been rewarded with a peerage for his government services and who owned land in three Welsh counties. Lord Newborough, aged 50, married the 13-year-old. Stella screamed that she would rather be a nun but to no avail. The couple stayed on in Italy, he quarrelling with her relations, she sneered at by local British expatriates for being 'a singing girl'. In 1792 the Newboroughs at last broke free and moved to Wales, where in her own words life became a perpetual fête as visitors by the hundred called on them. She still felt an aversion for her husband, yet when the only son by his first wife died and Stella learnt that her marriage was after all intended to be productive, she had two boys within a year. They delighted her. Stella's father and other relatives visited the Newboroughs in Britain, embarrassing Stella by turning up in sailor costumes.

On Newborough's death in 1807 Stella married again, this time a Russian baron (his were the Estonian estates). She went back to Italy to see her father at his request in 1818. Three years later, on the point of death, he sent her an amazing letter:

'Milady – I am at the end of my life without having revealed to anyone a secret concerning myself and you. It is this.

The day when you were born to a person I must not name and who has already passed away, a boy was born to me. I was asked to make an exchange, and in view of my financial circumstances at the time I fell in with the repeated requests, to some advantage. So it was that I adopted you as my daughter just as my son was adopted by the other party.

I see that Heaven has made good my shortcomings by raising you to a better position than that of your real father, even though he was of almost similar rank. This affords me some peace of mind as I end my life.'

Stella at once went to Modigliana for details that would allow her to understand this extraordinary confession. Anyone who could recall her birth and its circumstances was questioned. In that April of 1773, Stella learnt, two French people had arrived at the inn. They travelled as the Count and Countess de Joinville; the lady was very pregnant and gave birth the same evening. That the child should be a girl had sadly disappointed the husband – some matter of estates needing to be secured in the family. As it happened, Signora Chiappini also had a child that day, a boy. The Chiappinis were poor, the Count well off; a deal was proposed and a bargain struck. The girl thus became Stella Chiappini.

So who was her true father and where did he come from? What had he been doing in north Italy? Lady Stella Newborough now went first to France, to the Champagne province and a ruined castle that had belonged to the Joinvilles. She found they were long extinct, but those now entitled to use the name included members of the ducal house of Orleans. In Paris from July 1823 she pursued her enquiries by advertising. The trail stayed cold for some months; in response to the advertisement an elderly Orleans relative called to ask if her enquiries concerned money.

Then suddenly a breakthrough came. At Brisinghella, a dozen kilometers from Modigliana, for some days during 1773 a Count de Joinville had been held on orders of the Church. Stella took this as evidence enough to apply to the ecclesiastical court for her baptismal certificate to be changed. The Papal secretary of state allowed a search of Vatican archives, and in May 1824 the court ruled that there had been a child substitution at Modigliana, the count detained at Brisinghella having been largely responsible. This being the case, Stella was now Stella de Joinville.

As father Chiappini's letter had noted, she would be better off as a Newborough or a Russian baroness; but that ignored her determination. She was only half-way done.

Royal ambition

Henceforward Stella raised her claim to an entirely new order of magnitude. Looking for the boy whom she had been swapped for, she found him – Louis-Philippe of Orleans, born like her in 1773. Louis-Philippe would soon be king. His father had been the 'revolutionary' duke named Egalité, who despite supporting the Jacobites and voting for Louis XVI's execution had himself gone to the guillotine. His mother Adélaide was one of the richest women in France at the time of their marriage. This, then, was the couple travelling incognito in north Italy (the list of titles for Egalité in their marriage contract described him as Comte de Joinville). The husband's disappointment at having a daughter stemmed from the loss of entailed properties in Adélaide's dowry that a baby girl represented. It was simple. If further proof were needed, one had only to look at the portraits hanging in the Orleans' palace. When Stella and her Russian son visited there, both were struck by how like that family they were: Louis-Philippe strongly resembled father Chiappini. Other observers said the same.

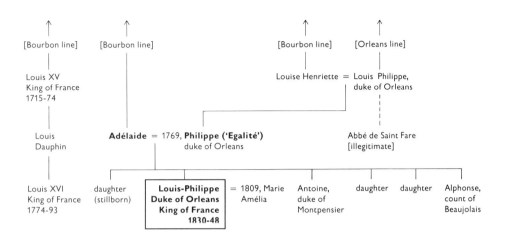

For the 'Elder Bourbon' line, see p.187

Styling herself 'Marie Etoile d'Orleans' (the 'Etoile' a translation of Stella), the claimant became relentless in pursuit of her quarry. A tell-tale phrase is heard: 'If I were the only person concerned'. Stella meant by this the future of her children, and the glory of belonging to a dynasty, but it all left her family quite cold: they escaped off home to Russia. Stella could not be stopped now. She did everything possible to obtain French endorsement of the changed Italian baptismal certificate. Mme de Genlis, governess to Egalité's children, was approached for help. Stella's own account of her life appeared in 1830. She drew support from adherents of the 'Elder Bourbon' royal line who stayed loyal to ex-king Charles X (Louis XVI's brother) and his grandson. These legitimists saw the Orleans family as usurpers, so it was right for that line to be vexed by an impostor. The hatred proved long-lasting: a Bourbonist play called *Maria Stella, or the Last of the Orleans* was staged in 1889, after Charles's grandson had died and the Bourbons had become Bourbon-Parmas.

What history allows

Stella chose to call Louis-Philippe 'the involuntary usurper of rights which henceforth he cannot keep without guilt', but her case is hard to sustain. Detailed historical reconstruction shows that neither Egalité nor Adélaide were in a position to have secretly visited north Italy during the spring of 1773. Their diaries are crammed with public appearances in France throughout April and May. Moreover, the birth of Louis-Philippe in Paris that October was attended by five people; a further three came into the room shortly after; baptism took place on the spot. The possibility (going by his record a fair one) that Egalité was travelling Italy with a pregnant mistress is also ruled out. And so indeed is any call for the child substitution itself: the ducal couple had four more children – two of them male – after Louis-Philippe. The entailed properties were safe.

Stella Newborough, disproved as a Princess of Orleans, may have been born into the nobility at some more modest level. The style of an ennobled de Joinville was used by at least one other family of the period. There would be no reason to doubt Chiappini's confession, nor to overturn the ecclesiastical court's ruling, if that humbler link were accepted. But if she knew this, she ignored it. Stella's need for something greater belonged with the way she experienced her own life. Her *Memoirs* say it best:

'To conquer, or die as I have lived! All or nothing!'

DOMELA

Harry Domela (b. 1904) came from a moderately well-off family of German settlers in the Baltic region (which in the phrase of the time made him an 'outsider German'). He attended a Russian-run school where he was bullied by the local boys. At the age of 15 he left to soldier with the German Freikorps, a paramilitary body that had recently put down a revolution in the Baltic, and as a result added to his unpopularity.

Germany between the two World Wars, the so-called Weimar Republic, suffered mass unemployment and inflation but Harry Domela was allowed to enter. He was untrained and too young to join the regular army then mobilizing to combat labour unrest, so he worked for a while as a gardener, and also as servant to a baroness, who taught him high-society manners. When she announced a cut in staff, Harry ran off with some of her spoons and was caught by the police. On this occasion he was let off and he managed to find other jobs until the government issued a ruling that made it very difficult for outsider Germans to get work. He drifted to Berlin and to a life on the streets. The winter of 1922–3 was a bad one for Domela and he felt desperate. When a tramp friend told him he looked like a count, an idea began to form.

Harry Domela was slightly built, blue-eyed and pale, and spoke with a lisp. The country swarmed with ex-aristocrats (the Weimar Republic had abolished titles of nobility). He looked and sounded like an aristocrat: why not live like one? However Domela soon ran into trouble, and served three separate prison sentences on charges of false pretences. He needed to raise his game.

When out of prison for the third time he decided to go south to Heidelberg, having heard about its student clubs and the élite drinking and duelling societies that still kept up their military and aristocratic image. One of these clubs befriended him: Harry said he was the Baltic Prince Lieven of Latvia, but soon the students were convinced he must be some greater personage, someone going incognito, because no one could reveal such ignorance of the military unless it were a front to hide

his true identity. And what noble family wanted to distance itself from the army enough to do that? Why, the House of Hohenzollern, formerly the rulers of Prussia. Their honorary title was allowed them only if all links with the armed services were broken. That explained Domela and his wish to seem ignorant: he was, in fact, Prince William of Hohenzollern, the Kaiser's grandson and probable successor if the monarchy were ever restored. The students were thrilled at their 'discovery' and treated him royally. When he went back north again it was with greater self-confidence.

In Erfurt Harry succeeded by his manner alone (a fawning hotel manager was sure that the visitors' book was about to get a royal signature). Soon, however, his policy of 'Never deny' became 'Affirm it'. Criss-crossing half a dozen towns in Thuringia, the Prince stayed at castles and stately homes, attended operas and soirées in his honour. People seemed ready to pick up his bills. All this was very risky – the real-life prince lived only a hundred miles away, Hohenzollern relatives even closer – and when the press wrote that Harry was seeing too much of the military his fraud seemed in danger of collapsing. One day he spotted a detective on the street.

By the summer of 1926 Domela had become trapped in his role. The hospitality-round was like a carousel: each time it stopped, another crowd of people eager for royal contact blocked his getting off. Uniformed staff snapped salutes. A social-democrat mayor talked for some moments with him and then fell silent, worried that this royal experience might lose him votes. It is a gallery of pictures from the Weimar Republic. One caricature of Marshal Blücher, bitterly opposed to President Ebert, was amazed to hear Domela say how well the President had served his country. Another landed militarist was given a lecture on how the unemployed could not survive on two marks benefit a day.

The eventual collapse began in classic fashion. Domela learnt from his hotel that they had a room booked for a Mr von Berg, which he knew to be the name of a senior official at the Prince's court. He fled at once, the detective after him. After persuading an army telephone unit to buy him a day's silence on the police lines, he fell in with two drinking companions at a Weimar wine-cellar. This was his final binge. Next day, having weighed up his chances of going on, he decided to enlist in the Foreign Legion (French occupying forces were in that part of Germany), but as he boarded the train he was arrested. Mr von Berg turned out to be a banker from Frankfurt.

Domela's trial made a sensation. Germany's Liberals seized the chance of scoring off the Nationalists who for two years had been his intimates (the left-wing press called them the 'Domelackeys'). Harry sat in Cologne writing his memoirs while the hearing was prepared. At his trial that summer, still in the blue suit he had worn for his impersonation and looked down on from the walls by portraits of the Hohenzollerns, he was given seven months'

imprisonment, changed at once to a suspended sentence. On 23 July 1927 Domela walked free, a film contract in his pocket and his book already serialized. Later, two plays were staged about him, one of them starring Domela in person (he tried to sue the man who played him in the other one).

The Domela affair brought the real-life Prince William and his family into a ridicule they did not deserve, or not until their lawyers stopped Prince William's photograph from being printed in Domela's book. The Prince's own story came to an end in May 1940 during World War II when he died from wounds in France and 50,000 people attended his funeral. Hitler was furious at this monarchist piece of theatre. He ordered all members of the House of Hohenzollern in uniform to be immediately dismissed from the armed forces.

The Tichborne Claimant:
mother's boy

Two men confronted each other at the Westminster session court on 10 May 1871. Only one of them was physically present, but the social extremes they stood at and which made their case a symbol of Victorian England had weight and reality enough for two. Witnesses counted by the hundred would testify for or against each man. Rival life-stories were in contention. The fight was on.

Roger Tichborne, heir to estates and a baronetcy, was born in 1829. His illegitimate mother Henriette was half French and kept him in Paris until his father, using a family funeral as excuse for the journey, smuggled the 16-year-old over to England and into Stonyhurst, the Catholic school. His mother's wishes were opposed again when Roger joined the army: much of what happened later can only be explained by Henriette Tichborne's need to settle accounts with her English family.

Young Tichborne was slim, with a long melancholy face and drooping locks. When he was 24 Tichborne fell in love with his cousin Kate. It would have been a sensible marriage uniting two estates together worth over £20,000 in annual rents, but there was some opposition and an enforced delay. At about this time Roger learnt that his regiment would not be going to India as he had hoped, so he resigned his commission and in 1853 left for South America. After ten months of enjoyable horseback adventures in Chile and Argentina he took ship at Rio to come home. The boat went down in a storm and no survivors were found.

Henriette refused to accept her son's death and advertised for news, offering a handsome reward. In May 1865 an Australian solicitor wrote to say that Roger Tichborne was living nearby at Wagga Wagga under the name of Castro; enquiries and answers were exchanged, as a result of which the man came to England in 1866. Henriette, a faithful old negro servant and the family solicitor recognized him; other relatives and acquaintances did not.

WILLCOCKS

People found it hard to stay angry with Princess Caraboo, but that could still leave them with a need to recover when she had fooled them.

Mary Willcocks (?1792–1864) was the daughter of a Devonshire cobbler who had a temper and a leather strap. With no schooling at the age of 15 Mary went to a local family as maid, quarrelled with her parents, and left Devonshire to walk all but the last few miles to London. The journey nearly killed her and after a spell in hospital she drifted. One employer taught her to read and write; others were not so kind. In 1813 she admitted herself into a prostitutes' home, mistaking it for a convent. A man from the Far East left her pregnant and with some insight into Oriental customs. The child died. The Eastern detail went into her stories, which all agreed were bizarre but harmless.

Each time she returned to her family home she soon became bored. On a visit in 1816 the talk was full of America. The fare to Philadelphia cost £5. Mary set out for Bristol, meeting some gypsies on the way. A means of raising her passage-money most likely occurred to her while she was with them.

In April 1817 Samuel Worrall, the magistrate of Almondsbury near Bristol, heard late one evening of a strange newcomer to the town. Soon the girl was at his door: a statuesque figure all in black, wearing wooden sandals and with her hair in a shawl. There was little communication at first. She was 'Caraboo', and when shown Oriental scenes in a book she recognized them. The floor was preferred to a bed. Mrs Worrall had a kind heart, and when Caraboo went to the Bristol poor-house after a few days she took her back.

For the next two months visitors flocked to see this Princess from Javasu. Mary invented religious rites, a language script with three dozen letters and some prettily exotic dance steps. Craniologists measured her head. She did a sketch map of her voyage to England – oddly, it included the island of St Helena, only known for being the exile home of Napoleon Bonaparte. Caraboo's exposure as an impostor did not take very long, but still the people called. How had Mary done it? Bristol became a joke for having been tricked. The Worralls however still loved her, and if passage-money to America was lacking, they could find £5. In July they put her on the boat.

For them personally, that drew a line under the affair, but Bristol the city still had something to prove. In September a local paper reported extraordinary happenings from (of all places) St Helena. It described how recently a longboat had been seen making for shore with a single rower. The governor went down to the beach; a female of interesting appearance sprang to land. She said that as her ship, blown off course, had neared the island she had been seized with longing to visit the home of the great Bonaparte. Since the ship would not stop, she had got into the longboat, cut its stays and pulled away. She was the Princess Caraboo.

An introduction to Napoleon followed once her language skills and knowledge of Chinese politics had convinced everyone that she was no impostor. Her story delighted Bonaparte, and soon he was beseeching the governor to allow her an apartment in his house. Bonaparte, hitherto a sulky and difficult prisoner, was completely changed. He was even writing to the Pope to have his marriage dissolved so that he could remain with his enchanting Princess – 'Her manner is noble and fascinating in a wonderful degree', the governor quoted him as saying.

Tichborne's 2-year-old nephew was the twelfth baronet. In order to claim his inheritance the new arrival had to start a legal action, which he did the following summer.

Castro/Orton: the claim

The claimant in court at Westminster was said by the defendants to be Arthur Orton, the youngest of twelve children of a Wapping butcher and born in 1834. At 17 and overweight, he was already known as 'Bullocky Orton' and weighed thirteen and a half stone. He became a merchant seaman, journeyed to Chile while still in his teens and there jumped ship. Small-town friends kept him alive and funded a return to England in 1851. The following year (leaving behind a girlfriend who planned to follow later) he went to Australia, working as a butcher under a new name taken from people in Chile who had befriended him. He married an Irish girl, then suddenly, and with a child due, found himself in debt. The solicitor whom

The first (civil) Tichborne hearing. Court scene, with the claimant under cross-examination.

The Princess Caraboo (opposite), as illustrated in a Bristol account of her dated 1817. Was she the love of Napoleon's later life?

(Top left) James Addison Reavis, Baron Peralta, and the Baroness Carmelita (top right), in about 1887. All the documents were in place for their claim to some eleven million acres of land in Arizona and New Mexico. Meanwhile a useful income was provided by tenants willing to purchase a quit-claim from them.

(Above) A scene from the film *The Man Who Never Was*: Ewen Montagu and his assistant (Clifton Webb and Robert Flemyng) beside the corpse of 'Major Martin'.

(Right) Mrs Anna Manahan (Anna Anderson), of Charlottesville, Virginia. In 1979 she declared her story to be 'nonsense' and told an interviewer 'throw it in the fire'.

The Romanov children of Russia, 1910: Marie, Tatiana, Anastasia, Olga and Alexis.

he turned to was given to understand that there was a little property back home, and that he had once been shipwrecked. A pipe carved with the initials 'R.C.T.' did the rest.

Henriette's support for the new arrival never wavered but it took several hard knocks. Castro wrote ahead that he had 'grown very stout', so to some extent she was prepared for changes, yet it was difficult for her to accept the new way he had of calling her 'mamma' instead of 'mother', the altered handwriting, the sketchy spelling. He spoke no French (their reunion in Paris caused him terrors), got the family estates wrong and could not say where his own regiment had served, but all these were explained away by Henriette as confusion in her poor dear Roger's head. Throughout she insisted that this man was her son. Then suddenly in 1868 the support was no more: Henriette died. There were enough adherents still to speak for him, but each had a different reason. Now when Castro hit the ball nothing came back.

The Westminster civil case had to confirm or deny that the claimant beyond a reasonable doubt was indeed Sir Roger Tichborne. To that end, although the case lasted 102 days, its task was straightforward. After hearing from one witness after another about the claimant's ignorance of Stonyhurst School or of the names of favourite Tichborne dogs, the jury was told that the true heir had initials tattooed on his arm where the claimant had none. That was enough: it decided there was a reasonable doubt, and its foreman duly stood up to announce as much. For the court president Lord Chief Justice Bovill, however, matters did not end with that verdict. He immediately ordered the claimant's arrest on charges of perjury. A second hearing, this time a criminal trial, began just over a year later and by comparison with the first case its task was extremely risky and complex. The complexity lay in the fact that the prosecution had to establish that the claimant was an outright impostor and to prove positively that he was someone else. The risk lay in the likelihood that it would fail.

Burden of proof

Originally the Crown hoped to prosecute for forgery (a felony) as well as for perjury (a misdemeanour). As the first case had shown, however, it could not do so, because the jury would not have been able to separate the issues. The Crown therefore went instead for twenty-three counts of perjury that meant going over virtually the entire ground of the first case again. There were fears that no jury would agree to serve when they realized what was at hand. Many of the 210 Crown witnesses had to be paid for and fetched at public expense from South America and Australia (the international *sub poena* did not yet exist). The claimant called even more witnesses – 300 in all. His counsel's opening and closing speeches lasted for forty-four days, the Chief Justice's summing up for twenty. This trial, the longest criminal case in British legal history, became a gigantic waste of public money (the estimated £150,000 would approach two million pounds in present values). Worse perhaps than that, justice may have miscarried: several of the perjury charges involved the claimant's being Orton, which in the view of some authorities was never proved.

Millions of people in England believed in the claimant. His case divided the country on class lines, from the hush of *The Times* newspaper to the shouts of a beer hall. Given a well-conducted defence of his claim, two or three of the jury might have refused to play along and to accept that he was an impostor. The man's mother had recognized him – was that not enough? The patronizing or sneering humour of several speeches in court could have fuelled a rebellion. Prosecuting counsel were booed in Palace Yard and at times needed police protection.

As it happened the Crown case survived the 188 days required but could claim little credit.

The defence lost its way and often its self-control too. The claimant was declared to be Arthur Orton and found guilty on all charges. 'False personation' immediately went into the statute book as a crime: English law wanted no more such cases to handle. Orton received a fourteen-year prison sentence, was released in 1884 and later sold his confession to a newspaper, withdrawing it almost immediately.

James Addison Reavis:
the quit-claim baron

Tucson, Arizona, in 1887. The territory still had a quarter-century to go before it would become a state. Things were on the move. America's peace terms with Mexico had added many acres of land to the whole south-west region, and these were available for government-settled farmers. Big men in industry saw prospects in Arizona: gold, silver and copper mines, civil engineering, railroads to be built.

The train brought a strange couple to Tucson that August. James Addison Reavis (1843–1914), a tall imposing figure with the air of a scholar, was already known in the territory as 'Don Jayme'. He had first come there eight years ago in pursuit of an extraordinary claim. Now here he was once more, back from Europe.

Early pay-offs

Land ceded to America under the Mexican peace terms would be given up to any claim able to show that it derived from a grant made by Spanish royalty at the time when Mexico was still an overseas colony. The Peralta claim held by Reavis met this condition. The Peralta family were descended from nobles created by Spain's King Ferdinand VI and from the old house of Navarre. An 18th-century line went overseas to Mexico, where Miguel de Peralta was created the first Baron Arizonac, a title carrying with it huge tracts of land. All the documents a claimant might need were in place. Somehow, via a shadowy middleman, James Reavis had acquired the deeds outright from a descendant of the Peralta family down on his luck, and four years back had filed his claim. Now it seemed this claim had both belt and braces, because with Reavis on the train was a wife, the Baroness Peralta. Carmelita (or Sofia Loreta Micaela, as family usage required) was declared to be the first Baron's great-granddaughter. She emerged as a rather stout young woman with captivating eyes.

Arizona said to itself that absurd claims by the dozen lay gathering dust at the land office, and that perhaps this was another Reavis bluff. Everyone recalled his thoroughness. They remembered too the sheer audacity that had him ride down Mexico way along with the land-office Spanish translator, verifying Peralta documents in the archives. And the flybills he had posted once he was back home. These advised one and all to settle with him promptly, because every man of them was a trespasser. Worst memory by far, though, was the size of that claim. Peralta land stretched 225 miles (583 km) east–west, 75 miles (194 km) north–south. It took in five counties, with Phoenix and six other towns, just short of eleven million acres or 4.45 million hectares in total. There was talk of Royal Johnson, the territory's surveyor-general and claims' assessor, being kin to Reavis or somehow in his pocket. Johnson certainly wasn't

MARTIN

The Allied invasion of Europe from the north African coast in 1943 looked at three possible routes. A foothold in Italy could be gained via Sicily; there was Greece, reachable from Crete; or a strike at Sardinia and Corsica would lead to southern France. At no other moment did psychological warfare have more to offer, with each side trying to second-guess the enemy.

Naval Intelligence in London came up with a plan named 'Operation Mincemeat'. Headed by Lt-Commander Ewen Montagu, who had the task of finding a corpse, the intention was that false clues of the invasion would be planted on this body. It would then show up in Spain (a neutral country in the war), from where with luck the clues would duly reach Berlin. The Germans were known to have an agent working out of the Spanish port of Huelva. So 'Major William Martin' would be washed ashore nearby as though following an air crash, with Allied documents in a briefcase chained to him.

Ewen Montagu found his corpse. The man was the right age and build for a Marines serving officer, and appropriately had died from pneumonia followed by exposure. His relatives, given assurances that the family's identity would be kept secret, went along with the deception.

Next, a number of convincing details were put together for Major Martin. He carried on him letters from 'Pam', his new fiancée, and her photo. There were bills from a tailor and from the jeweller who sold him the engagement ring (price £52.10.0d), also a bank's letter complaining about his overdraft. Two theatre ticket stubs were a last-minute addition. A man in Montagu's department resembled Martin, and his photo went on Martin's pass (corpses do not photograph well).

The briefcase carried word to General Alexander in Tunisia that invasion via Crete and Greece would use a feigned move as cover. This was a double bluff, because Alexander was told 'We stand a very good chance of making the Boche think we will go for Sicily'. In another letter Mountbatten introduced Major Martin to Eisenhower and the C.-in-C. Mediterranean as an expert in the use of invasion landing craft.

On 19 April 1943 the submarine Seraph left from Scotland. On board, Major Martin was removed from dry-ice pack and his 'Mae West' jacket inflated at 0430 hours on the 29th. After a few words from the service for burial at sea, the body was set adrift. Four days later the British naval attaché signalled from Madrid that a fisherman had recovered a British major just off Huelva. London had now to reply with well-judged signals of alarm which it realized would be intercepted – the attaché must demand back the documents, but must do so with discretion. By 13 May the attaché sounded hopeful of the Spanish knowing more about their catch than they would reveal; two days later, Spain's minister of marine left little doubt that the letters had been tampered with.

Their contents were at once known in Berlin. Admiral Dönitz saw Hitler about them on the 14th: the Führer was sure that the invasion would be via Greece. The German High Command moved troops away from the south coast of Sicily and ran down the island's defences. When the Allies landed there on 10 July they met with less opposition than expected. Countless lives were saved as a result of 'Operation Mincemeat' and William Martin, the man who never was.

hurrying with a verdict on the claim. Meanwhile, no doubt, Reavis as he had done previously would keep turning the screw, selling land tenants a quit-claim here or an easement there. The man could take ten dollars off some 'trespasser' patch farmer and think it a morning's work. Equally he could look to the Southern Pacific railroad and $50,000 interim payment for a right of way. Silver King paid $25,000 just to keep mining. There'd been town meetings about all this last time around. The Phoenix *Herald* had printed a headline 'Rascally Reavis Must Go', yet here the man was back again.

More at stake

Now it was a bigger affair in several quite different respects. Baroness Carmelita let herself be interviewed by the San Francisco *Examiner*. Asked about her origins, she said she was born in America and could scarce any longer call to mind her Spanish family. Her mother had died in childbirth, her father while back in Spain on business, leaving her to grow up as a ward in California. Somehow she had managed. Then, when a young woman, she had met Mr Reavis, who had been so interested to learn about her. They corresponded, met again, and married when she came of age. The two of them had just completed a marvellous European trip – in Madrid they found grandfather's will that left everything to his orphan Carmelita.

Reavis on his own account was grown bigger too. People no longer paid the baron off and good riddance; more and more they wanted him as their business partner in new enterprises. He made visits to Washington and to New York. With some top men he was planning to irrigate and develop the Salt Valley via a group of companies that had the celebrated lawyer Robert Ingersoll as president and was funded by fifty million dollars of equity capital. The Salt Valley settlers had already been offered preferential re-leases for purchase. And there was his baroness saying everyone would get rich, promising that not a single land tenant would be hurt.

Surveyor-general Johnson did his legal best when at last in 1890 he reported on Peralta. Much was wrong with the claim, he said: inconsistencies and errors had been found, the phrasing used Spanish incorrectly. He could not recommend it for Washington's approval. This made Johnson hero for a day, but there was no allegation of fraud by what he said, nor was anything finally settled.

Reavis at once sued the government for eleven million dollars. His land had been thrown open to settlement, sold off or reserved by lots, its major river wrongfully drained for irrigation purposes. Washington officials wondered how to stop the man. He had very powerful friends, one of them Collis P. Huntington, the California railroad millionaire, who argued that Reavis deserved to be supported as a man of vision. A Peralta Fund was set up to tide him over the long preparation for his law suit. Then, slowly but quite distinctly, the balance began to shift.

Reconstruction job

One year after Johnson's report a new organization came into being to handle the hundreds of land claims still on file with the US government. This body, the Court of Private Land-grant Claims, acted as both investigator and judge. Its lawyers assigned to the Peralta claim were Matthew G. Reynolds and Severo Mallet-Prevost, and they had more power than the former run-down land office ever knew. Together they set about constructing a life and works of James Addison Reavis. The task took them eighteen months, from late 1893 until June 1895. They learnt that Reavis came from a farming family in Missouri and that he had joined a Confederate regiment in the Civil War. During this army service he discovered he could copy his officer's signature well enough for a leave pass (fellow soldiers also enjoyed the benefit of this discovery). A year in Brazil taught him not just Portuguese but some Spanish too, probably rather incorrect Spanish. Then followed a time with a real-estate company, where he did more forgery. That was beginning to look like a talent. The next twenty years saw it blossom and bear fruit on behalf of the Peralta claim.

Over this period Reavis came up with many papers. His most recent strike (not for the first time) had been in Mexico. Peralta's original baron was appointed to the city of Guadalajara in 1742. The royal grant of land had followed, and Reavis claimed to have found there a copy-warrant dated 1778 approving the grant, together with probate proceedings of the baron's will and a complete family tree. He took copies of these items and had them certified as genuine.

Reynolds and Mallet-Prevost now journeyed to Guadalajara. Their handwriting expert studied the 1778 warrant: its script was a poor imitation of 18th-century style and its signature a forgery. The other items had taken a genuine document's first and last pages and inserted the forgery between them in such a way as to make it appear as though the genuine real-life parties (two brothers) were witnesses to it. Where words had been changed, chemical solvents could now dissolve the modern dogwood ink and restore the original iron ink below. A further group of papers had been written not with a quill but with a steel pen. Most damagingly of all, the expert was able to show that the original 1742 appointment was for a different man with a different title.

Mallet-Prevost then moved on to Spain. Here also were fraudulent registry-documents; but perhaps more useful was what the lawyer learned about Reavis's methods after a forgery had been planted. He always spoke of tight security at the church and state archives, of how only his personal contacts got him past the door. This was intended to add authenticity to his story and the forgeries. But in fact everything planted had to be 'found', and certified as genuine. Now Mallet-Prevost heard what went on. In Seville, at the Archives of the Indias, Reavis had been assigned a clerk to guide him to where documents were located and to keep an eye on him. Reavis always came back to the same locations. After some long while at this, the clerk fell ill and stayed away sick for two days. On his return, hoping Reavis's searches might be done, he was told that in case 77, drawer 3, bundle number 31 were the documents that his visitor required. He had never before seen these items, and suspected them now; but copies were duly made and certified. There were also occasions when Reavis would produce a sheet that had been folded (no papers in the archives were ever folded) or that was without a page-number (every archive-page was numbered). Then the clerk recalled how just on closing time items would appear from under Reavis's handkerchief. Eventually the visitor's search permit was withdrawn and a warrant issued for his arrest. Seville was too slow, however – the bird had flown.

A Federal case

Back in Arizona the lawyers turned to the baroness. She had in truth been born in California, though not to any Peralta. (Her father was a local man, her mother an Indian.) As stated earlier, she did grow up as a ward: Reavis had persuaded her guardian to sign an affidavit, 'in the interests of the girl', confirming the family tree. He had also made entries in the register of births and deaths at a California mission to tally with that tree. (Unluckily for him, the fathers kept a separate index volume so this tampering was detected.)

By the summer of 1895 both sets of lawyers at last were prepared. Reavis's case against the government occupied a fortnight. He lost, and was promptly arrested by the US marshal. At his own trial a year later, Carmelita broke down in tears after her twin boys had amused the court with their pranks. She knew nothing; she had believed the whole baroness story; now everyone was getting at her. Reavis was found guilty of trying to defraud the US government out of parts of its public lands. He received a two-year sentence and a fine of $5000.

The scheme that had taken most of his adult life and all his energy refused to lie down. On his release from jail in 1898 he told reporters he was 'still on deck', bound for New York 'to carry forward those irrigating endeavours'. But all the money had gone. Carmelita obtained a divorce in 1902. Later, both of them lived in Denver, Colorado, she surviving him by twenty years.

Anna Anderson:
the Romanov heiress

In February 1984 *The Times* of London announced that a Mrs Anna Anderson Manahan had died. Her photograph was above the obituary article: a dark, vibrant woman, wearing shiny jewellery. Next day a correction appeared in the paper. The photo was not of Mrs Manahan but of an actress with almost the same name.

This trivial mistake sums up Anna Anderson's story. We watch a woman playing the part of a Russian Grand Duchess for half a century, but even when she dies we cannot see what she really looked like.

The year 1913 marked three centuries of rule by the Romanovs in Russia. Tsar Nicholas, their final and reluctant emperor (he would have preferred to be a farmer), was enormously rich. Eight palaces together with huge estates made him worth an estimated 20 billion dollars before the royal foreign investments were counted. These were believed to include five million gold roubles at the Bank of England for each of his daughters: the Grand Duchesses Olga, Tatiana, Marie and (b. 1901) Anastasia. There was also his son and heir, Alexis.

A family in limbo

Close ties linked the five children with Europe's royal houses. Their paternal uncles were the Kaiser and the British King George; other uncles and aunts came on their German mother's side in the Hesse family. Tsar Nicholas never contemplated joining these relatives abroad in what might be his family's exile, even when World War I broke out and famine and unrest made a revolution almost certain. But in March 1917, his eyes at last opened, Nicholas decided to abdicate.

The provisional government held the royal family at their palace of Tsarskoye Selo until August, when they were sent to Siberia. Life was tolerable and the girls talked cheerfully of a life in England. The new Bolshevik government had no idea what to do with this family. During April and May of 1918 it moved them westward to the town of Ekaterinburg and into a rich merchant's property, the 'Ipatyev house', where conditions rapidly became squalid. Six weeks passed and the district came under threat from White troops fighting the revolution. By an account later taken as official, the local soviet authorized a hasty execution of the Romanovs. The entire family along with five of the staff were ordered downstairs to a basement room during the night of 16 July and shot.

Escape

'Anna Anderson' first comes to life nineteen months later when police in Berlin save her from a suicide attempt. For the period from Ipatyev's house to that date in February 1920 or even beyond it there are countless versions of what actually befell the Russian royal family, but as yet nothing – not even the 1989 announcement from Moscow of bodies found – completely disproves the one given by Anna after she had spent two years in Berlin's Dalldorf asylum following her suicide attempt. Anna let herself be identified as the Tsar's youngest daughter Anastasia. She declared the infamous last night at Ipatyev's house to have been 'not like that'. She claimed she was rescued by a man she later married and had a son with, and that they travelled to Romania. The man had died during street fighting in Bucharest and Anastasia escaped to Germany in search of her mother's relatives. Oddly, the world heard this account some months after a fellow patient at the asylum had identified her not as Anastasia but as the Tsar's *second* daughter, Tatiana. That itself makes the story suspect; also, she left Dalldorf asylum for the home of a monarchist émigré regularly visited by the former nobility and their hangers-on. This home was not the best environment for a girl with Anna's troubled pretensions (she had more spells in hospital during the five years to 1927).

Accounts given by other people are also suspect. Russia during the civil war was a time of great confusion. Much of what we hear from Red and White sources, from foreign diplomats, and from journalists on or off the ground has a ring of politics to it. At Ekaterinburg five successive on-the-spot investigations were run. Perhaps the family were killed only later and somewhere else. Witnesses disagreed as to how many were killed; the forensic evidence was doubtful; memories unreliable. Much later, in 1957, then in 1967 and again in 1970, a German court would declare the truth to be unknown. By this it meant that if the claimant Anna Anderson was unable to prove herself to be Anastasia, then her opponents equally were unable to prove the real Grand Duchess to be dead.

How much coincidence?

Back in the '20s, Anna's opponents came and went, some ending up with very mixed feelings. The Tsar's sister, Olga, longed to accept Anna. Eventually she said 'Not my niece', but stayed in anguished doubt all her life. The family's French teacher had a Russian wife who wept for joy at a first meeting and only changed her mind under pressure from her husband. A former maid of honour, sent by the Tsar's mother to inspect the claimant, began by denying Anna but later became one of her most enthusiastic supporters.

At these meetings with people who had known Anastasia when young, much of what happened only made sense to outsiders if an amazing coincidence were at work. One army captain was reminiscing about the Grand Duchess's wartime hospital visits, during which (though the captain did not mention it) a patient had been less than polite. The captain heard a sudden giggle and Anna say: 'The man with the pockets!' Then light dawned – as the patient had always stood hands in pockets while talking with Anastasia, they had given him that nickname. But this had been a private joke between the two of them; no one else could have known it, and indeed the captain himself had forgotten the episode until that moment. Then there was the Hesse family's secret: a peace-making bid had taken Anastasia's German uncle Ernest to St Petersburg halfway through the war. This was the last thing Grand Duke Ernest wanted to come out; he never forgave Anna for somehow knowing. To insiders, her revelations showed an ability to pick up vibrations from the unconscious mind. Yet in spite of these miracles Anna could be oddly ignorant on quite everyday matters. And why did she refuse to speak Russian?

Big business

In October 1928 Anna was on an over-publicized visit to America when a dozen of the Romanovs decided to call a halt to the claimant. They issued a formal document stating that the claim was a fairy tale. Before Anna returned to Germany there were signs of the fairy tale becoming a reality: she had herself made into a corporation, 'Grandanor', or the Grand Duchess Anastasia of the Romanovs, registered the following February.

From this point on, 'the Anastasia Case' increasingly takes over from the woman Anna

Anderson. In 1933 Berlin granted certificates of inheritance to the Tsar's surviving relatives. These papers covered money held for them in Germany (the amounts were trifling, about six thousand pounds in values of the day). One of the certificates carried the statement that Anastasia had died. Grandanor saw at once that if this were allowed to go unchallenged it would ruin all hope of the big pickings, which were thought to include forty million pounds at Baring's – a belief not denied to this day – in addition to five million roubles at the Bank of England and some rich American stocks. As soon as the German shareout began, application was made to court for the offending certificate to be revoked. Much later this grew into a legal action against one named relative: Barbara, duchess of Mecklenburg, a grand-niece of the Tsar's wife, chosen to represent all the certificate-holders. A first hearing opened in 1938. Allowing for wartime interruptions and other breaks, it ran for over thirty years. No other point of law was involved. The whole enormous business won Anna nothing at all.

During much of the time she lived in Germany, after 1946 as a hermit in the Black Forest gawped at by tourists. Two major films (one with Ingrid Bergman, the other with Lilli Palmer), nine full-scale biographies, uncounted plays and television documentaries appeared. Her royal supporters died or drifted away, leaving in effect only three: the German Crown Princess Cecilie, Prince Frederick of Saxe-Altenburg and his brother-in-law Sigismund of Prussia, nephew of the Tsar.

Goodbye nonsense

In 1968 Anna moved to America, settling at Charlottesville, Virginia, in a house with an overgrown garden and many cats. That December she married John Manahan, a retired history professor. Two years later the German court confirmed that the Anastasia Case would have no result.

Here at last, before spells of nervous illness returned, Anna seemed as Mrs Manahan to achieve a self-esteem. She was always good at letting other people do all the work (Prince Frederick for example spent years as her proxy at the hearing). Now they could have the whole 'nonsense', as she called her story in 1979. 'Throw it in the fire.' This most persistent of double identities, who was so often difficult and moody, as a third person could sit back more happily.

FURTHER READING

Ideas

Literature, history:
Carswell, John *Singular Travels, Campaigns and Adventures of Baron Munchausen by R.E. Raspe and Others*, London, 1948; Cohn, Norman *Warrant for Genocide*, London, 1967; Evans, Christopher *Cults of Unreason*, London, 1973; Fay, S., Chester, L. and Linklater, M. *Hoax*, London, 1972; Rieth, Adolf *Archaeological Fakes*, London, 1970; Schoenbaum, S. *Shakespeare's Lives*, Oxford, 1970; Thomson, Derick S. *The Gaelic Sources in Macpherson's 'Ossian'*, Edinburgh, 1952; Warburg, Fredric *All Authors are Equal*, London, 1973;

Science/Medicine:
Broad, William, and Wade, Nicholas *Betrayers of the Truth*, London, 1983; Gervaso, Roberto *Cagliostro, a Biography*, London, 1974; Hamilton, David *The Monkey Gland Affair*, London, 1986; Hearnshaw, Leslie *Cyril Burt, Psychologist*, London, 1979; Hixson, Joseph *The Patchwork Mouse*, New York, 1976; Jameson, Eric *The Natural History of Quackery*, London, 1961; Joravsky, David *The Lysenko Affair*, Cambridge, Mass., 1970; Joynson, Robert B. *The Burt Affair*, London, 1989; Kamin, Leon J. *The Science and Politics of IQ*, Potomac, Maryland, 1974; Medvedev, Zhores A. *The Rise and Fall of T.D. Lysenko*, New York and London, 1969; Zweig, Stefan *Mental Healers*, London, 1933;

Backhouse
Trevor-Roper, Hugh *Hermit of Peking*, London, 1978.

Money

Audit Commission for Local Authorities in England and Wales *Survey of Computer Fraud and Abuse (1987)*, London, 1987; Black, Charles, and Horsnell, Michael *Counterfeiter*, London, 1989; Bloom, Murray Teigh *Money of Their Own*, Port Clinton, Ohio, 1982; *The Man Who Stole Portugal*, London, 1967; Klein, Alexander (ed.) *Grand Deception*, London, 1956; Larsen, Egon *The Deceivers*, London, 1966; Miller, N.C. *The Great Salad Oil Swindle*, London, 1966; Norman, Adrian *Computer Insecurity*, London, 1983.

Objects

Archaeology:
Allegro, John M. *The Shapira Affair*, London, 1965;

Cole, Sonia *Counterfeit*, London, 1955; Klein, Alexander (ed.) *Grand Deception*, London, 1956; Rieth, Adolf *Archaeological Fakes*, London, 1970; Weiner, J.S. *The Piltdown Forgery*, London, 1955;

Autographs/Manuscripts/Books:
Barker, Nicolas, and Collins, John *A Sequel to An Enquiry into the Nature of Certain 19th-Century Pamphlets*, London, 1983; Myers, Robin, and Harris, Michael *Fakes and Frauds* (chapter by Nicolas Barker), Winchester, UK, 1989; Naifeh, Steven, and Smith, Gregory W. *The Mormon Murders*, New York, 1988; Partington, Wilfred *Thomas J. Wise in the Original Cloth*, London, 1946; Schoenbaum, S. *Shakespeare's Lives*, Oxford, 1970; Whitehead, John *This Solemn Mockery*, London, 1973;

Fine arts:
Arnau, Frank *Three Thousand Years of Deception in Art and Antiques*, London, 1961; Kurz, Otto *Fakes*, New York, 1967; Rieth, Adolf *Archaeological Fakes*, London, 1970;
Painting:
Arnau, Frank *Three Thousand Years of Deception in Art and Antiques*, London, 1961; Cole, Sonia *Counterfeit*, London, 1955; Irving, Clifford *Fake!*, London, 1970; Keating, Tom, with Norman, Geraldine, and Norman, Frank *Fake's Progress*, London, 1977; Kilbracken, Lord *Van Meegeren*, London, 1967; Lagrange, Francis, and Murray, William *Flag on Devil's Island*, London, 1962; Schüller, Sepp *Forgers, Dealers, Experts*, London, 1960;
Sculpture:
Pope-Hennessy, John *The Study and Criticism of Italian Sculpture*, Princeton, 1980; Sox, David *Unmasking the Forger*, London, 1987.

People

Barbour, Philip L. *Dimitry*, London, 1967; Davis, Natalie Zemon *The Return of Martin Guerre*, Cambridge Mass. and London, 1983; Domela, Harry *A Sham Prince*, London, 1927; Kurth, Peter *Anastasia: The Life of Anna Anderson*, London, 1983; Maugham, Lord *The Tichborne Case*, London, 1936; Montagu, Ewen *The Man Who Never Was*, London, 1970; Poole, Stanley B.-R. *Royal Mysteries and Pretenders*, London, 1969; Powell, Donald M. *The Peralta Grant*, Norman, Oklahoma, 1960; Rose, June *The Perfect Gentleman*, London, 1977; Sparrow, Gerald *The Great Impostors*, London, 1962; Summers, Anthony, and Mangold, Tom *The File on the Tsar*, London, 1976; Thompson, C. J. S.

Mysteries of Sex, London, 1938; Woodruff, Douglas *The Tichborne Claimant*, London, 1957.

General books

Haywood, Ian *Faking It: Art and the Politics of Forgery*, Brighton, UK, 1987.
Jones, Mark (ed.) *Fake? The Art of Deception* (British Museum exhibition catalogue), London, 1990.
Mills, John F., and Mansfield, John M. *The Genuine Article*, London, 1979.

Index

Bold number indicates an illustration

Fakes, frauds and forgeries